Praise for *Harlot's Sauce*
by Patricia Volonakis Davis:

"...a remarkable achievement..." - Maria Shriver

"A tongue-in-cheek, but thought-provoking description of 'real' Americans vs. 'first-generation' Americans. If we could all laugh at our convictions the way Ms. Davis laughs at hers, the world would be a safer and happier place." - Phil Collins

"Patricia becomes the girlfriend you cheer on, cry with, and just plain enjoy. She's brave, she's very funny, and she's written what is destined to become a best seller." - www.50fabulous.com

"...witty, human, readable" - www.bitchbuzz.com

"A rich, colorful tale. I laughed out loud." - Barbara Gates, author of *Already Home.*

"...inspiring, great read..." - *Greek Star*

"A great read, often humorous but always honest, Patricia presents what it's really like to be the new Italian-American daughter-in-law in a Greek-American family by opening doors most families keep closed." - Gil Mansergh, host, KRCB-FM's *"Word By Word: Conversation with Writers"*

"You'll love and identify with Patricia's insights, in retrospect, on life, love, cultures, friendships, conscious mothering, running a business in an adopted country, wifely duties, and a domineering mother-in-law, generously spiced with wretched dogs (and their owners), flying cockroaches, baseball bats, harlot's sauce, and a no-account woman who smells bad." - Lynn Henriksen, president, *Women's National Book Association, San Francisco Chapter*

"Ms. Davis takes the reader on a poignant and genuinely endearing romp, told with gusto and humor, that travels from an Italian-American neighborhood of New York to Greece to California, and along the way we get to meet an array of memorable people who shared her remarkable journey. Beautifully written, honest and provocative."
- Barry C. Hessenius, California Arts Council, *Barry's Blog*

Harper Davis Publishing

Harlot's Sauce:
A Memoir of Food, Family, Love, Loss, and Greece

Patricia Volonakis Davis is the editor-in-chief of ***Harlots' Sauce Radio*** (www.harlotssauce.com), a popular online magazine and podcast that inspires its readers and listeners to make "Something Delicious Out of Limited Choices," and is the source for the Gregory Randall Literary Prize. She is the author of *"If This Woman is Being Operated Recklessly,"* and other poems on women's issues. Her essays, stories, and celebrity interviews have appeared in various newspapers and magazines nationally and internationally. Ms. Davis emigrated to Athens, Greece in 1995, where she lived for seven years with her son and her Greek husband. She now resides in Northern California in Sleepy Hollow, "a perfect and aptly named place for a writer to write," says she.

For more information, visit www.patriciaVdavis.com
This title is also available as an e-book

Harlot's Sauce:
A Memoir of Food, Family, Love, Loss, and Greece

Patricia Volonakis Davis

Harper Davis Publishers

Harper Davis Publishing, Inc.

Published in the United States of America by Harper Davis Publishing

Davis, Patricia Volonakis.
Harlot's sauce : a memoir of food, family, love, loss, and Greece /
Patricia Volonakis Davis. --1st ed. --La Vergne, TN : Harper Davis, c2008.
p. cm.
LCCN 2008935347
ISBN: 978-0-9819153-0-2
1. Davis, Patricia Volonakis--Biography. 2. Italian American
women--Greece--Biography. 3. Americans--Greece--Biography.
4. Greece--Description and travel. 5. Intercountry marriage. I. Title.
DF747.A5 D38 2009
914.9504/76092--dc22 2009

Printed in the United States of America
Set in Italian Garamond

To Pete, my "Real" husband,
and to our sons,
Clint, Andy, Greg, Tim, Nick.
(I love you all.)

and
to Zeus, the dog.
(I won't forget you.)

Acknowledgements
Many, *many* thanks to:

The Angelidis/Iacovou Family for their assistance on the history of Cyprus, and Nicholas Stamatakis Ph.D, for his many email discussions on Greek history, culture and psychology.

Colin Jose and Jack Huckel of The National Soccer Hall of Fame in Oneonta, NY, for their invaluable research on the New York Cosmos.

Janis Chan, Joyce Maynard, Marlene Adelstein, Ali Bothwell Mancini, Nigel Voight, and Barbara Gates - six terrific editors; and Margot Van Riper and Susannah Greenberg - two fantastic publicists.

The people I worked with at Scholastic Inc., without whom this story would not have ended as it did.

The California Writers Club, The Women's National Book Association, and the *SF Bay Area Literary Arts Newsletter*.

Bill Russo, and everyone at the Dolce Channel, along with Maryann Maisano, Gaetano Iacono, and Anthony Skordi - three brilliant actors who made *Harlot's Sauce* podcasts extra special.

Ralph Epstein, Justin Oliver, David Hunter, and Paul Kaufman at the Fairfax Heath Club, who each have the wisdom of Socrates and the rock hard abs of Hercules! Thanks for all your advice about this book!

Some special women in Greece and the United States, who helped make this a 'spicy sauce', including: Eleni Angelinos, Michele Benza, Jackie Bissell, Pam Bourazanis, Jamie Brenner, Amber Burke, Carmen Colemere, Joanne Conner, Debbie Davis, Ellen Davis, Ann Del Castillo, Shailah Hathiramani, Maro Iacovou, Judy Konstantinidou, Audrey Kruger, Josie Lambidis, Nancy Leff, Randy Loukissas, Marie Marotta, Dolores Mosqueda, Jo O'Neill, Angela Papadopoulos, Kelly Preston, Breacis Rodriguez, Sofia Stathakis, Kim Tokas, Cristina Zaccarini...and too many more to list!

All my writers and staff at *Harlots' Sauce Radio*, all my 'neighbors' on VOX.com and the fans on my *Harlot's Sauce* page on Facebook - thank you

Joan and Manolis Maragoudakis, for more than I can possibly list.

And last, but not least, to the **First Lady of California, Maria Shriver,** for her generosity and encouragement. You are truly a muse for many of us who strive to "make something delicious out of limited choices."

Contents

Chapter One: Her Perilous Sail Begins

"A person needs a little madness or else they
never dare cut the rope and be free."
–Nikos Kazantzakis

Greece, 1980

Nothing about this trip was turning out the way I'd imagined!

That was the thought running through my head one night, as I was lying on my bed alone in my hotel room, on my first visit to Greece, which I'd embarked upon blissfully with Gregori, my Greek lover of three months.

First of all, during yet another evening with Gregori's relatives, I accidentally drank too much ouzo. (And if you've never had ouzo before — let me tell you — that can happen *quite* easily.) On top of that, because we "weren't allowed" to stay alone together, Gregori just dropped me off at my hotel afterward, and then left me there to return to his relatives. So I was abandoned, as well as drunk.

Overcome by misery, I pulled myself up and weaved toward the bath, where a shower, I hoped, would cheer me up and help settle the wooziness. It was only when I emerged, clean and maybe a bit more sober, that I noticed two uninvited guests waiting on the threshold of the doorway between the bed and the bath. At first I thought the ouzo was making me hallucinate. My visitors appeared to be some... sort of bug, but each was the size and color of a plum. They were shiny and slimy-looking, with long, wriggling, disgusting antennae. God help me — they were *roaches*. I'd never seen any that massive. As I stared in hypnotized revulsion, the giants moved. And when they did, I noticed something else about them that was different from any roach I'd ever seen. They had *wings*.

Suddenly, one flexed its wings as if it were showing off its muscles. I jumped back as it took off and flew out the window. But the second one — *oh, migod!* That one soared straight toward my bed and crawled up onto my *pillow*.

I screamed bloody murder, grabbed a towel, (because though I'd lost my sanity, I hadn't completely lost my modesty) and ran out into the hallway,

1

where I stood whimpering and shaking, rivulets of water from my hair mixing with the tears running down my face and onto the marble floor. At my scream, people came out of the adjacent rooms in their nightclothes. Alarmed by seeing a nearly naked, wet, and shivering girl in the hall, they rang for the night manager, who ran up to confront me.

"*Thes-pee-neece, tee ehete?*" said he, sternly. ("Miss, what's the problem?")

I started to babble, "There's a b-b-b-ug. In my room. *Big*. On my pillow."

At that, he got it. *Ah… not a Greek girl.* He spoke in accented English, then. "A *bahg*? What do you mean a *bahg*? Where?"

"In my room. I can't go back in there."

"You *mast* go back to your room. You are wearing only towels. You are making *paddles* on the floor."

"No, *please*. I'm afraid. If it has wings, it might have teeth. Could you go in and kill it for me?"

The people in the hall started murmuring. The manager's attention was diverted as he reassured them that there was no danger, just a foolish American girl who'd never seen flying cockroaches before. "You can go back to your rooms," he said in Greek. "Everything is okay."

Then he turned back to me. "*Leestin, Meess*, I don't know what kind of an animal there *ees* in your room, but I cannot go *een* there. I am not *permeeted*."

Another female guest at the hotel, who'd gathered that I was afraid to return to my room, or else was convinced that I was barking mad, handed me a robe and motioned sympathetically for me to put it on. I smiled at her gratefully and turned to the manager again. "If you can't go in my room, could you please ring my boy — my… fiancé?"

"Your fiancé? Where is *he*?"

Moments later, I was seated in the manager's office, in loaned nightwear, ringing up Gregori at his aunt and uncle's house. The phone rang endlessly and though I was no longer dripping wet, I could tell that the manager earnestly wished I weren't in his office.

Mercifully, someone finally picked up. "*Parah-kaloh?*" sleepily said whichever uncle or cousin.

"It's Patricia," I said timidly. "I'm *so* sorry, but I need to speak to Gregori."

"*Just a moment.*" There was another long silence as whoever it was went to wake up my erstwhile 'fiancé'.

2

"Hello?"

"Gregori, you have to come here. Right now. *Please*," I implored.

Twenty minutes later, Gregori was in the manager's office, listening, with startled eyes, to the hotel manager. I couldn't catch any of what he was saying, but I no longer cared. I was tired of everything.

The manager left us for a moment. I think he thought I was loopy. Gregori was staring at me the way I'd been staring at the bugs in my room earlier.

"He says you were standing outside your room, in the hall, naked and you were screaming."

"I was *not* naked," I said, indignantly. But then, I started to cry. "Listen, you didn't tell me I'd have to stay at the hotel alone. You didn't tell me we'd have to pretend to be engaged... all your other family 'rules', or any of that stuff about the Swedish girls. And you didn't warn me about those horrible bugs. I want to go *home*."

That declaration had Gregori conferring with the manager and they both went upstairs to my room. By the time I'd collected myself and followed them up, the beast on my pillow had been routed, my bag had been packed, and Gregori had even left out some clothes for me. After dressing, I handed the robe over to the manager who, still looking grim, had waited in the hallway. Gregori and I set for his aunt and uncle's house, where they made room for yet another sleepover guest.

In bed, in my borrowed room, I could hear them all in the kitchen. For some reason they'd switched over to English. They were talking about the night's events... and me.

"You should fly back to Athens earlier, Gregori," advised the youngest aunt sagely, "and spend a few days sightseeing, just the two of you, with no family around."

"Maybe that's a good idea," said one male cousin, "But while you're in Athens, think about whether it's a smart thing to get involved with an American girl. After all, she's a nice girl, but... she's not like *us*."

From the Long Island Sound to the Aegean Sea

*"She wanted something to happen—something,
anything: she did not know what."*
–Kate Chopin

My love affair with Gregori started when I was in the sixth grade. Gregori wouldn't actually be a participant in that affair until more than a decade later, however.

You see, my sixth grade teacher, Mr. Dubroff, introduced us to Greek mythology. Probably not every twelve-year-old was as eager as I to hear tales of Agamemnon's virgin sacrifice of his daughter Iphigenia, and Odysseus' personal war with the god of the sea, but I clung to Mr. Dubroff's every sentence. Every day I went home and repeated everything he taught us to my parents.

My father, Sicilian-born and thus also a fan of great epics, was impressed with my interest, so he came home one evening after work and surprised me with three volumes: Homer's *Iliad* and *Odyssey* and Vergil's *Aeneid*. He couldn't have known then that I'd consider them the best gifts he'd ever give me, or that his gifts would help me take the first steps toward my actual journeys to Greece. Nor could either of us have known that years later, his grandson, my son, in his own sixth-grade class, would also be reading *The Illiad*, but in Greek, and in the very land where the legends had originally been conceived.

From Mr. Dubroff's class on, I embraced everything to do with Ancient Greece. Reading about Greece in my room, in my parents' house on Long Island, New York, I traveled thousands of years into the past, to islands and peninsulas far away from my world of first-generation, blue-collar Americans, an insular world that was suffocating me. It's hard to explain why I felt that way, but I'll try.

First-generation, blue-collar Americans were only American 'sort of'. We were "Something-Hyphen-Americans." We had to have the hyphen, because only a part of each of us was rooted in The United States. Another part had never left the country in which our parents had been born, even if we ourselves had never *physically* been there. In order to differentiate what particular amalgamation of two distinct cultures we were, we branded ourselves 'Greek-American', 'Italian-American', etc.

4

That's why other American kids we went to school with, whose families had been in the States for generations, seemed peculiar to us. We called them "real" Americans. The real American didn't say he was, "Something-Hyphen-American," he said he was a "mutt." He didn't even know where his ancestors where from specifically, but he *did* know the precise location in the U.S. his family had settled back in the 1800's.

We were just as weird to those kids as they were to us. During roll call, when teachers would call out our names, like this:

"Patricia... She-fa-loh?"

"Uh... Jagah-deeev... ah... M... mak-ah-gee?"

"*Mmm*... Are-Gee- Ree... Pah-nah-gee-oh-top-poo-lohs? ...Is that right?"

The real Americans would turn and stare at us incredulously.

"What kind of name is *that*?" they'd ask, with dislike.

They'd mispronounced our family names, too (sometimes deliberately) and immediately shorten our first names to something more generic — a "nickname." Real Americans assigned us one whether we wanted them to, or not. Jagadev Mukherjee was eventually called 'Jack', and Argyri Panagiotopoulos caved altogether, becoming 'Angie Poulos' even before we got to high school. She was sneered at for it, though, because she wasn't fooling anybody. We all knew she was just like us—a bastard half-child of her parents' mother country.

I was one of the few who, to the irritation of many, stubbornly corrected people when they mispronounced my last name and insisted upon being called by my actual first name. (What was so hard about saying, "Patricia," anyway?)

Then again, we 'Hyphens' mocked the 'Real' family names just as much as they mocked ours. Their names were often no more than three syllables, first and last included. To me, a name like "Pete Davis" sounded like an alias.

And, boy — was it strange to hear those "Mr. and Mrs. Davis's" talk. Parents of the kids who were real Americans didn't speak broken English, but at least one of *our* parents did, and certainly all our grandparents did. In fact, the language our parents and grandparents spoke at home was likely another language besides English. Because we wanted to know which language, what sort of parents, and what type of food we'd be subjected to when we went to each other's homes, we'd always ask each other when we were first introduced, "*What* are you?"

Most of the time, when replying, we'd leave off the hyphen-American part altogether and just say, "Italian", "Polish", or whatever. Where we were from was vital information we needed to know about one another, even though we really weren't "from" where we said.

These Decrees of Identification applied to all of my schoolmates except for Margie Zimmerman. Because our area was primarily Christian and white, Margie only needed to be established as "white, but *not* Christian." So when kids asked Margie what she was, she just said, "Jewish." Now that I think about it, I became good friends with Margie almost as soon as we met, but we were in our late teens before I learned that her grandparents and father were from Germany.

"Jewish" was a separate subgroup. (I won't even get into the classifications we used for Asians and the occasional Hispanic or Black we came across.) It was unusual back then for a Jew to be in a lower-middle-class neighborhood. Most Jews who lived on that part of Long Island were white-collar, lived in the neighborhood that was better than ours, and went to a different school. But Margie ended up at our school because her parents were divorced. The divorce had changed Margie's mother's financial circumstances drastically, so Margie, her mother, grandmother and brother, didn't live far from my parents and me. I thought having divorced parents was another fascinating thing about her besides the fact that, as she first put it when we met in second grade, "I don't even know what 'a Jesus' *is*."

By the time we reached high school, there were more "Goldbergs" and "Friedmans," and a growing classmate population now being called "Afro-Americans." The "Real" Americans had a new label, too — "WASPS". We did mingle a bit, but we still made fun of each other. With a wan smile, Margie put up with 'friendly' Jewish jokes, and the WASPS, like our new friends, the brother and sister Kurt and Donna James, whom Margie and I met when we were in eleventh grade, took as much ribbing at this point in time as we first-generations did. When Kurt and Donna met up with us anywhere, we'd call out, "Here come White Bread and Mayonnaise!" and we acted repulsed when Kurt told us that their mother made mashed potatoes from a mix out of a box.

And I, like the majority of first-generation kids, was still most comfortable with friends whose parents were born outside the United States, because we felt we fit in nowhere, except with each other. We handled this by fluctuating between feeling out of place — or feeling superior. Real Americans seemed alien to us, but our parents and grandparents seemed alien to us, also. We ate different ethnic foods in our individual homes and spoke different languages, but we related to each other anyway, because all our parents had a tribal outlook and put similar restrictions on their American-born offspring as a result. They confined us to clannish enclaves and issued dire warnings about strangers wanting to harm us by giving us, "The Evil Eye". Every ethnic group had a name for this. Margie's grandmother, Bubbe, called it "*ayin hora*," my grandmother, "Nonnie" called it, "*malocchia*". (Kurt and Donna never even heard of it, until the rest of us brought it up.)

Our families' parenting methodology was the same, too. They mixed guilt into our baby cereal and spoon-fed it to us, always trying to get in one more mouthful, until we felt we'd burst if we swallowed anymore. As we grew older and tried to rebel, they'd bludgeon us with shame, dramatically shouting, "Oh, my God, I can't believe you did this! What will people *think*?"

If that didn't work, they'd beat us, or worse, stop talking to us altogether, until we surrendered to their commands. In between the beatings, shouting matches and guilt sessions, they'd kiss us, squeeze our faces, or even our backsides, because we were "so cute" they "couldn't resist." From one day to the next, we never knew if the adults in our family were going to adore us, or hold us in disgrace.

The things we loved about the United States — the freer lifestyle, the fast food, the technology, everything that came out of Hollywood — were the very things that made many of our parents uneasy.

Except for my mother and Margie's, that is. They loved the U.S. Margie and I ultimately concluded that we were actually "first-generations-and-a-half," because our mothers were born in what our grandparents called "America," too. But our mothers were an even more volatile, quixotic mix of the old world and the new. Because not only were their parents foreign, so were the men they'd married.

Though my mother called herself, "Nancy," she'd been christened, "Annunziata Santa," by my grandfather from Naples and my grandmother from Sicily. Nancy married "Giuseppe," who called himself, "Joe." Joe had an accent as thick as my grandmother's tomato sauce, because he'd been born in Sicily, too.

Yet, "they're ignorant and backward," was just one of the disparaging comments my mother would make about the Italians she knew. After one of these remarks, I finally pointed out that her husband — my *father* — was foreign, too.

7

"I know that," she snapped. "But he's *different*. Not like the rest of his family. They don't like me and *I* don't like them. They didn't want your father to marry me because my mother was married more than once. Can you imagine? Who do they think *they* are? And they didn't like it that I smoke, either. But your father didn't care. He used to light a cigarette for me right in front of all of them," she declared proudly.

On the other hand, when she met Margie's mother, she had this to say:

"She's a nice woman. The Jews are nice people but... they're not like us, you know. And I have to admit it surprises me a little that she's divorced."

Margie's mother, Alyssa, was another contradiction. She told Margie and me how she'd hated having to fast judiciously on Yom Kippur, even when she was a very young child:

"No food, no water — *nothing* — for twenty-five hours. I wasn't even allowed to brush my teeth!"

Much to Bubbe's dismay, Alyssa refused to subject her own children to this until they were, "old enough to understand and make the decision to fast, *themselves*."

Further heretical practices included putting up a small tree with lights every year, at the same time she set out the menorah, because, "My kids think the lights look pretty. And after all, what's the harm in a little tree?"

Alyssa was also adamant that her children should marry for love. "Don't do what I did," she proclaimed more than once, sometimes tearfully. "I married who my parents wanted me to marry and my husband and I made each other *miserable*. I finally got up the nerve to leave him and he made sure I paid for it. He left his own children *penniless*."

Despite her avowals regarding her children's future matrimonies, when Margie's older brother, David, announced he was engaged, Alyssa astounded everyone, including Bubbe, her own mother, when she asked, tentatively, "She Jewish, I hope. ...Right?"

She looked quite relieved when David answered, "Of course."

For Margie, this unanticipated preference on her mother's part was going to be a problem. By the time her brother got engaged, she and I were in college, though at separate schools. I was commuting every day to Suffolk College, but Margie had gone away to the University of Virginia, where, of all the people she could fall in love with, she'd fallen in love with Sean, a first-generation Irish-Catholic. He was as Irish-Catholic as they come, too. He had six brothers and sisters and went to church every

8

Sunday. He was also crazy about Margie and she about him. They wanted to get *married*.

"I didn't know it would matter to her," confided Margie to me, and I nodded sympathetically.

Margie and I had talked about our mothers and our relationships with them at great length over the years and we'd decided that they'd been affected by their individual childhoods far more than our own idiosyncratic upbringings had affected us. They'd been sorely pressured into getting married young and staying at home with kids. Margie and I had opportunities our mothers hadn't had, so we felt sorry for them and liable for their unhappiness. We couldn't fathom why we felt this sense of accountability. It never occurred to us once that they might have brought us up to feel it, because that was exactly the way they'd been brought up themselves.

At the end, we did love our mothers, but they frustrated us with their inconsistent values and long-held grudges. And every girl I knew had the same conflicted bond with her mother, except for Kurt's sister, Donna. Neither Margie nor I saw Donna's relationship with her mother as the only rational, balanced one to which we were exposed. Instead, we assumed that she and her mother 'weren't close', because the older Donna got, the less compelled she felt to please her mother rather than herself, and the more cautious about interfering in Donna's life her mother seemed to be.

Like the winter break after our first semester at college — I hadn't seen Margie or Donna since the summer before and neither had their parents. When the three of us met to make plans for what we'd do in the month before Donna and Margie had to fly back to their respective colleges, Donna said, "Keep in mind I'll only be here for a week. I'm going on a ski trip with some friends I met at school."

"Oh, my God! — you're not going to be here for Christmas?" I asked.

"Oh, my God! — what did your mother say?" added Margie.

Donna looked at both of us quizzically. "She said, 'Have fun and be careful.' "

I was puzzled now, too. "You mean... she's just going to let you go? She's not upset? She's still speaking to you?"

"I don't get it," Donna said. "Why should she be upset? It's not like I'm not going to see her again in May. That's only six months away."

At Donna's reply, Margie and I could only gawk at her.

"Oh, my God!" we said again.

Now, as Margie and I deliberated over the situation with Sean, she was biting her nails the whole time we talked. Our mothers' distinctive nurturing had left us just a tad on the anxious side. It was natural that we loved them and wanted their approval. What was not good was that we would eat ourselves up to get it. Margie's nails were bitten down so low they bled sometimes, and to combat *my* anxiety, I used to eat everything in sight. As a result, I was overweight and had gastrointestinal problems. Margie was pitifully thin and trying urgently to quit smoking. We were a mess, for sure. I guess that's why we'd clung to each other for so many years, like the only two surviving refugees of a war that had devastated our homeland. We felt such a solidarity that our only dissimilarity — our separate estimations on the 'Christ Concept' — had never come up between us in any substantial context. Until now.

I attempted the practical. "Do you think you'll be able to attend church with him if he asks?"

Margie looked surprised at the question, "Why not? I've been to church with *you*."

"Oh, sure," I replied sardonically. "And the first time you saw the statue of Jesus nailed to the Cross, you were petrified. You said you didn't sleep for a week."

"Well, I was alright when we went to Kurt and Donna's church."

I snorted. "That's a Protestant church. That's different."

Margie smiled. "It sure is. The experience was... more like a Scout meeting than a sermon." Tongue firmly in cheek, she said, "I didn't feel browbeaten after, like we're supposed to when we leave worship, you know? Their minister was *female*. And there was no incense."

We were on a roll now. I was laughing as I said, "I *know*. The incense at the Catholic Church almost gave Donna an asthma attack that one time she and Kurt came with us. And Angie Poulos told me that they use even *more* incense at the Greek Orthodox Church. Although, she didn't know why her church and the Catholic Church split, way back when. I've always wanted to know the reason."

Margie sobered suddenly. "I bet Sean knows. I wonder what he would say about Angie's or Kurt and Donna's church." She looked at me imploringly, biting her nails again. "I wonder if I should do this... marry him, I mean."

I said nothing. That was for her to decide.

She went on, "Do you know he feels guilty because we can't keep our hands off each other? He says his parents raised him that he should be a virgin until he got married."

10

"*Is* he?" I had to ask.

"Well... yes and no," she answered and then blushed. "I mean," she leaned in and whispered, "we have *oral* sex. But not intercourse. Sean says if his parents should ask him if he's a virgin, he wants to be able to answer them truthfully."

I nodded solemnly, "I see." Then, hiding my smirk, I leaned in, too and whispered back. "So... what do you think they're going to say when he 'truthfully' tells them you've had his dick in your mouth?"

*** ***

Margie eloped with her Irish-Catholic virgin and their families were pretty reasonable about it, all things considered. That changed when Margie became pregnant with a son. She and Sean had agreed to practice a blend of their religious customs with their children. But when they broke the joyful news to their parents that they were expecting, both sets wanted to know, "*Bris* or baptism?"

Margie was a wreck as she reported this to me, "We tried to say 'neither', but, I don't know... we just couldn't get that out. So we told them, 'both'."

"Both?" I repeated. "Will they let you have both?"

Separate discussions with priest and rabbi ensued, who bandied about divine phrases like, *"Covenant of Abraham,"* and *"One Holy Catholic and Apostolic Church."*

The young couple returned home, dejected. "They" weren't going to let them have both.

So they devised a daring scheme. They carefully researched a name for their new son and came up with "Jared," because it was biblical, but not specifically from the *Old Testament* or the *New*. After Jared's birth, they remained vigilant that no one from the Catholic side of the family saw him naked for his first few days.

"I don't want my mother asking us why we didn't have him circumcised in the hospital," Sean explained.

"And *she* would, for sure," added Margie.

Then, on the morning of the eighth day of his life, Jared was swabbed with iodine and had his foreskin removed. That same afternoon, he was swabbed with oil and splashed with water. Singing and praying accompanied both productions and the newborn's outfits (and diapers) were changed for each.

The plot was tough to pull off, but successful. Neither priest, with the paternal grandparents, nor rabbi, with the maternal grandparents, ever saw each other, nor knew there'd been any other sacred ritual. Moreover, Jared had a glorious childhood, rich in traditions from both sides of his family. Nonetheless, with so much duplicity entailed in having him, Margie and Sean never went for another child.

"I finally managed to quit smoking when I found out I was pregnant," said Margie. "But if I have to do this a second time and then for more than one First Holy Communion, Confirmation and Bar Mitzvah, I know I'll start again."

Donna and Kurt, with their usual "WASP-y" take on things, thought Margie and Sean's entire covert insurgency was absurd.

"I don't get it," Donna said, just as she and Kurt had dozens of times throughout our friendship. "Why the elaborate pretense, Margie? What terrible thing is going to happen if you and Sean *just tell* your parents what you want to do?"

Kurt nodded his agreement, "I mean, *holy cow —*" (another phrase we heard from them often) — "where is it written that bowing to our parents' wishes is compulsory no matter how old we get?"

And Margie replied to them just as she and I had dozens of times in the past, too. "Come *on*, you guys. That's just the way we do things. That's just what we were brought up to believe."

I understood perfectly why Margie and Sean felt they had to carry out their charade. I had my own struggles with my parents. One of the big ones was dealing with my mother's issuance of panicked edicts to me, owing to her unbridled fear of the unknown and my father's reluctance to intervene when she did. (Even when he might disagree with her.) To them, the world was a dangerous place for an eighteen-year-old girl. That's how I, who'd always loved books and school, ended up at a local junior college, rather than at any top-notch, four-year university for which my grades had qualified me.

When the time came for college applications, I asked for help with financial aid forms and here's what happened:

Mom: Are you out of your mind? We're not filling these out. You're not going to college.

Me: (shocked) What do you *mean?* Everybody goes to college!

Mom: (adamantly) Everybody does *not* go to college and *you're* not going!

12

Me: (horrified) Why *not?* Why can't I go?

Mom: Because you *can't,* that's why. You're not living on your own. You're too young!

Nonnie: (to me) "Why do you want to go to college? Why waste money? Get a job. Look at your cousin, Jeannie. She got a nice little job right after high school and now she has that new *Chevy.* She didn't need school to be smart enough to get a new car at her age. Wouldn't you rather get a nice job, a nice car and then get married?"

Me: (from horrified to terrified at that) Mom! Please!

Mom: (to my grandmother) Be *quiet,* Ma. Mind your business. (To me, shouting now) You're *not* going to college and *that's* the end of it!

Me: (to my father, in tears now) Dad! *Say* something!

Dad: (hesitantly, to my mother) I don't understand, Nancy. Why can't she go to college?

Nonnie: Uh-oh. *Holy shit!* Here we go.

Mom: (gaping at my father) Are you *kidding* me? (Shouting again) What — are you crazy, too? No! No! No! *No!*

So, I settled for going to a college close enough that I could commute. I could've gone away, of course, I was legally an adult, but my mother had threatened to disown me if I did and I didn't want to risk *that.*

I went to Suffolk Community College and held two jobs to pay for it, though it was hard doing that and carrying a full class load, too. So I had to take fewer courses per semester to keep up with everything. Margie and Donna would be finished with school long before I would, I knew. But I bought my own second-hand car and drove it back and forth from my parents' to my school, to my jobs, back to my parents' every day. And if I got home later than my mother anticipated I should, she'd be frantic that something had happened to me while driving and send my father out in *his* car to look for me, whom he'd find *for sure,* somewhere out on the opposite side of the highway, in a car crash. When I showed up at home, not dead, but just running late, she'd yell at me for worrying everyone. This happened more than once and got stressful after a while.

Nonnie said, "You're losing weight."

My mother said, "Of course she's losing weight. She's working two jobs, just to go to school. It's ridiculous."

I lost more weight and replaced my glasses with a pair of contact lenses.

My father said, "If God had wanted you to have contacts lenses, he would have put them in your eyes."

I gained weight back, lost it again, and popped antacids like M&M's. I argued with my parents and with my grandmother whenever she was there, which seemed like always, and stayed in my room as often as I could, doing homework, crying, or reading.

Ten years after I'd left the sixth grade, I was still in love with Ancient Greece. I'd been studying its art extensively at college now, memorizing the dimensions of the Parthenon's triglyphs and metopes. I knew which architect, long-gone to dust, had designed what significant bowl and statue. I'd learned how to tell the difference between Greek sculpture and Roman by the marble. I recognized clay vases and the painters of these by name, and from what parts of Greece they'd come. I'd had a full term's course on the life of Alexander the Great. I'd written papers on the works of Aristophanes, Euripides, Sophocles and more. From their tales I can still recite from memory which mythological son murdered his mother (Orestes), which "bad wife" was dreadfully misunderstood (Clytemnestra), who killed his own son and served him up to the gods as food (Tantalus), and on and on.

I was enthralled by it all and yearned to go to Greece. But, at twenty-one, my heroes and exhilarating voyages remained on the printed page. I'd hardly stepped a pinkie toe out of the area where I'd lived all my life, a limit which guaranteed that I still held naïve, judgmental attitudes about things and people I knew little about. I wished fervently that I could change my life, but had no idea how to make that happen.

And that was pretty much the girl I was when I met Gregori.

The Italian-American Meets the Greek

"I like two kinds of men — domestic and foreign."
–Mae West

It was 1979 and I was almost twenty-three years old. My parents had sold their house on Long Island and moved to Brooklyn to be near Nonnie. That gave me a good opportunity to get my own apartment. All right, it was only two blocks away from where my parents now lived, but it was a start. Now I was going to Queens College, pursuing a teaching degree, but having my own apartment meant that I could still only afford to attend part-time. So I had a fulltime job selling jewelry on The Diamond Exchange on 47th and 6th in Manhattan, and went to classes three nights a week. On Saturdays, I taught English as a Foreign Language at a language institute nearby. It was another tough schedule, but I felt better about myself than I had only a few years before.

Margie seemed happy, too. She and Sean married immediately after they'd graduated college and had Jared right away. Now Margie was quite content to, "stay at home with the baby for a few years and then we'll see," and Sean was working, believe it or not, with Margie's father, doing... who-knows-what.

"Doesn't matter what he's got him doing. He's finally helping out one of his kids, at least," huffed Alyssa.

Since Margie and Sean still lived on Long Island and our lifestyles had diverged, she and I didn't get to see each other often, though we still talked every day. However, Donna had moved to Manhattan after she'd graduated and was working in advertising, so she and I sometimes went out in the evenings when I wasn't in class, or met up for lunch in the city, down by Battery Park. And Kurt, who'd been a year ahead of us, was already working on his Master's Degree at New York University, so I got to spend time with him, too.

In fact, he and I even started a little 'thing', but it blew over rather quickly, and we went back to just being friends. To my mind, we were too different. I remember his telling me, "if you want to go away to school, stop crying about it, get the applications, take out student loans and *go*. Nobody can stop you but yourself." No matter how I tried to explain to him why I felt I couldn't do that, he simply never understood.

I'd also met another girl in one of my classes, Sharon, whom I'd introduced to Donna. We didn't know much about Sharon as yet, other than that she seemed sweet, but a bit 'boy-crazy'. What I mean by this specifically is that, as this was the pre-AIDS, post-women's lib era, she'd carry her diaphragm with her every time we went out on the weekends, "just in case she met someone," and talked about sex constantly. This was informative to Donna and me both, who were not nearly as prolific in that arena as Sharon was. We'd listen attentively as she entertained us with stories about her many trysts, which included a daring one at The New York Museum of Natural History. I still think of Sharon whenever anyone mentions the model of that giant blue whale they had suspended from the ceiling there.

15

On the night I met Gregori, Sharon and Donna had decreed I was spending too much time alone with my books and insisted I come out dancing with them. Sharon even bought me a new blouse to wear for the night out, a "late birthday present," she said.

"You look pretty," she cooed to me as she drove to the disco.

Donna looked back at me from the front passenger seat. "She does, doesn't she? You've lost so much weight since high school, Patricia, honestly. Your hair looks nice the longer length, too. And your own apartment!" she singsong-ed. "*Holy cow!* That's a big step for *you*, kiddo!"

"I guess so," I sighed forlornly.

Sharon giggled. "Now all we have to do is get her some good sex."

"Oh, be quiet, Sharon," I groused.

Donna laughed. "Yep. Especially since she broke up with Kurt. Did I tell you, Patricia, he's finally gotten over you and has been seeing someone?"

That comment, with its acerbic undertone, surprised me. "What do you mean, Donna? Kurt didn't have to 'get over me.' We went out for a while and decided it wasn't going to work, that's all. Kurt and I are still friends."

Sharon interjected, "You dated Donna's brother? I've met him. He's *so* cute."

"I never said he wasn't cute," I said defensively, "We just make better friends than we did boyfriend and girlfriend. He's not my type for that, that's all."

"What's 'your type'?" Sharon asked, curiously.

Not a 'Real' American, I thought. But out loud, I explained, "I guess I want someone who has things in common with me, like Sean does with Margie."

"You think *Sean* is like Margie?" Donna asked incredulously.

"In the important things, yes," I stated. "He... *gets* the way she thinks. But he's not like one of the guys we went to school with, who are so attached to what's familiar they're never going to leave the old neighborhood. He's special enough to be exciting to her, but enough *like* her to understand her."

Donna sounded genuinely hurt by my statements when she replied, "Maybe Kurt didn't excite you, Patricia, but he understands you, because he's known you for so long." She smiled at me now, to soften her words. "He understands your family is insane."

I shook my head. "That's just it, Donna," I said more gently now, too. "They're not insane. They're just... Italian."

16

"But *you're* not. You're American," Donna pointed out.

I looked out the side window and said forlornly a second time, "I guess so."

Sharon's next remark lightened things up. "Well, you just let me know, Donna, if that hunky brother of yours ever becomes available again. I'd do him in a heartbeat. Right in the backseat of this car, in fact."

"Hey — I'm sitting back here!" I said and we laughed.

Sharon and Donna were laughing again as they went off to dance at the club we'd chosen for the evening. I yawned as I watched them from where I stood off to the side. It was Friday. I'd worked all day and had to get up early the next morning to be at the language school. I wasn't in a partying mood.

"Excuse me, *meess*? Can I ask you a question?"

I turned. A squat, young man with a receding hairline, eye-catching smile, and a moustache like Groucho Marx, was leaning toward me. "Yes?" I asked, politely.

"Why *eesn't* a nice *gell* like you dancing?"

Whoa — witty pick-up line. And that accent — was it for real?

I didn't care to find out. "I'm sorry. I just don't feel like dancing right now."

His face fell. "Aw... too bad," he said, and walked away. I started to regret letting Sharon and Donna talk me into this. I looked to see where they'd gone.

And as I looked, I saw him.

He stood over six feet tall. He had a lean body, which he displayed well, but not too blatantly, in slim-fitting jeans and a white designer shirt. He'd left the two... no, *three*... top buttons of the shirt undone, so that all the women (including me) could admire how the glimpse of his tanned chest looked against the white cloth. He wore a thin gold chain around his neck, from which a cross, gold as well, dangled and peeked. The sight of that cross nestling in his black chest hair somehow generated lust in me, not piety. The face went well with the body. Chiseled nose and cheekbones, sculpted like those on the Greek statues of the chariot racers I'd seen in my art classes. Thick, smooth lips, dark brows, dark lashes, and eyes the color of Metaxa Seven Star Brandy. All topped by thick, curly hair, so black it reflected the lights above us as well as a mirror could.

He was looking at me. He started walking over.

Thank you, thank you, Sharon and Donna.

17

I feigned nonchalance as he came up close, bent down and whispered in my ear, "Why *eesn't* a nice *gell* like you dancing?"

What the...? They couldn't *be twins!*

Casually I asked him, "There was a short, balding fellow over here just a moment ago. Do you know each other?"

He gave me a rueful look. "That was my friend, Aleko. I'm Gregori."

Ah. So the opening line was something they'd come up with together, then.

"Is it rude to ask where you're both from?" I continued.

"Not at all," he responded, politely. "We're from Greece."

Jackpot.

I smiled at him. "Well, Gregori, I'm Patricia. I'd love to dance with you."

He didn't smile back, but he nodded and gestured me to the dance floor. As we wound our way through the other couples, I saw Sharon and Donna, who'd stopped dancing in disbelief as they watched *me*... with Gregori.

Being seen by my friends with someone who looked like him was exhilarating, but to be honest, the dance he and I shared was anything but. He didn't smile once, nor did he speak to me as we moved together. I got the impression he wasn't comfortable dancing, because his movements were a bit stilted. He kept his hands at his sides and did the same shuffling step, back and forth. He rarely looked down at me either, mostly gazed across the room as though he were waiting for the whole thing to be over. I worried that maybe he wasn't enjoying being with me, so I took a mental step back from my eagerness, just in case that were true. But I'd fretted for nothing, I guess, because at the end of the dance, he asked for my phone number.

Sharon sounded as ecstatic over this as I was. "He was *beeeeautiful*," she rhapsodized on the drive home. "And foreign. How sexy is that?"

Even Donna was bowled over. "That *accent*. It made even his little friend kind of cute."

I nodded my agreement vigorously. I'd finally met someone who, as I'd tried to explain to Donna, wasn't "the boy next door."

Little did I know that, in not wanting to, I'd done exactly that. He was just "the boy next door," in somebody else's neighborhood.

I couldn't wait to call Margie the next day and tell her. I couldn't wait until he phoned.

*** ***

18

On our first date, when I answered the door to Gregori, he stunned me anew with his looks. He was dressed impeccably, wearing a beautiful sports jacket and Italian leather shoes, which matched his belt perfectly. His socks bore the *Gucci* logo. I was impressed. It was a positive thing looking at him was such a pleasant pastime for me. There wasn't much else to occupy me at first. We went to a movie and having coffee afterward, once again, he didn't smile and barely spoke. When he did speak, it was only to say, "Did you enjoy the movie?" And, "I don't mind American coffee, but I prefer Greek."

But lowered eyes and banal commentary did not alter his effect on me. His inflections were so intriguing, that when he *did* say something, no matter what it was, it *sounded* fascinating. Nonetheless, it was a little tough groping for topics to get him talking.

Then I came up with, "What was it like for you when you first came to live in the United States?" That question was a real motivator.

"Horrible," he said. He shook his head. "I was thirteen. The *first* month I got here, I was on my bicycle, getting milk for my mother, when I got hit by a car. I got hurt badly and my bicycle was ruined. People jumped out of cars and surrounded me, asking questions, probably like, 'Where do you live? Are you hurt?' But I couldn't answer because I didn't know how to speak English. I couldn't even explain where I lived, so somebody could take me home." He shrugged. "Tough way to start out, yes?" Then he finally smiled a quick, sort of embarrassed smile. And when he did, I might as well have married him right then and been done with it, because that first smile hit me *hard*.

It was... an imperfect one. His front teeth, though white and clean, were as tiny as baby teeth and coupled by very wide gums. This one physical flaw delighted me. He wasn't conceited or aloof. He'd been self-conscious, that was all. Perhaps he was even *shy*.

Then there was that story he'd told. It was achingly familiar. My father told stories about how he'd struggled with the language too, when he'd first come to the United States. Anyone would have felt compassion when hearing about Gregori's experience, but to me, it was heart crushing. Because his story was like my father's, Gregori was *like* my father, I imagined. And he was shy. A virtue and an endearing quality, both assigned hastily to him by my green little brain. Simultaneously, this association with my father that I'd clicked upon made Gregori less of a foreigner to me than some of my American-born counterparts.

Like Kurt again. I remember the day I decided Kurt and I would have to go back to our previous platonic relationship. One of my boy cousins from my father's side came to visit me at my apartment and Kurt was there. I introduced him as "my boyfriend", and my cousin decided this warranted he hug Kurt. But before he could get close enough to do that, Kurt jumped back as though he'd been scalded. Then he held his hand *waaay* out in front of himself, ostensibly to shake hands, but in actuality to approximate the distance he required between my encroaching cousin and himself. What's more, I'd never seen Kurt and his father hug, either. They shook hands, too, like business associates. It struck me as jarring that he'd rebuffed my cousin's warm exuberance. I was used to men kissing each other, giving each other light, playful slaps on the face (and other body parts). Not an hour after he'd done that, the three of us decided to order pizza. As my cousin and I were deep in discussion about where we should order it from, Kurt said, "What difference does it make? Pizza's just pizza."

When I scowled at him for that, my cousin laughed and said, "Man, Kurt, are you in trouble. Saying that to an Italian girl, that's like *blasphemy.*"

Ironically, just as I was thinking back to that, Gregori asked me, "Do you consider yourself more American, or more Italian?"

"More Italian," I said immediately, and then added my usual postscript, "I guess."

"Do you speak Italian?"

"I took a few years at school."

"Your parents didn't teach you?"

"No, because my mother doesn't speak it much, either."

"But, her parents were born in Italy. Why didn't they teach her?" he asked.

"I don't know."

"Yet you still consider yourself Italian."

I rephrased it, "No, I *feel* more Italian. The American culture is so different than what I'm used to from my parents. Americans have different family values than we do... they eat differently, they dress differently—"

"I know!" he jumped in. "The first time I saw a group of American businessmen, I couldn't believe how they were dressed. Their ties didn't reach their belt buckle and their shoes looked like... what crippled people have to wear to walk better."

That description made me laugh. Encouraged, Gregori went on earnestly, "And they don't let you touch them. I swear, Patricia, when I

20

came from Greece and went to school here, I had to remind myself not to touch anybody. In Greece, everybody touches everybody."

Still laughing, I said, "Italians do that, too."

"But, here's what I don't understand," he continued, at ease by now, "they're comfortable letting strangers see them naked. When I go to the gym, nobody has a towel around their waists after their shower. They have business conversations, they shake hands with each other, and they're *completely* naked. They don't like to be hugged, but they don't mind strangers seeing their…" he gestured toward his trousers and shook his head.

I understood his way of thinking. Public nudity, even in communal locker rooms, was something we first-generation Italian-Americans were taught was a mortal sin, too. That and not wearing shoes, which my grandmother admonished us, "only 'gypsies' did."

Once again, I was reminded of poor Kurt, sitting happily bare-assed in my kitchen, reading one of his course books on investment banking, and me hissing at him to put some clothes on. "I don't get it, Trish. There's no one here besides us," he'd said.

"It's a cultural quirk, all right," I chuckled with Gregori. Then smiling wickedly, I added, "But maybe the reason they feel so comfortable naked, is because they look so much better like that than they do in those clothes."

He laughed uproariously at that and I was pleased he approved. But if anyone else had been sitting with us, they would have pointed out how smug we sounded.

"What about your family?" I asked, "I know you said you have an older brother who lives in Yonkers near his wife's family and your mother and father live in Queens, with you. Is there any family left in Greece?"

He made a circling motion with his open palm I'd learn was a Greek gesture that signified, 'surplus'. "Plenty. In Greece, Australia and South Africa, too. My mother has thirteen brothers and sisters, and my father has ten. All on both sides had kids. I also have an aunt and uncle who live in Astoria near us. You?"

"I've got lots of aunts, uncles, and first cousins, too. The cousins I'm closest to are three of my girl cousins on my father's side, Marie, Marietta, and Josephine. Marietta and Marie are both first daughters of two of my uncles. It's an Italian tradition to name first children after the grandparents on the father's side. Josephine was a second daughter — she's Marie's younger sister — so she was named for her grandmother on her *mother's* side," I explained.

21

"That's the way to do it. That's what we do, too."

"My mom bucked the system, though," I told him. "She said, 'We've got *four* Mariettas plus the original. It's ridiculous. My daughter is getting her own first name.' "

"Your mother said that? Strange."

When we discussed my mother's freer-thinking perspective, his manner was cool, whereas mine was admiring. The implications of that still didn't hit me when he added resolutely, "My son's name will be Nicholas, after my father."

I just thought, *How sweet that he loves his father so.*

"What about grandparents? Are any of yours still living?" Gregori went on.

I nodded, "One grandmother."

"Mari-etta?" he said the name with that charming intonation again.

"No, Graziella, my mother's mother." I chuckled as I thought of her. "In English, she's called 'Grace', and that's a real misnomer." When I saw he didn't get my meaning, I elaborated, "She's about as different as possible from the way my other grandmother was."

He tilted his head, questioningly, "How so?"

I smiled and leaned back. He was going to enjoy this story. "Well, for starters, she swears. All the time, in fact."

He laughed. "I have an aunt who does that, my Uncle Sotiri's wife, Marina. It's really amazing the things she'll say."

"My grandmother, too. And she's been married four times."

The smile fell from his face instantly. "*Four* times?"

I giggled gleefully and ticked off her husbands' names on my fingers, "There was my real grandfather, Carlo, then 'Grandpa' John, 'Grandpa' Sal and another 'Grandpa' Sal. She's still married to the second Sal. My cousins and I all call him, 'Grandpa' Sal *Two*."

Gregori shook his head in disbelief. "I don't think I even know anybody who's been married four times. No one in my family has ever been divorced." Clearly he didn't see the amusing side to this and it surprised me. My friends unanimously agreed my grandmother led an exciting life for her age.

"Oh, she didn't divorce them all," I corrected Gregori, drolly. "The only one she divorced was my real grandfather. Her second and third husbands died. Contrary to popular family rumor, she didn't kill them, though."

He looked shocked. "What do you mean?"

My tone should've indicated I was joking. Perhaps there was a language barrier. I tried again.

"Well, 'Grandpa' John died before I was born, so I got this story second-hand, from my aunt. She told me that one night, my grandmother — we call her 'Nonnie', by the way — made 'Grandpa' John's favorite — spaghetti with *salsa puttanesca*. Do you know what that is?"

"I know *puttanesca* sounds a lot like the Greek word for 'harlot'."

Grinning, I said, "The meaning is the same in Italian. *Salsa puttanesca* literally means 'sauce of the harlot'."

"An appropriate name for your grandmother's sauce."

That stopped me short. "What do you mean?"

He waved a hand dismissively. "Bad joke. Go on."

I wasn't *that* naïve. I got what he meant, but I chose to give him the benefit of the doubt. So I went on as though he hadn't spoken, "Harlot's Sauce is a spicy tomato sauce invented by prostitutes in Naples. They cooked it because it could be made quickly, you know," — I winked at him — "between clients. Since they were poor, they couldn't add meats to it, but even with a limited choice of ingredients, those women were able to create something delicious. The sauce became popular all throughout southern Italy. My grandmother added meats to create her own adaptation, and everybody in my family loves it. 'Grandpa' John loved it, too. She made that sauce for him the night he died. She found him dead at the dinner table, faced down in his plate of pasta."

Gregori whispered almost fearfully, "What did she put in it?"

"Oh, for Pete's sake," I finally said. "She didn't *poison* him, if that's what you're thinking. She just put his plate of pasta in front of him; went back in the kitchen just for a *minute*, because he asked for some grated cheese to go with it. Which, knowing her, she probably left off the table deliberately, since she hates cheese so much. And when she came back—"

"She hates cheese?" Gregori cut in. "How is that possible? I thought all Italians like cheese."

I shrugged. "Not my grandmother. My father doesn't, either."

This news was evidently astounding to Gregori. "*Both* of them? What do they eat, then?"

"The same things we eat. Just without cheese."

"*My God,*" he said. I could see he was a man who understood the value of food.

"Do you like pizza?" I blurted.

23

"I do," he replied. "I'm particular about it, though. That probably sounds silly."

I shook my head and looked at him, somewhat dreamily. "It doesn't. Not at all."

Gregori stared back with his own kind of interest, momentarily. Then he cleared his throat. "*Um...* how did your grandmother's third husband die?"

That brought me back. "Oh. Well... there was a stray black cat that got into my grandmother's kitchen one day."

"*Uh oh.* Bad luck," he said.

Now that was more like it. He was finally getting caught up in my 'Nonnie stories'.

Pleased, I said, "That's exactly what my grandmother thought. She was convinced it was that black cat that caused the first 'Grandpa' Sal to have his heart attack. Luckily, he recovered and when he came home from the hospital, she did her best to care for him so he wouldn't have another. Her methods to accomplish this were not the best. She was determined that he stop smoking, but he was seventy-five, had smoked all his life and refused to give it up. So they fought about it. *All* the time. Even the neighbors complained about their shouting matches. One day, he got sick of her nagging, packed up and went to his son's house."

"So they *did* get a divorce," Gregori said.

"Not exactly," I said wryly. "They were in... negotiations, which my grandmother insists were about a reconciliation. But those 'discussions' were stressful for him, too, and he had another heart attack. Sadly, this one was fatal. And you know what my grandmother said when his son called to tell us?"

Gregori shook his head.

"She said, 'You *see*? Those *bastards*. I bet they let him smoke.' So it became the family joke that she'd killed those two husbands."

"That's some story," Gregori said.

I smiled grimly this time. "It gets better. His children had the locks changed on the house she and 'Grandpa' Sal had shared. She went home one day and her key wouldn't work. So she walked to a pay phone and called our house. My father answered and Nonnie told him to send my mother over to help her break in. My father didn't want my mother to help."

"I'm not surprised," interjected Gregori.

I nodded my concurrence and continued, "So Nonnie said, 'Listen, you *son-of-a-bitch*, they're trying to steal my house. You tell my daughter to get over here, or I'm going to break a window with my shoe and these *bastard* neighbors of mine, who can't mind their own business, are going to call the police! Do you want your mother-in-law to go to jail?"

Gregori was looking quite forbidding. "Your grandmother called your father a 'son-of-a-bitch'?"

"She calls everyone that," I said airily. "She even calls her own kids that sometimes."

"What did your father do then?"

"What *could* he do? It's his mother-in-law, after all. My mother drove over to help, as she was told. And Nonnie was right — the neighbors did call the police." I said laughingly, "I would've loved to have seen what my father would've done if they'd actually arrested my mother and grandmother."

"That would have been something, all right."

"But my grandmother must've suspected 'Grandpa' Sal's kids were up to something, because she'd been carrying the deed to the house in her handbag. It had her name right on it. She pointed that out to the police officers. There was nothing they could do after that. You can't get arrested for breaking into your own house. As a matter of fact, they even helped pick the lock."

Gregori just stared at me after I finished the story. I could tell that he didn't think it was at all funny. I was surprised. Kurt had almost split a gut when I'd told it to *him*.

After a moment Gregori asked, "You said your father's family is from Sicily. What did *they* think of your grandmother?"

I shook my head, "They didn't like her. Or my mother. They didn't want my father to marry my mother."

"I'm not surprised," Gregori said again.

His censure at last penetrated my hormone-clogged interpretations. I gave him a steely look then and said smoothly, "Oh, but my father didn't care one whit what his family thought. He adored my mother *then* and he adores her *now*. As far as my father's concerned, my mother comes first, whether his family approves or not."

Gregori raised an eyebrow. "Really?" he said.

"Absolutely," I affirmed.

Based solely on this, we could have learned so much about who we each were and what we'd become later in life. Instead, the entire time we were together that evening, my foremost thought was not on *why* he was wearing

25

that brooding expression, but on how much I liked the way it looked on him. *He's gorgeous* and *he's Greek!* was the refrain playing in my mind.

He also made up for some of his condemnation of my parents by siding with them when I told him they hadn't wanted me to go away to school. He didn't approve of my family's matriarchal structure and their not teaching me to speak Italian, but keeping me home for college, he did. Strangely, this gave me a sense of relief.

"Of course they wanted you to stay at home. Why should you want to go away from your parents, anyway? There's a lot that can happen to a young girl when she's away at school. Not that I'm trying to give you the evil eye."

I looked at him in surprise. "People believe in that in Greece, too?"

"Who doesn't?"

"My American friends laugh when I talk about it."

"What do *they* know?" he said.

So there it was. Gregori was perfect for me. I didn't want a 'real' American boy who didn't understand *any* of what I'd grown up with and valued. I wanted to keep the great traditions from my background, discarding only the bits that restrained me. But a boy who'd be happy living out the whole of his life in the vicinity where we just happened to be born, never learning or seeing anything new, was not for me, either. Gregori was an exquisite combination of the intrepid, yet comfortable. Precisely what I thought I wanted.

As for him, when I asked him later on what he'd found appealing about *me* when we first met, *he* said, "Your breasts."

So I suppose we deserved each other. It was a match made in heaven, or more like Zeus's Olympus, with all the elements of Greek tragedy and comedy.

A few months later, we were lovers. (Unhappily, that part of our relationship — for me, anyway — was a lot like our first dance. But I assumed this would fix itself as we got to know one another.)

And soon we were planning a trip to Greece together.

My first trip to Greece. I couldn't believe it was happening at last.

Chapter Two: The Island of Rhodes

"Many cities of men he saw and learned their minds,
many pains he suffered, heartsick on the open sea . . ."
–Homer, *The Odyssey*

Get a Room

I wondered if it could possibly be as beautiful as I'd dreamed.

The answer was, *yes*.

First, there were the colors. Most notably, the color of the sea. The color of the sea in Rhodes was… exactly blue. That was it. Not a touch of green, just primary, translucent blue. It looked like India ink, even up close. When I sunk my legs down into the Aegean, I was astonished that the color blue coated me and changed the tone of my skin.

The water was also cold. A bit too cold for me, but Gregori loved it. "Who wants to swim in bath water?" said he.

Personally, I prefer warmer water, but still, it was perfect to cool down my skin after a swim, when I lay on the sand, letting the sun bake me and the sea salt dry in powdery rivulets on my skin. The water was also so clean that when I swam out, I could see the rocks and the kelp deep below. Tiny black fish swam past, unperturbed, but quickly scattered if I raised my foot. I scooped the water up into my hand. Instead of blue, the water in my palm was perfectly clear.

There were so many shades of blue in Greece. The sky was another, lighter and pristine. In Rhodes (*Rodos*), as in all of Greece in the summertime, the sky was never any other color and bad weather never interfered with outdoor plans. I learned later that even when it did rain in Greece, in the wintertime, it was as operatic as everything else about the country and the people. It came down suddenly, pouring a deluge and flooding the streets. Then just as abruptly, it stopped. The sun burst out and brilliant red poppies and silver snails made an instantaneous, dramatic appearance.

The sun in Greece shone not just from the sky, but from everywhere. It didn't only reflect off the flowers, leaves, buildings, and sea; it seemed to erupt from within them, making every object blindingly vibrant. The sun was the reason houses and churches were painted in such a vivid palette, or else just stark, chalky white. It affected the paint over time, until the brightness became warm and faded and the white of the stucco buildings appeared to meld with nature's choice of tones for the earth, sea, and sky. Those hues of blue, golden yellow, terracotta, magenta, pristine white, would become indelibly inked on my heart.

I started to climb one of the enormous, black lava rocks that jutted high above the water.

"Watch out for *ahee-nous*," said Gregori. "I don't know how to say them in English, but they're sharp and they go in your feet if you walk on them."

He was pointing to a smattering of black shadows that were sticking out from the parts of the rocks that were underwater: spiky sea urchins. They were a metaphor for this first holiday in Greece. Enjoy the unusual and the beautiful on offer, but... be careful where you step.

Gregori's and my first "romantic holiday" to Greece together was like a prophecy from the Oracle at Delphi of what married life would be like for us over the next two decades. But the bad bits of that trip were so flavored with the thrill of my finally being in Greece, that I never analyzed what they might mean in a permanent relationship. I was in love, not just with a Greek, but with Greece and the island of Rhodes.

At six o'clock in the evening, in the summertime, the sea in Rhodes was at its warmest, having been heated by the sun all day. But as the sun set sometime around nine in the evening, the air quickly lost its warmth. The nights were cool and occasionally breezy, with a deceptively soft wind called *mel-tee-mee*.

"Make sure you bring a sweater when we go out at night," Gregori cautioned me. "The coolness can be uncomfortable after such hot days. And you'll get muscle stiffness from it. It's just like air-conditioning. If I sleep with it on all night, I always get stiff the next day."

"You don't like air-conditioning?" I asked.

"Not many Greeks do. Very few homes or hotels, with the exception of the hotels that cater to American tourists, are air-conditioned. That's why Greeks here keep their shutters closed at night, too. The *mel-tee-mee* has the same effect as air-conditioning. We knew a woman who woke up paralyzed from stroke. When her family saw that she'd slept with her shutters open, they knew her stroke had been caused by the cold draft coming in."

"Oh, come on, Gregori," I scoffed gently, "she didn't get paralysis from a draft."

Gregori insisted earnestly, "She *did*. It permanently froze her muscles."

I couldn't resist teasing him over this. I said mischievously, "*Wow.* It makes you wonder how all the Cubbies fans in Chicago are still able to move, doesn't it?"

It wasn't a joke to Greeks, however. I soon learned that 'Chill Fear' was engrained in them. Babies in carriages were remarkably well covered and perspiring and people did keep their windows closed tightly at night to keep out that draft. I suppose this explained why there were no screens on the windows of many of even the most luxurious homes or hotels. Why bother to have screens when you had no intention of letting in air?

What I didn't know was that screen-less hotel windows would play a significant role in my visit to Rhodes that summer, which would connect to Gregori's hard-pressed ideal not to oppose the dating conduct standard expected there at the time.

When Gregori invited me to travel to Greece and meet his family, I was over the moon. To a Greek, meeting family meant that the relationship was "serious." Then Gregori informed me I'd be staying in a hotel on my own and he'd have to stay with relatives at their home on the island. He worked his way around to telling me this by unraveling "the code."

"Rhodes is my uncle's home. He got married a few years back and has two young daughters now," he explained. "I *have* to be their guest, or they'll be offended."

"Don't they get any relatives visiting them?"

"Sure they do. Like I told you, my uncle has twelve brothers and sisters, including my mother. All of them and their children visit, because it's where they were born. They don't *all* come at once, but every summer, there are some who stay with my uncle. It's the way we do things."

"Every summer?" I repeated, amazed. "I guess everyone helps with the extra expenses for the larger meals, the laundry and so forth?"

He seemed taken aback by that. "Of course not. It's not acceptable to take money from family when they're staying with you. They're *guests.* Maybe some of the other women help my aunt cook and clean, but they can't offer money. That would insult my uncle."

I thought about all this. Then I said, "Listen, I don't think I'd feel comfortable staying at your aunt and uncle's house. I'd rather stay at a hotel."

"Oh, that's perfect then," he said, sounding relieved. "Because you see… *you* can't stay at my uncle's house. I mean… we're not *engaged*, so I have to stay with them and… you have to stay in a hotel by yourself."

"But surely, since I'd be going there *with* you, they'll expect us to want to stay *together*, at a hotel?" I asked, thoroughly confused.

"*No*, we can't do that. Then they'll assume we're lovers." He was getting exasperated that I just wasn't following this. "We're not supposed to be obvious about that, so they can pretend not to know. Because we're not engaged," he repeated. "And if we ever… *wanted* to be engaged, they'd remember that we were lovers *before* we were engaged."

I was really at a loss. "Which would mean…?" I prompted.

He'd shifted from exasperated to ill at ease. "Which would mean that, in their eyes, you… weren't a nice girl. Because you let me… *you know*. They'd have a hard time accepting you as my wife. They're… old-fashioned."

I could feel my face get red at that. "Let me just see if I've got this. They *know* we're lovers, but if we don't stay together at the hotel, they can pretend *not* to think I'm not a nice girl? Because if they already *know*, doesn't that already make me, 'not nice'?"

"Aha! But if *I* don't stay with you at the hotel, they'll get the message that *I* see you as a 'good type' of girl, a girl I might want to *marry* someday. Don't you see? I'm doing it for *you*."

I stayed silent, thinking. I knew some relatives we had in Italy held similar beliefs. Furthermore, my own grandmother warned me that girls don't go away with their boyfriends if they wanted that boyfriend to marry them. "He's from the old world. I know how they think. Why buy the cow when he can get the milk for free?"

Yes, she'd *really* said that.

I thought back to that now, as Gregori put his arms around me to reassure me. "Come on… it'll be all right. We'll find ways to be alone together. It will be fun. You'll love it. I promise."

What could I say if he put it that way? I smiled hesitantly, "All right, Gregori."

He kissed me. "Good girl."

And that was one reason I stayed at a hotel, alone, when I was on my first trip to Greece *with* my boyfriend. But there was more to this that I only found out after I got to Rhodes. It had to do with the Swedish girls.

The tourism laws in Greece allow a ten percent overbooking for hotels and airlines in order to offset any cancellations. That summer, Americans were beginning to discover what Europeans already knew — Greece was an ideal holiday spot. The unanticipated American tourists meant *no one* had cancelled. As a result, travelers were turned away from hotels and flights out, despite having confirmed reservations. The tourist police were going mad trying to find places to put the extra people, who were sleeping on benches in parks, or anywhere else they could find; their luggage propped next to them.

Gregori didn't tell me about this situation before I left the United States. He didn't want to scare me off, he said. But he hadn't managed to book me a room by the time I arrived. Luckily, a cousin of his, Mihali, who lived on the island, had done some masonry work at a hotel not too far from Gregori's uncle's house. This gave Mihali, in Greek slang language, "*meh-son,*" meaning a 'connection' at this hotel. The "*meh-son*" was the sole reason I was able to get a room. Unfortunately, the only room available was a chambermaid's room, which had a bed and sink, but no bath or toilet. I had to use the employee toilet down the hall. The day manager assured us I'd get a "better" room the next day. After a ten-hour flight from New York to Athens and waiting in the Athens airport for my connecting flight to Rhodes for another eight hours, I longed for a shower. It wasn't to be. But at least I wasn't sleeping in the park. That's why the moment I got the room, I dropped my cases, changed and Gregori took me to the beach.

The next day, a single-occupancy room became available. It wasn't much bigger than the maid's room, but it did have a shower with a private toilet. And a large window… with no screens, naturally.

This was the first thing I pointed out to Gregori when he brought my luggage up. "What if I want to leave the window open to get some air?"

"You know what I told you about that, but if you insist, just leave the shutters open."

"But mosquitoes will fly in."

"Mosquitoes? There are no mosquitoes here." I must have given him a dubious look, because he amended, "Anyway, even if there are, it's windy at night, like I told you. The mosquitoes don't fly when it's windy. Now, I'm sure you want to get unpacked, have a shower. I'll meet you downstairs."

I smiled at him shyly. "Why don't you just wait here, if you like? I won't be long."

An odd look crossed his face. "*Er…* look. Because I told the desk clerk I was your fiancé, he let me bring your cases up, but I'm not supposed to be up here. Two people are not allowed to stay in a single room."

31

"Doesn't the hotel know we only got the single room because there was nothing else available?"

"Yes, but they've had big problems with foreign woman renting single rooms and there's a new rule. It's because of the Swedes."

As Gregori shed light on that cryptic statement, I detected that potentially 'loose' women were a source of preoccupation for Rhodians. That was because they had first-hand experience with the havoc wreaked by such females, in the form of — *Ta Da!* — the Swedish female tourists.

Swedish female tourists, according to the Hellenic standards back then, were, to use Gregori's phrase once again, "not nice girls," because their country had no double standards in sexual deportment. Gregori told me that these 'wenches' were mesmerizing the poor local boys. And *that* was because all 'good' Greek girls knew better than to indulge any sexual appetite they might have, as this would ruin them for marriage. A dire fate, apparently, from which Gregori was clearly doing his best to spare me.

But the Swedish female tourists "looking for a good time" had no fear of being pronounced unmarriageable. I guess, unlike my grandmother, they prescribed to a different old chestnut, "Why buy the whole pig, if you only want a little sausage?"

The young Swedish girls would partake with abandon of Greece's handsome and horny men. The siren-like Swedes lured the local males into their 'single person only' hotel rooms, their unusual-in-the-Aegean, blue-eyed, blonde-haired beauty making it *impossible* for the Greek men to resist. Consequently, the willing-to-frolic foreigners were creating an inequity in the summer social lives of the Hellenic youth. Greek girls were left with no male companionship. They felt rejected and started to get ideas that their parents didn't like.

It put the hotels in a fix, too. Other hotel guests, who weren't there strictly for bonking and binge drinking, would complain about the noisy local boys going in and out of the various rooms all night. As a result, the *Ministry of Tourism* passed a new law which decreed that no foreign women could have any male locals up in her single-occupancy room.

Needless to say, staying at the hotel by myself, and now discovering that Gregori and I wouldn't even be able to make love there, put a completely different slant on our holiday. It was now like a high school class trip, with the activities of Gregori and me, along with the rest of the boys and girls, being watched very carefully by two diligent chaperones—the Greek government and Gregori's relatives.

Relatives, Relatives, Relatives

> *"My uncle's dying wish — he wanted me*
> *on his lap. He was in the electric chair."*
> –Rodney Dangerfield

They were charming, welcoming, and endless. Gregori had a great number of family members on the island and an even greater obsession with pleasing them. There were his uncle and aunt on his mother's side and their two young daughters. Living in a flat upstairs above them was a single uncle. There was the cousin, Mihali, with the hotel *meh-son*. (I remembered his name, at least.) Mihali lived further out, in a small village, with his wife, two children, and his parents. He had siblings, too — two brothers with wives, children, and a sister and her brood. Then there was an ancient, adorable couple who... I never did get it straight how *they* were related. Those were just the relatives who *lived* on Rhodes. There were also visiting aunts, uncles, and cousins from Australia and South Africa, and Gregori's brother and sister-in-law, from the States. I don't know where the local relatives managed to put all these visitors, as the only visitor not staying with a family member was me.

Just trying to keep their names straight was mind-boggling.

Gregori held my arm as he introduced me, "Patricia, this is my cousin Mihali's wife, Soulah. Next to her, on her right, is my Uncle Niko's wife, Roulah. On Roulah's right, is their *koumbara* (best man's wife), Noulah. Across from Noulah, we have Roulah's brother's fiancée Voulah. And, of course, you know my brother Gerry's wife, Thoulah."

Soulah, Roulah, Noulah, Voulah, and Thoulah. He wasn't pulling my leg.

There were also two female cousins from Australia, both named Vasiliki, after their grandmother, of course. But one went by 'Viki' and the other by 'Kiki'.

"That way we know which one you're talking to when you call us!" they said.

There were also a great number of *Marias,* just like in my family and amongst the men, there were *Gregoris, Gerasimos,* (which was Gregori's brother's full name*)* and *Nikos* everywhere, some of whom even had both the same first *and* family name. The way the 'Gregoris' and the 'Nikos' of the same first and last name were told apart in conversation, was to mention who their dads were. But this can only work for a maximum of three generations in the same family. Depending on how long you live, there'll eventually be someone in your family with your first name *and* the same sire's name.

Niko's wife, Roulah gave me this grammar lesson, "The family name ending has a masculine and feminine form. The ending difference indicates *possession*, meaning that daughters only, *belong* to their fathers. And if a woman takes her husband's name, the difference between her version of that last name and his specifies that she's owned no longer by her *father*, but by her *husband* now."

One of the Australian cousins, Kiki, (or was it Viki?) added, "Yes, but I just read that some prominent women in Greece have begun to reject the use of the 'possessive' form of their family names, insisting they also be called by the masculine form."

"That's just what we need, Viki — socialites and politician's wives changing the Greek language," Gregori remarked.

It sounded like Gregori was only joking with Viki, but his Uncle Niko admonished him, "You're a chauvinist, Gregori. You get that from your father."

"My father's not a chauvinist," Gregori responded firmly.

When Niko lifted an eyebrow at Gregori, I saw the family resemblance. "*Isn't* he? He yelled his head off at me once, because he saw me helping your Aunt Roulah do the dishes."

"Niko, that's enough," Roulah stopped her husband. "You don't want Patricia to get a bad impression." Then to me, she said, "Don't pay attention to Niko. He likes to tease. Gregori's father is a very nice man."

Though Gregori had been reproached for his remark to his cousin, everyone in the company agreed with his statement that the American custom of calling someone after their father, as a 'Junior', was, "a practice which makes no sense at all. How can one name a child after oneself?"

I think I was the only one who saw that pronouncement as incongruous.

Names in Gregori's family were, without a doubt, important to everyone. They were explained to me with the same degree of solemnity as biblical 'begats'. I found myself memorizing the elocutions thereof, just as I'd memorized science classifications in high school — fretfully and with little success. Thankfully there were 'godparents' or friends of the family so close that they were given the titles, *Thio*, meaning "uncle" and *Thia*, meaning "aunt." This became my saving grace. I called everyone who was older than I, *"Thio"* or *"Thia."* It was respectful and saved my brain cells from fatigue.

The conversation that first evening was conducted in English for my benefit. Almost everyone spoke English, although they all had different accents depending on where they'd been educated or where they lived. And everyone of Gregori's parents' generation spoke Italian fluently.

"We speak Italian because Mussolini took over Rhodes during World War II and made us all Italian citizens," *Thio* Niko informed me.

"Did he?" I asked. Once more, I was intrigued by Greek history. I knew about ancient Greece, but this more recent past I didn't.

Thio Niko badgered Gregori again, "What's the matter, Gregori? Too lazy to let the young lady know the history of the island where you were born?"

Gregori grinned at his uncle's taunts this time. "*Sigah, Thio.* (Give me a break, Uncle.) She just got here yesterday."

Niko turned to me again, "We were taught Italian at school and were forbidden to speak Greek."

I frowned. "You mustn't have liked that."

"No," he agreed. "But apart from that, the Italians were benevolent conquerors and did much to enhance *Rodos.* Gregori will take you sightseeing and show you the improvements your ancestors made here, like the black and white stone mosaics they created in the streets. We became very friendly with the Italians. Some of us even intermarried with them."

I smiled at that last bit.

Gregori added, "Many of them never wanted to be allies with Hitler, anyway. In fact, after the Italians surrendered, the Germans started shooting them as traitors. My father was seventeen at the time. He never viewed the Italians as enemies. He hid two Italian soldiers in the basement of his house."

"How brave of him," I breathed.

"Do you speak Italian, Patricia?" interjected Roulah.

"Just a little," I said ruefully.

"Her parents never taught her," Gregori curtly informed his aunt.

"I wonder why not? I'm teaching my daughters to speak it. So far, they're doing quite well."

Roulah's daughters, Maria and Katerina, were aged four and six respectively. They spoke Greek, naturally, but like their parents, they also spoke excellent English. Now, here they were barely in school and already learning a third language. Well, didn't I feel stupid?

Gregori looked at his watch. "It's getting late. I should take Patricia back to her hotel. *Thio*, may I use your car? I'll be back in an hour."

I stood up to say good-bye to everyone. I guess this meant my first full day in Greece was at an end. But at least it was taken care of that I'd met Gregori's family.

Roulah kissed me on both cheeks. "See you tomorrow," she said.

Tomorrow?

*** ***

Once I was introduced as "Gregori's possible-intended-Italian-girlfriend-from-America-whose-father-had-been-born-in-Sicily," we were invited to every relative's home. Gregori said we "had" to accept each invitation. These visits took up many of my fourteen days there. I couldn't understand why it was necessary to spend so much time with relatives, especially as Gregori had been there for two weeks with them before my arrival. If we weren't visiting family, we got to go to the beach, but most likely we'd meet up with more relatives there. If they asked us politely what we were doing that evening, Gregori would invite them to spend the evening out with us, too.

"Otherwise their feelings would be hurt," he said again.

And because they were "old-fashioned," Gregori scrutinized every outfit I wore and let me know what was 'too revealing' or in any other way not suitable to wear in front of them. This inspection of my clothing was mandated by another commonality Gregori and I shared. We'd both been 'ethnically-conditioned' to give the utmost respect to something that Italians and Greeks both call, "*figura*", which means "impression". For Greeks and Italians, toilet training of their children is not as imperative as *figura*-training. Our parents hammered it into our souls that we'd better project the most laudable staging of ourselves to everyone outside our immediate family, *if we knew what was good for us*. We learned young that creating a bad impression to outsiders was no less depraved than murder.

Growing up, when we were visiting, Nonnie would make a fist at her grandchildren, put it in her mouth, then bite down on it with a fierce expression on her face, as a signal to us that meant, "If you make *male figura* (a bad impression) in front of these people, so help me God, I'll *kill* you

36

when we get home." This terrorized us into behaving. My mother inherited this technique and used it very effectively, as well.

Good impressions were created by many behaviors, including what we said to people, how we responded to what was said to us, what food we ate or didn't in their homes, and the food we presented to them in *ours*. Naturally, the clothing we wore also played a big role in this production. Hence, Gregori's critique of my outfits when going to see his relatives, and my submitting to his assessment seemed routine to me.

Custom also dictated the family treat us wherever we went, because as also rationalized for me previously, "we were guests." I began to wonder if Gregori was overly fond of his relatives, or just plain cheap. Every evening out with 'flesh and blood' meant he never had to open his wallet. But it also meant that the dining choices weren't up to us. The older folks were fiendishly enamored of a new food craze sweeping the islands, called "toast." It was two slices of white bread, between which was a bitter, white cheese and one slice of what tasted like three-days-old ham. This was placed between two metal plates and heated until the cheese melted. It was innovative to the island Greeks in the 1980's, but to me, it was just a ham sandwich. And we'd had so many of them since I got there that my system clogged up with no hope of ever functioning properly again.

Nonetheless, I certainly didn't want to be rude to anyone, so we went out to dinner with them all, eating whatever they suggested. And we did the best we could with the few evenings we did manage on our own. The island's ambience was a great help.

The port of Rhodes, called *Mandraki*, is magnificent. Whenever I think of it, I remember how it shone at night. Outdoor cafes lined the front of the Venetian-style buildings built by the Italian dictator's architects. The bright café lights reflected onto the pale color of those buildings, making them shimmer gold, a glow that spilled onto the sidewalks, into the water and onto the boats docked there. There were people sitting outside at the cafes, or walking with their families, or lounging on the yachts docked by the restaurants. Tourists and locals laughed in a symphony of languages, jubilant at the privilege of being in this breathtaking and celebrated setting. On this side of the port, it was all 'Sound and Light', like the title of the nightly program at the 14th Century Castle of Saint John, for which the island is famous. But further along the marina, the gleam from the buildings filtered into the water beyond and thinned out to vanish into the darkness of the night sea.

The moonlight picked up here, taking over the surface of the water. Silvery now, cool and hushed, a dark-haired mystery woman, rather than the gilded-haired, merry one across. On the brunette side of the port, there were three ancient windmills. The sea breeze would catch in their mill vanes and they'd rotate leisurely, beckoning to lovers to come onto the silky shadow of the pier. One time, when we were alone, Gregori and I walked there, holding hands. We sat on the rocks beside the mills and looked out at the satin dark sea, under the black and light-specked sky. The breeze stirred soothingly and rippled the water, a sail from a boat, the ends of my hair, the lapel of Gregori's summer jacket.

I snuggled up to him as he put his arm around me and pointed to the entrance of the harbor, "See those two tall columns? Thousands of years ago, the feet of the Colossus of Rhodes were planted on them. The columns are the only thing left of that statue. Before the Italians came, the island was overrun with snakes, but they got rid of this problem by bringing in the deer. That's why you see the stag and the doe statues now on the columns where the Colossus once stood."

As Gregori talked about the island's history and told me stories of his childhood there, music drifted out to us from the *tavernas* across the water. If a song was a favorite of his, he'd sing some of it, translating the words. He was entrancing as he sang those ballads to me and I wished we had the privacy at night I'd thought we'd have.

But Gregori's family took priority. We also had no rental car for private jaunts. Gregori said they were ungodly expensive. What this all meant in one sentence was that the only place we could make love was on the beach. And as romantic and erotic as that might sound, sex on the beach with Gregori was not what I thought it would be, either.

Seaside Rendezvous

"What's the Greek name for swine's snout?"
–Robert Browning

To begin with, every other young couple had the same idea for the same reasons we had.

"There are so many people here," I pointed out quietly, as we walked in the dark on the sand.

"*Shhh.* I know. Don't worry, we'll find somewhere," Gregori whispered back to me.

"Why are you whispering so low? I can hardly hear you."

"Because we don't want to disturb others and you never know — one of my cousins could be here too. I don't want anybody to recognize us."

"Oh, come *on,*" I said, finally losing my patience, "Do you think they'd call out if they did? They're not here so they can be on the lookout for *us.*"

"*Shhh!*" he repeated, this time more adamantly. "Here… here's a spot."

"The sand is wet. I wish we had a blanket."

"Did you expect me to bring a blanket when my uncle and I came to pick you up for dinner? Don't you think that would have been a little obvious?"

"I just think the sand's going to scrape. It might feel yucky, too," I said uncertainly.

"Take off your clothes and lie down. I'll make sure you don't feel 'yucky'," he promised silkily.

When it was over, he murmured, "*Now* how do you feel?"

I just smiled. I didn't want to hurt his feelings with the truth, which was, "like my backside has been exfoliated."

Then…

Slap! Slap! Slap!

"What are you doing?" asked Gregori.

"It's the damn mosquitoes."

Now it was his turn to lose patience. "I told you — there are no mosquitoes here!"

"Oh, really?" I retorted, "Then I guess I've been getting bitten sadistically all week by non-existent things!"

"*Shhh!*" he said, for the third time. "I hear something. …It's the tourist police! They've come to chase people off. Get dressed, *quick!* They'll shine their lights right on us!"

"*What?*" Panicked, I fumbled for my clothes. "You might have mentioned that earlier," I said frantically.

"*Hurry up!* They're coming!"

Overall, my biggest temptation was celibacy.

At least I had some fun on the beaches during the day. They were each so dazzling in their own way, that's it's impossible to describe them all. And there was so much going on there, I don't know where to start.

Just as Gregori hadn't told me about the hotel issues and the tourist police, I discovered he also left out some other pertinent facts. Such as that the same Swedish women who came to Greece to cavort with the denizen males sunbathed topless. Observing this would be another novel experience for me, the callow "little American," which is what he and his family had taken to calling me.

On this trip, I'd gone from being an ordinary American, to a specifically christened "*Amerikanaki*", which in Greek, means, "little American". They weren't labeling me "little" because I was young, or short. It wouldn't have mattered if I'd been a six-foot-four, seventy-year-old. Because the Greeks I met back then thought I was naïve in my knowledge of the rest of the world, and gullible, to boot. This made me easily dismissible, hence "little."

Yes, *Amerikanaki* was a slight. But I have to admit, it was an apt description of me, which made it doubly irritating. I'd never seen women bathe topless before, it was true, but I learned that it was common practice for many females in various parts of Europe, though Greeks themselves hadn't yet adopted it by 1980. The Swedes didn't seem to notice this, or the natives' reactions to it, including Gregori's family.

The older, married Greek men, like *Thio* Niko and cousin Mihali, did their best to ignore the half-naked girls gamboling around them. But when one of the young Swedes walked over to a outdoor shower nearest the family blankets and splashed water on her naked breasts, I saw *Thio* Niko's face redden. Mihali deliberately turned his back, muttering something about "foreigners." Only Gregori's older brother, ogled openly, until his wife, Thoulah, slapped his arm, "*Stop* that, Gerry!"

The married Greek women, like Roulah and Soulah, had another reaction altogether. Their popular pastime was to discuss the foreign girls' breasts. Transfixed by the variety in shape, size, and fullness, they'd make hand motions mimicking cones and spheres. They'd put their arms out away from their own chests, to demonstrate fuller breasts or their thumbs and forefingers close together to illustrate petite ones.

The single Greek cousins would scowl whenever a topless Swedish girl walked past. However, I got the impression that rather than being scandalized, it was more that they were feeling left out of all the fun. Especially if the 'imported competition' was accompanied by a handsome Greek male, which they usually were.

I pointed out to Gregori, "I don't think the Swedes are sunbathing topless in order to provoke anyone. I think they sunbathe topless because it's their culture's standard."

When he heard this, one of the South African cousins, Gerasimo, derided me, "And how did you come to that conclusion, *Amerikanaki?*"

That term was really getting on my nerves, but I managed to be polite. "It's not too hard to work it out, Gerasimo, after seeing Swedish mothers in mono-kinis walking hand-in-hand with their children and chubby, wizened-up Swedish grannies, sunning themselves topless, too."

Gregori found my riposte amusing. He laughed, showing those little white teeth, now even whiter against his tan, which made him all the more handsome. As for him, I'd been wondering why he switched from regular sunglasses to mirrored ones every time we went to the beach and then took long walks along the shore — by himself.

Then Thoulah made the mocking comment, "I see Gregori has his *perving* glasses on again," and I understood he'd deliberately worn mirrored glasses in order to hide where he was aiming his eyes. He'd come back from these walks, saying nothing, but looking distinctly 'bothered'. Of all the reactions to the topless Swedes, I hated my own boyfriend's the most. It was devious.

But there was comic relief from the bathing beauty parade in the exploits of the *kamakia.* They're like the Greek equivalent of ...gigolos, except *kamakia* didn't sell their bodies, they *donated* them, as long as sex was unconditional and a beautiful girl took a while to let him bed her. To a *kamaki,* (which is one *kamakia)* the chase was half the fun.

Gregori smiled as he explained that, *"kamaki"* in the Greek language means "spear." Specifically, the metal shaft designed to impale underwater octopi.

I just rolled my eyes at him, which made him laugh once more.

None of us woman on the beach could prevent our glance being momentarily snagged on the miniscule swimwear of a *kamaki* swaggering past our line of vision. This was more by reflex than desire. Physical fitness was not a prerequisite for *kamakia,* so it was hard not to do a 'double-take' when a *kamaki* swaggered by. We had to be sure we'd *really* seen what we thought. But a woman was in for it if a *kamaki* noticed her 'interest' and considered her a fish worth spearing. He'd amble over, determine what foreign language she spoke, and, impressively enough, be able to converse with her a bit in whatever language that was. When the *kamakia* spoke English, they sounded like this:

"Where you from, *preety gell?* What your name? I am *Takis."* (Or *Laki,* or perhaps, *Panos,* all male nicknames, short for an auspicious variety of multi-syllabic first names.) "You like have a swim with Takis? What you say, pretty *gell?"*

Every *kamaki* used the same basic dialogue. But the ones who were scrawny, hairy, or paunchy, would puff away on cigarettes, gesturing with them as they spoke. They assumed a cigarette as an additional prop to the swimsuit added *machismo* and detracted from their less desirable corporeal aspects. The more externally appealing ones, however, being assured of their perfection since birth by every female relative, did nothing more than direct an intense look at their prey, then flash gleaming teeth in a smile. These particular *kamakia* proved trickier to pry loose, because they could boast a certain appeal. Especially if an uninitiated tourist was on a short holiday and didn't know these same men worked the beaches all summer, in persistent pursuit of new plunder. It was these fishermen who had the most chance of going home with an unwary octopus, hit well, softened up and dangling from a string, ready to be fried.

The *kamakia* knew to stay well away from me, however. Though I might have been considered spear-worthy if I were alone, since I was single and foreign, I was well guarded by a Greek and they knew it. Gregori made a critical miscalculation, however, when he told me to bring a one-piece swimsuit "for when we were with family." Since I was the only female on the beach under sixty not wearing a bikini or topless, I became the 'something different', attracting the attention of — you might have guessed — the Swedish men. They looked like replicas of Kurt, only with suntans, and though none of them approached me, their light eyes followed me everywhere I walked. It infuriated Gregori.

"Did you have to pick a white one-piece bathing suit?" he demanded, pulling me aside, away from where the relatives could hear.

"What's wrong with white?" I asked, my feelings hurt. "It looks great with a tan."

"Your nipples are showing through," he snapped. "I can see two dark spots, like bulls-eyes."

My mouth dropped open. "You can see no such thing! This suit is lined!"

He insisted, getting angrier by the minute. "Oh, yeah? Have you seen what you look like when it's wet?"

I was mortified. "I'm not discussing this with you anymore." I stomped back toward the blankets and sat down in a huff, next to Kiki and Viki.

Kiki eyed me with amusement, "Have a row with cuz, did you?" she asked.

I shook my head in exasperation, but said nothing. Then I put my towel around my shoulders, because now I felt self-conscious in my most modest swimsuit.

Viki sighed, dragged on her cigarette, then philosophized in her laconic Aussie lilt, "Greek men. They're just like the sun and the ouzo here. Great in small doses, but too much and you can get truly sick."

I eyed her curiously. "What's ouzo?"

She exclaimed, "*The-ah mou!* (My God) You've never tasted it? You've *got* to!"

"I know!" Kiki added excitedly, "We'll go to *bouzoukia* tonight! No trip to Greece is complete without dancing at *bouzoukia* and drinking ouzo, Patricia. It'll be so much fun!"

"Fun." *Sure.*

Aristophanes would've loved to add my next theatrical misadventures to his plays named after nature: *The Birds, The Wasps, The Frogs*. He would have called this one . . .

The Bugs

> *"Open your mouth and shut your eyes
> and see what Zeus will send you."*
> **–Aristophanes**

The music was fantastic and deafeningly loud. The tavern where it was played teemed with people and cigarette smoke. I found out that going to *bouzoukia* meant going to hear live Greek blues music, called *Rembitiko*, which featured the *bouzouki,* a string instrument similar to a mandolin.

As the singer and the musicians put everything they had into their song, a waiter led us to a corner where more than a dozen of us were crammed around two tables made to fit four apiece. Despite our close quarters, in order to be heard, we had to lean in close to each other and yell.

"Oh, come on, *Thio,* not toast again! Let's get something else," shouted Gerry.

Kiki nodded her agreement. "Yes, let's! And don't forget ouzo," she shrilled. "With plenty of ice!"

43

My first taste of Greek ouzo. I liked it. It had a refreshing anise flavor and seemed quite smooth and light. I finished my glass.

Gregori glowered at me. He was still annoyed because of the bathing suit incident that afternoon. "Don't drink too much of that stuff. It's stronger than you think."

I was about to tell him to 'stuff it', but before I could open my mouth, Viki jumped in as my champion, "Oh *piss off,* Gregori. Can't she have any fun?" She stood up and practically pulled my arm out of its socket as she got me up with her. "Come on, Patricia — let's dance!"

Stunned by his cousin's outburst, Gregori said nothing, as Thoulah and Kiki jumped up, too.

"All *right!*" Thoulah caterwauled. "Let's go!"

With me in tow, they pushed their way through the crush to the miniscule dance floor directly in front of the musicians. The singer was wailing now, a song I recognized as one that Gregori had sung to me, about a man who'd lost his home and his freedom, "*. . . And you never cried for me, Mother Greece, selling your children as slaves!*"

We danced in a circular line, holding hands with dozens of other happily swaying people. A man at the front of the line was waving a white table napkin jerkily, as he slid and hopped to the tune. It was all I could do to keep up with the intricate steps. When it was over, we returned to the table breathlessly and drank more ouzo, while Gregori eyed me wrathfully.

After my second glass, I stood up to use the toilet and had to sit back down immediately. I'd made a mistake. Ouzo was not 'light'. I was exceedingly dizzy all at once and not pleasantly. It was as if I'd suddenly contracted the flu.

Now what to do? I didn't dare stand up again. I tried signaling Gregori discreetly, but he was ignoring me deliberately. I knew he'd have a fit if I disgraced myself in front of everyone. Trapped by manners, I became more fog-headed as everyone around me shouted, ate, smoked, and drank. I'd stopped drinking the ouzo, but I wasn't getting any more sober. The alcohol was still working its way through me. The situation was becoming dire, so I had to take action. I leaned over to Thoulah and managed, "I'm not feeling well." Thoulah took one look at me, then turned to Gregori and announced at the top of her voice, "Gregori, I think Patricia's drunk."

Great job, Thoulah. Gregori looked just as angry as I thought he would. He came around the table and lifted me out of my chair. I swayed dramatically and some of the relatives chortled good-naturedly.

Gregori was not pleased at all. Turning to Viki, he scolded, "This is all *your* fault. You knew she never had ouzo before."

Viki was not intimidated. "She only had two glasses. How was I supposed to know she was a two-can screamer? Besides, what's all the fuss about? So she'll go to her hotel and sleep it off. It's not like she's got anything better to do once she gets there."

It might have turned into a full-blown argument if I hadn't chosen that moment to hiccough and moan, "Gregori, we *have* to go right *now*."

Still holding on to me, Gregori shouted to Gerasimo, "Give me *Thio's* car keys. I'll drive her to her hotel and meet you back here."

Gerasimo was leering as he threw the car keys to Gregori. "Sleep well, *Amerikanaki*," he bellowed mockingly to me.

The ouzo was good for something, at least. It gave me the nerve to curl my lip at Gerasimo.

Gregori steered me out of the restaurant and once we were outside, much to his distaste, I got sick. He berated me the entire drive to the hotel and when we entered the hotel lobby, even the concierge could see I was smashed, because he let Gregori take me upstairs, despite the new law. I couldn't have made it without help. I leaned heavily against Gregori the whole way up on the lift and into my room. Once there, he placed me on the bed and placed a towel on the floor.

"Here — aim for this if you have to be sick again."

I felt wretched. My stomach and throat hurt from being sick and my thighs were stinging where the sand had scraped them two nights before. Pathetically, I said to Gregori, "Don't leave yet. Stay with me just a little longer."

He was in no mood to be compassionate. "Isn't it bad enough that you did this in front of my family? Do you want me to leave them at *bouzoukia*, too? Twelve people with only one car? That would make a terrible impression."

Figura and guilt, jointly. A method of obtaining my compliance that always worked, whether it was my parents or my boyfriend who used it on me. I didn't ask him to stay again.

"You'll be all right in the morning," he said gruffly. "Get some sleep."

Then he left.

You know what happened next. I came out of that shower and there they were — two vermin from Greek hell, sent to my room by Hades himself. And after making a complete fool of myself in front of Gregori's aunt and uncle at *bouzoukia*, I ended up sleeping at their house. Where, because I'd woken everyone, they were all up in the middle of the night, sitting in the kitchen, smoking, and giving Gregori advice about me.

It was Gerasimo who'd said, "She's not like us," and my heart sank when I heard it. As hard as I'd tried to make a good impression and let Gregori see that I'd make him a good wife, it was a shortcoming still to some of his family that I wasn't Greek.

At least Viki defended me. "She's had enough, that's all. Of relatives, of staying by herself at the hotel. What kind of holiday is that?"

Then I heard Gregori's voice. "That's not it." He mused, "Everything's gone wrong since Patricia got here. First there was no hotel, then she got sick, now cockroaches. I think her grandmother put the evil eye on this trip. She didn't want Patricia to come."

"Oh, *God forbid*. Light a candle at the church before you leave, just in case. You don't want *that* on you, especially on the plane," cautioned one of the aunts.

I sat up in bed. '*The evil eye*'. *Why hadn't I thought of that?*

We left for Athens the next day and three days later, we were back in New York.

Chapter Three: The Evil Eye

*"I only have one superstition: I touch
all the bases when I hit a home run."*
–Babe Ruth

Why Gregori and I Lit a Candle — Just in Case

"So, let me get this straight — you had a crappy time together in Greece, but you're still seeing him, because you think somebody, possibly your grandmother, put 'the evil eye' on the trip?"

It was Donna who'd asked the question. I was back at work and it was one of those perfect, late summer days that don't come along often enough in New York City. She and I were taking advantage of it by meeting at our usual spot in Battery Park, eating sandwiches outdoors and enjoying the view of the Statue of the Liberty across the water.

I nodded. "We lit a candle at church before we left Rhodes, just in case, to get rid of it."

Donna just looked at me as she chewed thoughtfully. Then she swallowed and said, "You know, I've been hearing about this 'evil eye' thing ever since high school. Somebody would say something to set you guys off on it and Margie would shriek and knock wood, you'd make the Sign of the Cross, and Angie Poulos would spit three times, which I always thought was pretty gross. I'd ask you about it and you'd all *always* say the same thing," she continued in a mimicking tone, " 'It's just something we grew up with,' like you were in some kind of exclusive club. So, once and for all — what the hell *is* 'the evil eye', Patricia? Explain it to me." Then she folded her hands and sat back, waiting to be instructed.

I took a deep breath. "Well, let's say you have a headache…" I began.
And here's what I told Donna:

A headache might be brought on from too much reading or a second glass of wine. Or it *might* be evidence that someone gave you 'the evil eye.' Maybe you're wearing your especially nice bracelet, when your neighbor comes by for coffee. She takes one look at it and feels envy, but she doesn't say she's envious. Instead, she says, "Is that a new bracelet?"

You say, "Yes, an anniversary gift from my husband."

She says, "Oh. An anniversary gift. How nice."

You'll notice she didn't say, "An anniversary gift, *bless your heart.*" Or even, "An anniversary gift. How nice. *Toof-toof-toof.*"

By not blessing, or making spitting sounds after her compliment, she's giving you clues that she's *jealous* and might mean to give you 'the evil eye.' If you don't take action against this, you, or even your husband who gave you the bracelet, might get a headache. If it's a powerful 'evil eye,' you might even discover that the only reason your husband bought it for you in the first place, is because he's having an affair.

Headaches and infidelity happen. But those of us who understand 'the evil eye' know they're not chance accidents. Your head was fine until someone thought about you in a bad way. That thought's aura penetrated your skull, causing head pain. Your marriage was also secure, until someone's hateful thought engendered an unholy desire in your husband's private parts. Now if you've got something really spectacular, like an especially wonderful husband — *watch out.* The better off you are, the more jealous others feel and the stronger the degree of force behind their 'evil eye.' Your husband could even *die,* which, depending on your point of view, might be even more appalling than his having an affair. All because of 'the evil eye.' *Toof-toof-toof.*

(I added the spitting sounds there, so Donna would be safe.)

Once she knew that key way 'the evil eye' transmitted, I gave her a rundown of some other ways people can become liable to risk:

1) Anyone wishing you ill can transmit 'the evil eye' by writing you a nasty letter. 'Chain' letters that threaten dire consequences if you don't send out copies are also versions of 'the evil eye.' But take note: overly kind letters from people who aren't close to you that don't bless you along with the 'good' wishes should also be suspect. Nobody you don't know very well is ever really *that* nice.

2) Strangers who stare at you for long periods of time are not just rude, they're *toxic.* They're staring because you have either something they admire, like a beautiful smile, or something they *don't,* like a smelly cigar. Whichever it is, they want to hex you by staring at you — *hard* — until they can convey their 'evil eye.' That's why you should always have your talisman with you when you're going anywhere there'll be strangers.

"What do you mean, a 'talisman'?" interrupted Donna.

"I'll get to that," I said, and went on:

48

3) There is another type of 'eye' and it's the most potent one, because we give it to *ourselves*. If we indicate, in any way, that we're not grateful for the things we have, or we prefer something else, we might incur 'The Wrath of God.' 'The Wrath of God' is worse than 'the evil eye,' because no human can prevent or remove it, once it's been invoked.

For example, if you say to your sister, "How lovely your hair looks today, *God bless you!* I can't do anything with my stupid hair."

The next thing you know, you wake up in the morning and your hair is falling out in great clumps. Vitamins won't help and 'evil eye removers' won't, either. This is a *special* form of 'the eye.' *You* caused it yourself, by making God angry. You weren't thankful enough, so you're being punished. Now you'll just have to live with it, until God decides you've learned your lesson.

Some people believe they can circumvent punishment from God, by prefacing their wishes with *conditionals*. I remember my grandmother saying, "Next year, *if I live*, I'll go see my sister in Italy."

See how that one would work? By phrasing her desire to go to Italy with, *"if I live,"* she was letting God know she was taking nothing for granted, nor making *any* demands.

God's 'eye' cannot be prevented or removed. However, 'fellow-human-being-inflicted evil eye' can be warded off with talismans or charms, like the following:

- A small, blue glass eye, a pair of red plastic horns, a cross or other religious symbol, sometimes worn *along with* red plastic horns or a blue glass eye.
- A bulb of garlic.
- A house entranceway painted blue.

Donna broke in again, *"Huh.* So that's why Angie's mother had garlic bulbs all over the house. I always thought she was afraid of vampires."

I nodded and continued with another vital point in my lesson:

People who enjoy cursing others especially like to inflict 'the eye' on newborn babies. To protect an infant against 'the evil eye,' you can pin one of those blue glass eyes on the baby's diaper. Babies in India get tiny black dots placed behind their ears. There are options from other nations, too.

At this point, Donna smirked, "So, I guess if I ever have a baby I'm really fond of, I should put all the talismans from everywhere in the world on her at once, for 'extra-strength' protection?"

I said with frustration, "You *see*? This is why I didn't want to discuss this with you. You're making fun of it. You sound just like Kurt."

Donna apologized and fought hard to stifle her smile. So I went on:

Suppose we weren't assiduous enough in our preventive methodology and have let 'the evil eye' slip past — how to get rid of it? This was Nonnie's cure:

A) Take a small curved dish filled with water and place it near the afflicted person.

B) Sprinkle a drop of oil onto the water's surface. If the oil separates into two drops, you've pinpointed 'the evil eye'.

C) Bow your head and whisper a prayer. As you pray, the two drops of oil will 'magically' pull together to make one drop. Shortly after that, your subject's 'evil eye' should disappear.

"But the easiest thing to do," I concluded, "Is what Gregori and I did. Light a candle at a church. That's *always* effective. You can also ask a priest or rabbi to bless you, if you've been exposed to 'the eye'. I'm not sure if a Muslim cleric will do so, as well. They might."

That was enough for Donna. In as cutting a tone as I'd ever heard from her, she said, "Well, I'll check, Patricia, at my local mosque. I won't bother to go to any Protestant denomination churches for blessings against 'the evil eye', though. You know why? The ministry there maintain that a belief in God and having free will and thought are not mutually exclusive."

"I knew you wouldn't take this seriously," I said.

"Well, *come on!*" Donna exclaimed. "Garlic? 'Beezlebub-Chasing Blue' doorways? Oil drops separating in water? For *godssakes,* didn't you take freshman physics? Tell me — do you *really* believe all of this?"

I shrugged. "It's possible. The Greek-Orthodox Church accepts it and so does the Catholic Church."

"And since when do *you* hold everything the churches say as true? You were one of the first people I know to make fun of some of the stuff you learned in your religion classes."

I had no response to that. She was right.

She heaved a sigh, stood up and dropped her sandwich remains in the trash bin nearby. "Let's examine your evidence here, shall we? There was no hotel room for you. Then when you got one, bugs flew in. And then, you got sick on ouzo. Was there anything else?"

"No."

Like a lawyer, she interrogated her witness. "The other tourists you said were sleeping in the parks — did they all ultimately get perfect rooms?"

"No."

"And what about those two bugs that flew in? Repulsive, I admit, but were they the *only* flying cockroaches to be found anywhere on the island?"

"No. They were pretty much everywhere."

"Well, then perhaps all the others flew in at once, like a satanic plague, the moment you stepped foot on Rhodes?"

"*No.*"

"Of course they didn't!" Donna said tartly, pacing back and forth as she spoke. "The window was open with no screens on it, it was dark out, the bugs saw the light in your room and flew in because you were in the shower and there was no one around to scare them off. That's *all*. And do you honestly think, even if your grandmother could put 'the evil eye' on you like you say, to prevent you from getting a double room, because she didn't want you to have sex with Gregori" — she shook her head at this — "she'd have the ability, just by her sheer *will*, to overbook every hotel in Greece and force all those poor tourists to sleep outside?"

I grimaced. "You don't know my grandmother's will. And my mother didn't want me to go either. That gives any 'evil eye' double-whammy power."

"Patricia! Be reasonable, *please.*"

"Okay, it does sound stupid when you put it like that. But why did I get sick then, on the ouzo?"

Donna stopped pacing to look down at me, "If *I* know the answer to that, so should you. It sounds like you ate nothing but ham, cheese and white bread for ten days. Your stomach must have been a mess. I bet you couldn't go to the bathroom the entire time you were there."

"Donna!" I said, scandalized.

"Oh, *please.* Everybody who knows you well *knows* you've been constipated and queasy ever since you came out of your mother's womb and spent the next twenty-odd years in that household. You've got the most

51

reactive digestive system of anybody I know. A diet like that, coupled with all the stress of meeting the family — over and over *again* — staying alone, the lousy sex, the bathing suit argument, the mosquitoes and the cockroach on your pillow and then you drink alcohol — *80 proof* alcohol? No wonder you threw up."

It made sense. There was nothing I could say.

She went on, "You are an intelligent person. Don't you see how dangerous this sort of magical thinking is?"

I looked at her quizzically, "How so?"

"Because it obscures facts," she stated ardently. "In this case the facts are that you were left alone at a hotel, because you were Gregori's second choice. He'd rather have stayed with his family than spend more time with you."

I shook my head, "That's not true at all, Donna. He did that because they're... very traditional."

"That's not 'traditional'. That's hypocritical. They *know* you're sleeping together. You went off together to Athens by yourselves with their knowledge. And besides, even if you're right, then why didn't he take you to another part of Greece where there wasn't any family?"

I could feel my back going up. "Because he wanted me to meet them. We're getting serious."

Donna's lovely green eyes widened at that. "Are you for real? I thought this was just a fling. How can you think of getting serious with a man who dictates what you should wear, how much you should drink, what you're going to do on your first vacation together and where and how you make love?"

"I don't see him that way at all," I said hotly.

"Yes, you do," she shot back. "You just don't *want* to, for some reason I can't figure. That's why you'd rather believe everything that happened on your trip happened because of this 'evil eye' nonsense. You know, Patricia, I love you dearly. I was so happy when you and Kurt starting going together. I'd hoped it would last and you and I'd be sisters-in-law someday. Now I'm starting to think my brother had a lucky escape."

And I was starting to think that maybe Donna and I wouldn't be friends for much longer.

I looked at my watch. "It's getting late," I said stiffly. "We'd better head back."

Donna phoned to apologize the next day. I was so glad. I didn't want to stay mad at her. Even though I felt Margie and I had more in common, I loved Donna, too. We never brought up that conversation again. And I admit that, even as far back as then, there was a part of me that knew she'd brought up many solid points. But why I preferred to think that 'the evil eye' was at work, rather than that Gregori and I might not be as suited as I'd hoped, was simple. I'd already decided he was perfect for me and evidence to the contrary wasn't going to shake my conviction. As far as belief in 'the evil eye' was concerned, once I took it into my psyche, it was in forever, I thought, no matter what I might tell myself. But as time went on, my frightened convictions and firm verdicts would diminish with exposure to new experiences and I would choose to reexamine everything I'd been taught and believed. Sadly, Gregori would never make that same choice.

There were also inklings that I would change going forward. Because it wasn't just the commonalities we shared that made me feel drawn to Gregori. I liked that his perspectives challenged me to examine my own on many issues. For example, it was he who made me see I had a duty as an American to understand the foreign policies of the United States and add my voice to them. I remember the conversation that brought this sharply to my attention. Gregori brought up the U.S. Embassy in Iran hostage crisis and asked my opinion on the shah of Iran:

I hesitated. "I guess I don't know enough about him to have one."

He was floored. "Don't you know why those Americans are being held hostage there?"

I got defensive. "Even if I did, what can I do about it?"

His answer was scathing. "How can *any* American, whose government policies determine the fate of people all over the world, not know what her country is doing? Do you exercise your right and opportunity to vote?"

I felt my face burn with shame at that rebuke. I read newspapers... occasionally. And... now that I was thinking about it, I realized I got most of my political opinions from what I heard my parents say. I can give reasonable excuses as to why the rest of the world seemed so far away, why, true to my *Amerikanaki* nature, I trusted I could rely on my government to decide our national and foreign policies without my having to worry myself. But I won't. I'll just say that discussion with Gregori forced me to recognize that I was even more provincial than I'd suspected and that this was not just a hindrance for *me,* but actually had far-reaching consequences. His commentary taught me to take a hard look at the world and not live in blind, privileged comfort. At that point, I saw him as almost *heroic,* for what I believed was his open, probing mind.

All these rationales ensured that, despite our disappointing first holiday together, I continued to see Gregori after we returned. Often we had lots of fun. And yet, the more earnest we became about a future together, the more time we spent bickering. We'd even joke that we got along best only when there was a 'full moon'. Our debates were over weighty subjects, such as whether or not females should be allowed to fly planes, to petty ones, such as whether Greek or Italian olive oil was best.

I thought he was respecting my intelligence. It never occurred to me that these symposiums we were having were part of my training program to becoming his wife. Gregori thought our union would work because my questions meant I was studying to learn things *his* way. Our contrary opinions didn't seem to be flagrant clues that we weren't meant to marry. Through our infatuated eyes, they were impassioned, sociological debates, or just minor annoyances. They added spice.

However, I do have to admit that there was one thing about Gregori that puzzled me. Despite the fact that he'd lived in the United States since he was thirteen years old, he hadn't embraced any of its culture. He was still 'purely Greek'. He preferred Greek restaurants, Greek music, Greek people. He compared the United States unfavorably to Greece and endlessly lamented that life could be so much better, *if only things were* as they were in Greece. This was irksome sometimes, but I had no idea how much it would affect our future.

I also wouldn't find out until later, that Gregori deemed me what the Greeks call *"apli."* That meant I was a girl who didn't have high expectations, a 'simple' girl. Being thought of as *"apli,"* is usually a compliment, but not when it's applied as Gregori was applying it to me. To him and his family, my *'apli*-ness' signified that I was *pliable.* While they were under *that* mistaken assumption, I was under my own false impression that though Gregori could be obstinate, it was only because he was so *confident.* Given time and love, we'd both learn to compromise and make each other happy. If Margie and her Irish-Catholic husband could do it, why couldn't we?

Boy, were we fooled.

Other people besides Donna were not. One of them was my father.

Women's Work

"My Heart Belongs to Daddy"
–Cole Porter lyrics

It took three more years of part-time school for me to finish up my bachelor's degree and for Gregori to propose. While I'd been going to school, he'd been grappling with what he wanted to do. He'd dropped out of college, so he became a dental technician for a while. But that salary wouldn't get him very far once he moved out of his parents' place. Like many Europeans, since he was single, he still lived with them. He finally decided to buy his own medallion taxi, as two of his friends, Aleko and Leonides, had. They'd told Gregori it was a lucrative business and urged him to give it a try. Buying a taxi took all Gregori's savings, so I was twenty-six before I had my two long-awaited rewards — my first college diploma and Gregori's engagement ring.

My father was happy about my graduation, but *not at all* about my impending marriage. It wasn't often that Dad got a bee in his bonnet, but when he did, there was no living with him.

It might have started when Gregori voiced his objection to female pilots. My father, the only one in my immediate family who'd supported my idea to go to college and who'd married, over the objections of *his* family, ironically, a chain-smoking, opinion-touting feminist, perhaps had a foreshadowing of troubles to come.

Or maybe it was because my mother took one look at Gregori and flatly told me, after he'd left, "He's not for you."

We might as well admit that mothers *do* have a sense about these things. It probably comes from us having been connected to their navels at one time. Take it from me, no matter what sort of relationship you might have with your mother, if she tells you your man is wrong for you, save yourself and him years of aggravation and just break it off. I didn't, obviously, so maybe my dad felt the need to reinforce the maternal offensive.

Another possibility might've been that my father made up his mind about Gregori upon meeting his parents. *That* meeting made an impression on everyone involved.

In the four years I'd known Gregori, I'd found his parents, Niko and Demetra, refreshing, because they was so unlike my own parents. In my family, it was mostly the women who made all the commotion, in Gregori's, it was the men. While Gregori and I were dating, I spent lots of time at their apartment in Astoria, because it was much closer than my place to work and school. Sometimes as I walked up their block, I could hear Niko shouting, his voice carrying outdoors and three buildings down. He wasn't scolding anyone but the politicians whose exploits he was reading about in his beloved Greek newspaper.

"Oh-lee klef-tehs eenay! Eh, Demetra?" ("They're all thieves! Right, Demetra?")

And Demetra, while keeping her eye on whatever she had on the stove, would nod. Gregori's mother was the quietest person. When she did speak, it was in a child-like voice, the high-pitched tone of which she said was the result of a hysterectomy surgery gone bad years before. That seemed strange, but when I tried to ask her about it, Gregori signaled to me by putting his finger to his lips. Talking about that surgery was forbidden. I'd find out why.

Occasionally Gerry and Thoulah would come by for dinner, too. Then the noise generated by the three men was beyond belief. They were mostly discussing politics, but it would get so riotous that one day the tenant in the apartment below stopped me as I was going past her landing to find out what they were fighting about upstairs. "Should I call the police?" she asked.

I sighed. "They're just discussing Greece."

"Oh, my!" she exclaimed, "Has the government there been overthrown?"

The fact that Demetra remained serene and focused on whatever she was doing while the men carried on this way was remarkable to me. My mother would have clouted them on their heads with her macaroni pot. I wondered if Demetra ever chafed at the aspect that her husband and sons lorded it over her. But things are never the way they seem.

After Gregori and I got engaged, Demetra and Niko were invited to my parents' for a coffee. They couldn't speak English that well, but like many of Gregori's other relatives, they spoke Italian. This made it easy for my parents and Gregori's to communicate, though it was harder for me to follow their conversation. That's why I almost missed an imperative part of the exchange between the two fathers. They'd been getting on well, chatting about their respective 'old countries'. Until my father got up to help my mother clear.

And Niko said, "*Che cosa stai facendo? Quello è lavoro delle donne.*" ("What are you doing? That's women's work.")

I wasn't sure I'd understood Gregori's father correctly. My father's annoyed reply, also in Italian, clarified things. "A *real* man helps his wife when she needs help."

Demetra laughed as though she was used to her husband being a 'prankster'. But Gregori's dad wasn't joking, and my father knew it.

Meanwhile, Gregori had no chance of understanding anything being said. He didn't speak any Italian, so he was off on some other train of thought. It was his mother's edgy laugh or the tone he picked up in the men's voices that made him tune back in. He smiled over at me and asked, "What are we discussing?"

I hesitated. "... I think we're talking about... household chores."

My mother cleared her throat rather noisily, but said nothing.

Gregori and his parents left shortly thereafter, Gregori's dad and mine both saying a brusque "good night," Gregori's mom, a bit red-faced, thanking us for the company, and Gregori still looking confused. Neither of my parents said anything to me, but when my mother and I got up to wash plates, my father made his evaluation of the episode plain. "*I* will do the dishes. You and your daughter..." he motioned for us to leave the kitchen, "... go inside."

And that was that.

They Would Not, They Could Not (With Apologies to Dr. Seuss)

"I've had a wonderful evening.
But this wasn't it."
–Groucho Marx

The next fiasco occurred at Gregori's parents' home.

It was the cheese.

Nonnie was also present at this in-law get-together. Though she was my mother's mother, it was she and my father who had in common that aversion for cheese. They couldn't stand the smell of it; they didn't want it in any food, whether it was chunked, baked, sliced, or sprinkled.

57

Whenever my father peeked at a dish containing cheese, he'd shiver, "*Ugh! That's horrible!*" as though there was a severed horse's head in the oven, rather than just some chicken *parmegiano*. And whenever my grandmother smelled just a *whiff* of cheese, she'd screech, "Pee-*eeeww!* It's *sickening!* It smells like filthy feet!"

Given the intensity of their dislike, I thought it prudent to tell Demetra that my father and grandmother *unequivocally* didn't like cheese. My future-mother-in-law remarked that since Italian recipes used cheese, she was surprised they didn't like it. I took that as an offhand comment, not a rebuttal. And I did something then that I was to spend a great deal of time in future doing. I tried to shed light on a point-of-view for Demetra.

I said, "Many Italian dishes aren't made with cheese."

Demetra said, "*Mmmmm.*"

In conversations that I'd had with others, a response of, "*Mmmmm,*" usually meant "I see," or, "I agree." Therefore, that's how I translated Demetra's "*Mmmm.*"

It took me years to figure out that Demetra's "*Mmmm,*" meant, "I'm just pretending to listen, because I Don't Want to Hear You."

That day in her kitchen, when I talked of Italian foods from different regions, *ad nauseam* and she replied, "*Mmmm,*" not only did it signify that she wasn't listening because she didn't want to hear me, it also meant she'd already planned a menu which contained cheese in a big way. It was *moussaka*; a Greek dish made with layers of eggplant, potatoes and minced meat, baked in a cream sauce. Delicious, but only to *some,* because the cream sauce is flavored with plenty of *cheese.* Gregori's mother was known for her tasty *moussaka,* a merit of which she was proud. The detail that two of her four dinner guests "would not, could not" eat cheese, "could not, would not" deter her from presenting her best recipe, the scent of which unambiguously wafted through the communal hallway of their building.

"I smell cheese," pronounced my father the moment we stepped in. He looked at me as though I were Brutus. "*Jee-zus Christ,* Patricia! Don't tell me they don't know I hate cheese!"

"I told them, I swear!" I whispered urgently.

My grandmother wailed, "It *stinks* in this hall! Oh, *God,* what are they trying to feed us?"

"*Shhh* — be *quiet!*" my mother hissed. "Somebody's coming! Don't make a scene, I'm warning you *both!*"

Just then, Gregori opened the door. "Welcome!" he said, "Come in." Smiling, he motioned us all inside. Then he noticed the long faces. "Is something wrong?" he asked.

"Well—" began my grandmother.

"—No, nothing," said my mother at the same time. She sniffed the air in a show of appreciation. "*Hmm.* I smell... cinnamon, I think. Is your mother baking?"

Gregori laughed. "No. The cinnamon you're smelling now is in the meat sauce she made. Greeks use cinnamon to spice the sauce, like you use pepper in Italian tomato sauce."

"What else is in it?" demanded my father.

"What do you mean?" asked Gregori.

I looked at Gregori pleadingly, in a fruitless effort to avert catastrophe. "Gregori, I told you and your mom that my father and grandmother don't eat cheese. Yet we're smelling cheese. If there's cheese in what your mother made... that's going to be a big problem for them."

Then Gregori did something I didn't expect. He fibbed. With a straight face, he looked at us and said, "Cheese? No. *No* cheese."

"*Hah!*" exclaimed my grandmother, "You're joking, right?"

Before Gregori could reply to *that*, Demetra sailed in from the bedroom. "Hello!" she said, in English, "Sorry to be late. My husband *ees* come from work just now, he make a shower, and then, we eat."

In came Niko a few minutes later, bobbing his head in greeting. "Hello... *buena sera.*" Then he clapped his hands together once in anticipation and said to his wife, in Greek, "Is the food ready, Demetra? Shall we eat?"

Demetra nodded and motioned us all to the table. My father and grandmother looked like they were about to do the dead man's walk.

My mother's polite exclamation, "Oh, doesn't the table look nice?" was the one positive note in the air.

Still oblivious, Gregori proffered, "My mother's been working since yesterday, getting the apartment and the dinner ready. She was... we all were... looking forward to your coming."

"We were looking forward to it, too," replied my mother, valiantly. "Thank you for having us."

This exchange seemed to remind Nonnie and Dad of their social obligations. They sat at their places, hands folded, eyes down, like chastised children.

Gregori's mother sliced up huge pieces of *moussaka* for everyone and plopped them on our plates. This time, from directly in front of them, the cheese scent beset my father and grandmother. However, whether it was my mother's daggers glance at him or my beseeching one, my father shuddered a deep breath and picked up his fork. *Bless him*, he was going to tough it out.

Nonnie didn't do as well. Granted, she didn't push her plate away and exclaim "ugh!" as she ordinarily would. But she couldn't bring herself to swallow any of it. To her, it was just too vile. Pasting on a smile, she looked at Gregori. "You know what?" she said, "This has cheese in it, doesn't it?"

Once again, Gregori lied. "Cheese? I don't think so."

"Well, I *do* think so," said Nonnie, still smiling. "And I don't eat cheese."

Until that moment, Niko had been intent on his own *moussaka*, a dish he thoroughly enjoyed. Now, however, he looked up from his plate at his wife, then back down at his half-eaten food, as he asked. *"Tee eh-hee oh moussakas?"* ("What's wrong with the *moussaka*?")

Demetra hastened to reassure him. She motioned to my grandmother and spoke in Greek, too. "Nothing. It's only that she says she doesn't like cheese."

Niko looked at his wife in disbelief. "She's Italian, isn't she? Italians like cheese."

Then he made an error in judgment. Accustomed to his wishes being acted upon by the women in his family, he presumed that my grandmother would also comply with his requests. Smiling, he coaxed her in Italian, *"Signora, mangi un poco. Il formaggio è buono per voi."* ("Come on, now, Mrs. — eat some. Cheese is good for you.")

The gaze Nonnie leveled at him erased all doubt that the word 'obey' was not part of her vocabulary. She reiterated, this time in Italian, too, so it'd be clear to everyone, *"Non mi piace formaggio."* ("I don't like cheese.")

Niko blinked. He hadn't expected a veto. Yet, he said nothing — *Thank you, God* — and just resumed his meal. Despite the elbow-nudge from my mother, my father soon joined the uprising and abandoned the *moussaka*. Then he spied the salad. There was still hope to fill his stomach with something. "Patricia, would you pass me the salad, please?" he asked.

Knowing he preferred vinegar on salads, I notified him, "It has lemon dressing on it."

"That's true," acknowledged Gregori, "but Greeks also use vinegar on salad like Italians. My mother uses lemon, because she knows I can't stand the smell of vinegar." He continued, eager to have a topic for conversation, "But people still try to give me things with vinegar in it. They say 'it only has a little' or sometimes," he was warming to his subject now, "they even *lie* and say there isn't any on the food." He shook his head and looked at my father as he went on. "Like they think I'm stupid and can't tell that there's vinegar in it. To me, it's so *strong* I can't miss it."

It took him a moment to figure out why my grandmother, father, mother, and I were staring coldly at him. When it clicked, his face went pink.

"Who wants dessert?" asked his mother.

*** ***

I was the whipping boy the next day. "My parents were offended. Nobody ate." Gregori railed.

"I *said* that my father and grandmother don't eat cheese. How can you serve things to people you know they won't like and expect them to eat them?"

"You have to at least *taste* it. That's the way Greeks do things."

"But my family is *not* Greek and they don't think like that. They weren't trying to offend anyone. *They* were offended because you tried to force them to eat something they hate."

To Gregori, it was beyond rude to imply that his mother's food was hateful. So he retaliated, "I ate some of your mother's sauce and I thought it was horrible. You know I don't like that Italian red sauce, but I *ate* it, anyway." The look on his face illustrated how revolting he'd found the experience.

It was one I couldn't forget, either. My mother had been making Nonnie's sauce one evening when Gregori and I dropped by. Compelled by Greek etiquette, he commented that it "smelled delicious." Having no idea of "the way Greeks do things," my mother offered him some. According to further instruction in Hellenic politesse, Gregori was now obliged to eat. So he did, treating us to a sham performance of gastric ecstasy. Immediately after, he got sick. (And *no* — my mother hadn't put anything in the sauce.)

"Oh, I *remember*," I assured him. "What were you *thinking*? My mother is not impressed by who likes her food."

"Well, my mother is!" Gregori yelled.

"Then she shouldn't serve what people won't eat!" I yelled back.

So it would go. His view, then mine. Or rather, the 'Greek' approach, then the 'Italian-American' approach. When they were the same, we were okay, but when they weren't, we argued. I defended things I wasn't even sure I agreed with, because I resented Gregori's arrogant ruling that "the Greek way" was the right way and everyone else's was wrong. What we didn't see was that only *our own* estimations should have been important. Did either of us have our own individual position on *anything?*

*** ***

After the *moussaka* episode, my father concluded I was making a poor choice of husband. He was going to let me know that, in no vague terms. In the first part of this crusade he tried 'reason'. He'd always thought my apartment was an unnecessary display of independence, so he seldom visited me there. Despite that, two days after that dinner, the buzzer sounded. When I flipped up the call switch, my father's voice came through.

"It's Daddy. I want to talk to you."

Uh oh.

What followed was an hour of my father detailing every reason it would be a mistake for Gregori and me to marry. He spoke gently, though. It was unusual that he wasn't trying to force me to change my mind by scolding that I lacked common sense. So I did listen, but like Demetra wanting to serve her favorite recipe, I didn't *hear.* The few phrases that did sink in, such as "taxi driver," "anti-American foreigner," only served to accomplish what Donna had by her criticisms. They made feel protective of Gregori. Besides, the man telling me all this wore a blue-collar and was foreign *himself,* so why would I accept those as deficiencies?

When Dad saw his talk had failed, the bee in his bonnet went from buzzing to vicious. He elected another tack: If I can't get *her* away from him, I'll drive *him* away from her.

And so, Dad began the second part of his crusade like a quest for the Holy Grail.

Chapter Four: Exorcism, Sicilian Style

"You can get more with a kind word and a gun than you can get with a kind word alone."
–Al Capone

Fighting for Greece

The first strike was at the next family get-together. We were at Nonnie's and her table was crowded with cousins, aunts, uncles, all talking at once, as usual, when my father suddenly called out to Gregori. Involved in conversation with a cousin, Gregori didn't hear him right away.

Dad snapped his fingers and whistled loudly. "*Yoo-hoo*, Gregori! I'm talking to *you!*"

Gregori and everyone else stopped speaking to look at my father. "Yes?" asked Gregori, politely.

My father leaned back in his chair. "Let me ask you a question," he began. "You know I was born in Italy, right?"

"Of course."

"And you were born in Greece."

"That's right."

"But I consider *this* my country. *Yessiree*, there's no place like the United States," declared my father.

I had a sick feeling this was not one of dad's usual sermons. He had a certain flare in his eye. "Don't you agree that this is the best country in the world?"

Everyone's attention was on Gregori, who knew he was walking into a trap. He nodded cautiously. "It has its good points and bad, like every other country."

"*No.*" My father tapped his finger on the table for emphasis. "There is no other country like this one. It's the best." *Tap-tap-tap.*

Gregori said nothing.

"So," my father went on, now pointing his finger directly at Gregori, "my question to you is this — if there was a war between the United States and Greece, which side would you fight on?"

The silence in the room took on a different feel. Old Westerns. The gunfight scene. Then, one of my cousins snorted. "Come on, Uncle Joe. Doesn't his grandmother live there?"

There was a burst of laughter. I had a fleeting hope that my father's gauntlet would be dismissed as "teasing."

But Dad wouldn't have it. "That shouldn't matter. He lives in *this* country. He has opportunities in *this* country." He banged his hand on the table with every sentence and the gleam in his eye sharpened. "So I'm asking this man a question and he should be able to answer it."

"Yes, I can answer it," replied Gregori, seriously. "I don't think I'd be able to pull a gun on anybody in Greece."

My father raised his hands in mock resignation. "Well then, Gregori, *you* don't belong here."

At that ruling, there was tense silence again. This time, it was my grandmother who broke it with the words, "Who wants dessert?"

Soccer, Ed Sullivan, and Takis Paralikis

"Eddie? Keesa me goo-night."
–Topo Gigio

To appreciate how cleverly my father orchestrated his next strike, you'll need some details about his chosen setting.

Loving all things American, my father became an enthusiastic baseball fan upon his immigration to The United States. But he'd been brought up playing and watching soccer. He counted himself blessed that living in the U.S., he could enjoy both sports.

My father made ends meet by overtime at his regular job as a butcher at a local market and then Saturdays at a second job. But Sunday was his day off to relax and watch those sports. I used to love to sit with him when I was a little girl. He had trouble explaining baseball to me then, but soccer was easier to understand and much more visually dramatic.

At my parents' home, uncles, cousins, and friends huddled around the television when a soccer match aired from Europe. They'd jump up and shout in Italian when a player nearly made a goal, intercepted a goal, or ran with the ball close to the goal. As these activities encompassed most of any match, the action in the living room was as intense as the performances on the screen. And should a player achieve a goal, the stadium announcer would echo, **"GOOOOOOOOOOOOOAAAAAALLLLLL!"** The camera would pan close-up to the player who'd scored. He'd be running jubilantly across the field, head flung back triumphantly, until he and his teammates crushed together in a massive embrace of male exultation. The stadium would be thunderous, the announcer commentating at the top of his lungs, frantically. The play would stop for two minutes or more to allow everyone to bask in the screaming and sweaty clinching.

And at our house, the clan would be shouting, "GOAL! GOAL! *Madonna mia, che fantastico* **GOAL!!!!!**"

But if the scoring team was the opposing team, the play the result of the opposition's brilliance, the men in our house would gaze at the screen as though witnessing death. There'd be groaning and hand clenching, as the wrong team and wrong fans celebrated. Sometimes, a spate of loud jeers in Italian would ensue, "*Stupido! Che katso fai?*" (Best not to translate that.)

No matter if our team won or lost, there'd be a din coming from the men that wouldn't subside until the match was over and some female would shout, "Okay, time to eat!"

If luck came my way, the match was taped from an Italian station and the local station would also air a short clip of an Italian children's show, which featured the puppet mouse, *Topo Gigio*. Oh, he was *so* cute. I'll never forget the Sunday evening in 1963 when my dad called to me, "Patricia, look who's on *The Ed Sullivan Show*."

It was *Topo Gigio!* I didn't know my beloved puppet mouse could speak English, too.

When I watch soccer now, the fun I had as a little girl with my father and uncles together, watching soccer and *Topo Gigio* comes back brilliantly.

By the time I met Gregori, there was cable television. The Hellenes in New York had the "Greek Channel," and *The Takis Paralikis Show*, based right there in Astoria, where Gregori and his family lived. Taki was a short, middle-aged fellow, with large ears and slicked-back black hair and eyebrows that reminded me of another puppet, Bert, from *Sesame Street*. He read the Greek news in a monotone. Next was a succession of local Greek merchants' adverts, owners and their families carrying platters of *gyro*, flashing diamond rings or posing in fur coats, all from their shops located nearby. Gregori would say, "Look — there's *Panagiota*'s Uncle Kosta, eating at *Baba Giorgi's*. He's at the same table where we sat last time."

After, they'd show the soccer match from Greece. Gregori and his friends reacted to soccer the way my father and uncles did. I'd enjoyed watching soccer with my father and now I enjoyed watching with my fiancé.

Which is how we inadvertently helped my father instigate the next segment of his crusade.

Gregori had gotten the hint that he wasn't my dad's preferred choice and was willing to try to change my father's mind. Men have always bonded over sports and it was something to start with, that he and my dad were both keen soccer fans. We could all go to a match together. Wouldn't that be fun? Unfortunately, where Gregori was hoping to forge a connection, Dad saw an opportunity to recommence his offensive.

The match we went to see was the New York Cosmos against the Greek National Team, at Giants Stadium. It was July 1, 1981, and there were over 42,000 spectators in the stands, a sizeable attendance for a soccer match taking place in the United States. It was quite a treat for Gregori that the Greek National Team would not only be *in* the United States competing, but against one of the best teams the U.S. had to offer. Gregori also invited his brother and sister-in-law to come along. Gerry and Thoulah were a presentable couple suited to the task of swaying my dad's opinion in Gregori's favor. Gregori had planned well. However, as with all best laid plans, things went awry. As soon as we sat down, it started drizzling. Just a little at first, then steadily, as the match wore on. Cold damp would not be the primary discomfort of the outing, though.

"Why are we sitting *here*?" demanded my father. "We're with the Greek team fans."

It wasn't too difficult for him to work that out. We were surrounded by hundreds of people, all speaking Greek, wearing blue and white, waving Greek flags and shouting, *"Ellas Ole! Ellas Ole!"* which means, simply enough, "Greece! Olé Greece!"

I spoke so only my dad could hear. "Dad, be nice. *Please,*" I implored.

Though I'd kept my voice down, Dad saw no reason to do the same. "I thought we were sitting in the Cosmos section. I'm rooting for the Cosmos. I'm a *Cosmos* fan!"

Our companions discreetly ignored my dad's outburst, but strangers around us stared warily, as my father mutinously took his seat. Dad noticed he'd attracted an unanticipated audience. He settled down… for about nine minutes. Because approximately eight and one-half minutes into the match, Roberto Cabanas of the Cosmos scored the first goal. Pandemonium ensued. Cheers from the Cosmos' side, hisses from the Greek National Team side. All sitting with us were disappointed that the Greeks hadn't been the first to score. All, that is, except one.

"Hooray for the Cosmos!" my father applauded. He raised his fist high above his head. "Cosmos! Cosmos!" he chanted. With a leer, he turned to Gregori, clapping him on the shoulder. "That was some goal, wasn't it? Come on, admit it."

Gregori wasn't particularly rooting for the *Ethniki;* he liked the Cosmos, too. But like me, he didn't know how to handle my father. His conduct was downright risky. Soccer is taken seriously in many parts of the world. *Very* seriously. Fans are notorious for fighting, with sometimes deadly results. My father was well aware of this, which made his actions even more disquieting.

Gregori answered him cautiously. "It was a fine goal, yes. Roberto Cabanas is a good player."

"He's a brilliant offensive weapon. With him and Chinaglia, the Cosmos *will* win." My dad's voice had risen enough that people around us turned to look intently at him again. Hoping to avert trouble, Gregori said nothing.

Ardizoglou of the *Ethniki* made a shot for the goal, but it was saved by Birkenmeier.

My father's, "Bravo!" was drowned out by the surrounding moans.

My attention was so fixed on my dad by this time, I was missing the match. I didn't see Jeff Durgan of the Cosmos being issued a 'caution'. I don't know what he did, but whatever it was, it got a big "Boo!" from the *Ethniki* fans. Dad was booing, too, which momentarily confused me. Then I saw his 'boos' were for the referee who'd penalized Durgan. This time we got serious glares. A man sitting below us muttered, *"Mahlahkah."*

I knew what *that* meant. *"Mahlahkah"* was one of the first things I'd memorized in Greek. It isn't flattering. My father's unrestrained support of the Cosmos was not being taken well by Greeks sitting near us.

Sarganis came in with a brilliant save. The crowd surrounding cheered and applauded.

"Shit!" said my father.

Once again, people in our vicinity turned to scowl at him. I had a bad feeling about how all this was going to turn out. Gregori had been thinking the same, because he leaned over to me and asked quietly, "Can you get him to stop? He's going to get us killed."

I didn't know what to do. "Dad, *please*," I whispered, tearfully, "please stop."

My distress silenced him for a while. Maybe he hadn't made out that I was also being affected by his miscreant performance. He'd been aiming to get at Gregori and was succeeding. Gregori and Gerry kept glancing at the fans around us, wondering when, not *if*, we were going to get an unpleasant reaction to the heckling coming from our section. The only one of us who seemed oblivious to the unfolding drama was Thoulah. She was a Cosmos fan, too, though she had the good sense to be more discreet about it.

"Oh, *look!*" Thoulah murmured to me, "They've put Seninho in! *This* should be something!"

The Portuguese Seninho was famous for his great headers and left-footed shots. He was so popular a player that he was known only by the one name, just like Pelè and Cher.

"*Seninho! Seninho!*" chorused the Cosmos fans from across the stadium.

"Seninho!" chimed in my father from his seat amongst their opponents. "Whoa-*Ho-Ho! SEN-eeeeeeen-YO!!!*" His subdued manner hadn't lasted long.

A save by Sarganis again. A cheer from the *Ethniki* side.

And a "*Boo!*" from my father.

So it went. I was holding my breath for whatever would generate more recklessness from my dad. And it happened. Near the close of the match, just as I was beginning to think we might escape unharmed, Giorgio Chinaglia of the Cosmos scored a goal. The Cosmos were ahead 2-0.

Dad jumped up to issue his final battle cry. "HOO-RAY for the Cosmos! The Cosmos win!"

Another step closer to throwing all our lives away, he waved his arms wildly and spun, addressing the crowd around him, "The *Americans* win!" He gestured to the ground, "*This* is America!" He pointed to his chest, "I'm an American!"

My father is a portly little fellow. The sight of him then, all five feet-six inches of him, jumping, belly jiggling, would have been hilarious, if it wasn't so maniacal. His outburst of, "I'm an American!" in his broad Sicilian accent, could be rationalized only as spontaneous onset of schizophrenia. Not only that, he was grossly misinformed. With the exception of four American players, The Cosmos line-up read like a roster of U.N. delegates: Vladislav Bogicevic, Yugoslavian, Andranjek Eskandarian, Iranian, Hubert

Birkenmeir, German, Julio Cesar Romero and Robert Cabanas, from Paraguay, Wim Rijsbergen, Dutch, Francois Van Der Elst, from Belgium, Chico Borja, from Ecuador, Seninho, Portuguese, Steve Wegerle, South African and Bob Iarusci, Canadian. And more irony — Giorgio Chinaglia, who'd scored the final goal for the Cosmos? He was an *Italian.*

Fortuitously, the Greeks seated near us were more familiar with the Cosmos' birthplaces. The furious looks they'd aimed at my father changed to looks of confusion. I can't really be sure about this, but perhaps they even recognized that Dad's accent couldn't be from *any* part of the United States. After some whispering amongst themselves, it appeared they'd concluded he was deranged. They turned away cautiously and left us alone. We were reprieved.

Gregori figured we'd take advantage of that immediately. "Match's over," he said, tersely. "Time to leave."

As we got to the car, my father clasped his hands and rubbed them together.

"Well!" he grinned. "That was a great game, wasn't it?"

The Greek and the Wolf

"A four-letter Italian word for 'good bye'? — BANG!"
–Carroll O'Conner as 'Archie Bunker'

Despite Gregori's forceful condemnation of my father's Machiavellian methods, he wasn't backing out of our wedding. The date drew nearer and my father grew desperate.

One evening, Gregori and I were at my parents', having a pleasant time discussing the reception. My mother and I were *'ooh-*ing' over photos of bouquets made of oriental hybrid lilies and Gregori sat smiling at us.

And my father was steaming. His lone, enraged bee had multiplied to a full hive, all madly droning inside his head, until he was mad from it. He had to do something, *anything,* to stop their ceaseless din.

"You know what, Gregori?" he blurted out, interrupting my mother's question about seating arrangements, "all this here we're doing now," he gestured at the photos on the table, "reminds me of when *we* got married." He put his arm around my mother and beamed innocently.

That carefully artless look had me eyeing him with misgiving as he continued, "*Yessiree,*" he chuckled, "we had so much planning to do, too. We couldn't decide which caterer we was gonna use. One was this H-Irish guy . . ." (My father always puts an 'h' sound in front of English words that start with vowels) ". . . and the other caterer, well, he was a Greek."

My mother frowned in confusion. "I don't remember a Greek caterer—" she began.

"—But you know," interrupted Dad again, "my father didn't want us to use no Greek caterer. No, *siree*. You know why?"

My stomach sank. *What now?*

He paused for effect, then delivered his *coup de grace,* "Because his motto was, 'If you see a Greek in the woods, standing next to a wolf, you shoot the Greek and keep the wolf.' "

I was staggered. I never expected he'd utter something so atrocious.

My mother was first to speak. "Holy *God!*" she exclaimed. "*How* could you say such a thing? What the *hell* is w*rong* with you?"

Dad did look shamefaced. Just a *bit.* But he wasn't about to take his words back. He'd tried everything within the boundaries of reason and quite a bit beyond. Nothing he'd instigated had been effective. His last resort was to take out the 'big guns' — unadulterated bigotry — and aim straight at my future husband. This time he'd achieved a direct hit. Gregori was silent, but livid.

I stepped into the fray, trying to salvage the unsalvageable. "Ha ha," I laughed, nervously. "He's joking. Honestly, Gregori, it's a *gag.*" I swallowed and went on doggedly, "Just recently... listen to this, you'll think this is interesting... my father and I were reading, *A History of Sicily* and it explained how all the people living there consider themselves Italians, but that they're all originally from somewhere else. They'd all paint the roofs on their houses a different color, depending on where they'd come from." I stopped here to clear my throat, as Gregori stared at me in stony silence. "And when we looked up our family name, they'd had a *blue* roof." I looked at my father, "And what did the blue roof symbolize, Dad?"

My father stayed silent.

"*Dad!*" I tried again. "*Tell them* — what did it symbolize?"

Mutinously, he mumbled, "Greece."

I'd worked up a sweat waiting for that answer. "Greece! Right." I slapped the table and appealed to Gregori. "That's why this is *funny.*" I looked at my mother for help now, too. "Right, Mom? Because the grandfather Dad mentioned — his name is *Greek*. It's Appollonio, for 'Apollo'. See? It was a *joke*. Ha ha. He got us, didn't he? Good job, Dad." I held my breath, waiting for results.

"If it was a joke, it was certainly a poor one," my mother replied angrily, still frowning at my father.

Neither Gregori nor my father spoke.

Dad didn't get the reaction he'd strived for. Gregori did not storm out. In fact, my frantic intervention was proof that my father's 'proverb' only accomplished the opposite of what he'd been trying to accomplish. My fiancé's and my father's dislike for one another was now official and since Gregori hadn't started the trouble, he and I were now solidified as a unit against my father's 'side'.

Don't imagine that my father was the only force trying to break us up, however. There was another stalwartly against our union, Gregori's best friend, Leonides. His resolute code was that Greeks should *never* marry outside their own. Like my father, he too, had a rationale.

Birds of a Feather

> **"I was born a Greek and I will die a Greek.
> Mr. Pattakos was born a fascist and he will
> die a fascist."**
> –Melina Mecouri, *upon her exile by the Greek junta*

After just one hour in Leonides' company, my mother had this to say: "Show me who you go with, and I'll tell you who you are."

(My family had an endless supply of maxims.)

Though I didn't agree with her assessment that Leonides and Gregori had to be alike as they were friends, I did agree that Leonides himself was... not admirable. His one concession to his adopted country was to call himself "Louie" and that was only because, "Americans are too stupid to pronounce my real name." Leonides ridiculed and despised all things American. Especially me.

I pointed this out after Gregori and I returned from Greece still a couple and Louie didn't seem happy about it. We were sitting at a booth at the Neptune Diner in Astoria, where Gregori's friends always gathered. Aleko was with us and Louie would be meeting us, there, too.

I said to both Gregori and Aleko, "You know, I don't think Louie likes me."

They exchanged a look. Then Gregori sighed. "It's not that. He just believes that Greeks should only get involved with Greeks."

"Why?" I asked, already hurt.

Aleko jumped in. Even though I'd chosen to dance with Gregori rather than him that first night, he'd never held it against me. He was always a gentleman. "Don't take it personally, Patricia," he entreated me. "Like a lot of Greeks, Louie feels that his culture is threatened by outsiders. Greece was conquered by foreigners for thousands of years. And everything Greek — the history, the culture, the religion, were all repressed by the regime in charge. Not only did they force us to change our way of life, they looted Greece of its ancient treasures."

That I knew from my studies at college. The removal from The Parthenon of sculptures now known as "*The Elgin Marbles*" when Greece was under occupation by the Ottoman Empire was a perfect example of what Aleko was talking about.

Gregori nodded and picked up what Aleko had been saying, "Then there was World War II, when Mussolini took over the Ionian Islands, like Rhodes. The Greeks there were made mandatory Italian citizens. So Greeks secretly taught their children Greek in *kreef-toh skoh-lee-oh*, which means, 'hidden school', that would conceal them from enemy spies. After World War II, we had a king for a while and then we suffered through a military dictatorship from 1967 to 1974."

"Which was backed by the United States," Aleko interjected flatly. "And all of us — Gregori, me, Louie, were there for the beginning of that. It was hell and we eventually had to leave. We came here to the United States, the country that started the trouble in Greece in the first place. Some, like Louie, still resent it."

I shook my head. "I can't imagine how you must have felt when your country was taken over like that."

"I'll tell you how it felt," Gregori offered. "I was twelve years old when it happened. We didn't have a television back then. We tried to find information on the radio, but they'd stopped all broadcasts. Just like *that*, the radio went dead. My parents, my brother, and I ran downstairs to my grandparents' place, because their radio could get the *BBC*. The *BBC* reported that there'd been a military coup by the hard right-wing and that, at that very moment, tanks were rolling down the streets of Athens, into the main square." He looked at me, remembering. "We were scared. We didn't know what was going to happen to Greece. That night, the adults made a plan that Gerry, who was already in high school, would stay in Greece with my grandparents until he graduated. I hadn't started high school yet, so I'd go with my parents to my uncle's house in the United States. And... that was it. We had to leave. And while my parents were planning this and listening to the broadcast, Gerry and I had to keep watch for anybody who might tell the police we were listening to foreign radio. People were being taken away to prison for less. They'd even arrested Mikis Theodorakis."

I looked at him in disbelief. "Not the composer who wrote the music for *Serpico* and *Zorba the Greek?*"

Aleko nodded, "Yes, the same. He was very popular in Greece, naturally, and he vehemently opposed the junta. The coup had occurred because elections in Greece were nearing and *NATO* suspected that the King of Greece would be voted out by supporters of the left, so they authorized their own takeover with their chosen leader, Yiorgos Papadopoulos. He did represent the right, but it was the *very far* right." Aleko's voice seemed to stick at this next part, "Papadopoulos proclaimed an 'emergency' state of martial law and thousands of socialists had to go underground. Anyone who opposed the new regime was exiled or arrested. Mikis Theodorakis was one of them. Within eight months of its existence, the junta published its first list of forbidden artistic works, including several hundred titles of classical Greek tragedies and not surprisingly, Mikis Theodorakis' music."

"How *awful*," I said. "I had no idea."

I was beginning to have some sympathy for Louie's perspective. Just as I thought of him, he arrived with his girlfriend, Helen. He gave a curt nod in my direction, while Helen smiled a shy, "Hello." We made room for them in the booth and as soon as Louie was seated, he began speaking in Greek.

"*Reh*, Louie," Helen chided softly. "Speak *Eengleesh*. Patricia is here."

Louie frowned and kept speaking in Greek.

I marveled at how polished Helen always looked. Everything from her hair to her nail color to her matching lipstick was so perfect, it was hard for most people to take their eyes off her. She spoke accented English like the rest, but on her it was even more charismatic, because of her throaty voice. She was five years younger than I, and Gregori had told me that Louie started dating her when she was only sixteen and he was twenty-two. She'd also attended classes at Queens College. On the occasions we'd run into each other there, I never once saw her wearing a pair of jeans.

73

Louie ordered his usual two double cheeseburgers and French fries, Helen just coffee. Both she and Louie lit cigarettes as they waited for their orders to arrive.

"So what were you all talking about?" Helen asked.

"We were telling Patricia about the junta," Gregori told her.

Helen exclaimed as she inhaled around her cigarette," Oh, *The-ah mou!*" She blew out the smoke. "Patricia, you can't imagine it. My parents wanted to stay, but after a while, we left, too. Life was *so* different. We had to start every school day by writing a page on why we were proud to live under the 'leadership' of Papadopoulos. Then the government said we weren't allowed to have more than three people in a room at the same time, because more than three signified a political protest meeting. So if you had more than three people in the family, you couldn't even *eat* together." By the time she finished recounting this, she had tears in her eyes. "It upsets me just thinking about it."

Louie sneered over at me, "*Your* countrymen were responsible for that."

"*Sigah,* Louie," protested Aleko on my behalf. "Patricia was just a little girl then, too. What could she do?"

Louie just grunted. The arrival of his food saved me from any more indictments. After that, we saw nothing of his face for a while. He kept it down two inches above his cheeseburgers, as he doused them liberally with salt and ketchup and then tucked in.

I turned to the other three. "How did the dictatorship end?"

Gregori answered bleakly. "How do they ever end? In bloodshed, that's how. On November 17, in 1973, a group of students protested against the government by taking over their university, the *Athens Polytechnic*. The junta responded with a brutal force of soldiers and tanks. Two dozen students were slaughtered and hundreds of others were wounded. There are recordings and films of them begging for mercy. "

That account gave me chills. "Oh, how horrible. For something like this to happen in *Greece*, of all places. What happened after that?"

Gregori went on, "Papadopoulos was overthrown by another general, and the following year, this new arm of the dictatorship plotted a putsch on nearby Cyprus. There was an assassination attempt on Cyprus' president, so he fled to London. With the rationalization of protecting Turkish-Cypriots, because the island was now leaderless, Turkey invaded Cyprus. The northern portion of Cyprus became controlled by Turkey, a circumstance that exists to this day. That same year, the Greek junta dissolved and the socialist politicians came back to restore democracy. And Mikis Theodorakis, who'd been exiled, also returned to Greece. His music is now the symbol of the *Greek Resistance*."

I said sorrowfully, "That's some experience to have lived through."

Helen nodded. "No Greek will ever forget it. We struggled hard and long, Patricia, but there are no more kings, dictators, or foreign governments ruling Greece. Today, Greeks do everything they can to safeguard every aspect of Hellenism, especially the democratic government."

So Louie's friends were using the Greek 'siege mentality' to justify his objections to me and my relationship with Gregori. When I took into consideration all that Greece had suffered politically, Leonides' resolve to preserve his rich culture by marrying *only* a Greek girl and wanting his best friend to follow suit, was comprehensible.

But maybe that wasn't his real reason. Leonides' standards were exacting regarding *which* Greek girls would suit and once his task to devour every scrap on his plate was achieved, he elucidated his qualifications for me. The whole time he talked, one speck of cheeseburger remained glued to the corner of his mouth.

"A wife has to be at least five years younger than a husband," he declared. "The younger she is, the better."

I knew I would regret it, but I asked anyway. "Why?"

"The younger she is, the less she expects. She thinks you're smarter than she is and it's always the smarter person who's in charge."

"Why not just marry a stupid person, then?" I asked flippantly.

That got a few chuckles from Gregori and Aleko, but Louie responded seriously. "A stupid wife is bad for your kids. You just want her to be inexperienced. That way you can train her any way you like."

"What does the wife get from this arrangement?" I had to find out.

Louie looked surprised that I didn't know. "She gets what every woman wants, of course — free room and board and never has to work a day in her life."

There'd be no point in arguing with those assumptions. But from the way he told it, it sounded like his future bride would work *every minute*, as a cook, housekeeper, nanny, and chauffeur for his children.

I sat looking at him and thinking. This was Gregori's closest friend. There had to be *something* redeeming about him that Gregori admired. And of course, there was, right there in front of me. My mother saw it, but I didn't.

That's why when Louie finished his diatribe, I still questioned, "But, wouldn't you want qualities in a wife you could identify with, so you'd enjoy being in her company?"

"Sure," he answered promptly. "She'd have to be sexually attractive. And pretty. As pretty that is, as a *Greek* girl can be, because that's the trouble. Greek girls aren't as pretty as foreign girls. That's why *some* Greek men," he glared briefly at Gregori, "are getting themselves mixed up with them."

So *that* was Louie's rationalization for how I'd gotten Gregori in my clutches, tempting him away from his duty to procreate with a Greek. As far as Louie was concerned, there was nothing else to recommend me as a wife for a Greek male except my looks. Another objection he had was that I was living on my own. That advertised that I wasn't a virgin. If Louie's best friend *were* going to settle for 'used goods', at least they should be Greek goods. Even a Greek harlot probably had someone to teach her to cook Greek food, somewhere along the line. But I didn't know even the rudimentary things about being a Greek wife and would have to be taught. That would require effort and it might not even take. By then, Gregori would regret his lapse into lust because he'd no longer be enthralled with me physically.

I'd never met anyone like Louie before, so I couldn't see him for what he was or that his type was not restricted exclusively to Greece. I just felt bad about the way he viewed me and I did my best to show him that I'd make a great wife for his best friend. It puzzled me that my efforts were in vain. Louie simply couldn't abide me, no matter what.

When Louie got up to pay his bill, it hit me that everything he'd said about his future wife's credentials, had been said right in front of his at-least-five-years-younger, moldable-to-suit-his-ways, 'not as pretty-as-a-foreign-girl' Greek girlfriend.

As Donna and Kurt would say, *Holy cow.*

Apprehensively, I turned my eyes toward Helen. Just as you'd expect, she looked murderous.

Aleko again tried to heal an injury that Louie had caused. "Ignore him," he said to Helen. "We never pay any attention when he gives his nationalistic lectures."

"*Bah!*" Helen spat furiously. "He's not a nationalist. He's a *kolo-tree-peeda!*"

Gregori and Aleko burst out laughing at that.

"What does that mean?" I asked through their laughter, but Louie came back to the booth. After we left, Gregori told me that *kolo-tree-peeda* means "asshole."

Not long after that, Helen dumped Louie for someone she'd met at college. Louie was enraged by this and even Gregori and Aleko couldn't understand it.

"I thought they made such a nice couple," Gregori said, and Aleko nodded his agreement.

How strange to be the only one not surprised.

Gregori tried to reassure me that Louie meant nothing by his contempt toward me. "To his way of thinking, *you're* not his friend, I am. He just wants what he thinks is best for me."

So that meant that Louie, being Gregori's friend, was treating me, Gregori's girlfriend, disrespectfully, because he wanted what was best for Gregori? It made no more sense when Louie acted like this toward me, than when my father behaved as he did toward Gregori.

Louie continued his campaign against our marriage right up until our official engagement. What could he do at that point? And since he'd tried to be a true friend to Gregori in the best way he knew how, Gregori asked Louie to be his best man. Unbelievably, Louie accepted.

Incredible, isn't it? With two diametrically opposing breakdowns of the relationship, my dad and Leonides had both arrived at the same conclusion: I was "too American" to make a suitable wife for Gregori.

The number of our friends and family who openly opposed our union was growing. Sick of everyone sticking their noses in, I became hell-bent on marrying Gregori, *no matter what.* Gregori seemed to take the same stand. But there was one person who said something about our engagement that did make me doubt myself briefly. And that was Kurt.

Kurt had finished his master's degree and gotten a job with a multi-national firm that was sending him overseas. Donna was hosting a going-away party for him. At first, Gregori refused to go. It was my fault. I thought everything should be aboveboard between us, so I'd told him that Donna didn't think we were suited and that Kurt and I once dated. He didn't take this information well, especially that second part.

"Did you sleep with him?" he demanded.

I couldn't believe the question. "Gregori! It was *before* you and I met. We're just friends now."

He was never able to wrap his head around that. From then on, every time I mentioned Kurt, he'd say, "you mean, your ex-lover?" Or if I mentioned Donna, it would be, "you mean, the *puttana*?" (whore)

So when I told him about Kurt's farewell party and he said, "I'm not going," I finally got angry.

"Fine, don't come," I said, "But *I'm* going."

When he saw I was serious about going without him, he decided he'd come, too, just to keep an eye out.

Kurt picked this up straightaway. Gregori gave him a terse handshake when I introduced them, but said not one word. Then he sat down in a corner and remained there for the rest of the night.

Kurt sounded amused at first, as he observed Gregori observing us. The moment we had a chance to talk by ourselves, he pointed out, "He's watching us like a hawk. You told him about us, didn't you?"

I shrugged. "I just thought...'honesty is the best policy' and all that."

"He didn't take it well, I gather?" His voice was still jovial. "You know, I went to school with a number of Greeks. I have to say, not one of them came across as medieval as your fiancé."

I didn't know what to say to that, so I shrugged again.

Abruptly Kurt sounded almost angry. "Well, I knew you'd rebel eventually, although I have to admit, I didn't expect this'd be the way you'd do it."

Puzzled, I looked up at him, "What do you mean?"

He didn't answer. Instead, still in that same clipped tone, he continued, "I bet your parents don't like him. They couldn't. Why would they like that he's going to be in charge now, instead of them?"

Startled by that, I asked him again, "Kurt! *What* do you mean?"

And again, he didn't answer, just stared down at me with the most intense expression I'd ever seen on his face.

His eyes are just as beautifully green as Donna's, I thought. *Why hadn't I ever notice that?*

An image flashed into my head then, of Kurt and me, lying in my bed together, naked, he stroking my hair. I got a sudden, clenching fright in my stomach that I'd made a dreadful mistake. Feeling the blood drain from my face at that disloyal thought, I stepped back from him at once.

Still looking at me sharply, Kurt murmured, "Are you sure you want to marry him?"

"Yes," I whispered, all but terrified, "Very much so."

For a split second, I thought he'd argue that with me. Then his expression changed and he stepped back, too. "In that case, be happy. You deserve to be happy. Remember that, Trish. I mean... *Patricia*." He smiled at me softly, then walked away to attend to his other guests.

Gregori and I left shortly afterward.

Kurt moved overseas. It would be years before I'd see him again.

*** ***

Happily, at least Gregori's parents were looking forward to our wedding. As long as it was held in the right church, that is.

Chapter Five: High Church, Low Church

*"We are all tattooed in our cradles
with the beliefs of our tribe."*
–Oliver Wendell Holmes, Sr.

Mom, God, Neighbors and Catholics

My mother had gone to Catholic school and hated it. She never gave us details, she'd just joke, "They call them 'nuns' because 'none' of them are Christian." Nevertheless, she was born Catholic and it would've been outrageous back then, to raise her children any other way. So raise us Catholic she did, 'sort of'. God she accepted, but religious dogma she did *not*. I found that out when I was seven.

I attended public school, but every Saturday morning, I went to the Catholic Church for "religious instruction." I didn't mind sitting through the lesson and seeing some of my friends from regular school. When I got home after my first religion class, my mother was sitting at the kitchen table, smoking a cigarette.

"Well," she said, "What did you learn?"

That was curious. It was my habit when I came home from school to tell my mother what had happened at school that day. If she were inclined, she'd listen. If not, she'd say, "Tell me later. I'm busy right now." This time, though, she was waiting for me to come home, so she could ask me what I'd learned in religion class.

So I told her. "The teacher taught us today that we're Catholic. We believe in One God, The Holy Ghost, and Jesus, the Son of God."

My mother took a puff of her cigarette and nodded. "Okay. What else did she say?"

I tried to remember everything. "*Ummm…* she said that not everybody is Catholic. But that the Catholic religion is the One True Religion and our God is The One True God."

My mother took another puff. "And what do you think?"

"What do you mean, Mom?"

She leaned forward. "I mean, do you agree or *disagree?*"

80

This was *more* than curious. The lesson hadn't been presented as though I were allowed to dispute it. No one had ever invited me to disagree with a teacher before. Yet, my mother had asked for *my opinion* and she was clearly waiting to hear it. I pondered carefully before I spoke, wanting to give this occurrence its deserved reverence. And while I was thinking, I remembered something I'd worried about fleetingly as the teacher spoke.

"Well, Mom," I said, in the most grown-up fashion I could muster, "here's my question: Not all my friends were there. Margie wasn't because she's Jewish, right?"

"That's right."

"Margie's my best friend and you said her mother's nice, too, right?"

"Yes. Go on."

"And Alice Wilson — you don't know her, but she's in my reading group at school. She was at religious instructions today, but her twin brother wasn't."

"Why not?"

"Because Alice's mother and father have *different* religions. Her brother is following her mother's religion, but she's following her father's."

"That's an interesting approach."

"The teacher said that the Catholic religion is the *best* and that Catholics are good people. And... it sounded like she meant that other people who *aren't* Catholic aren't good people because they don't have the *best* religion like we do."

My mother frowned. "People who aren't Catholic aren't necessarily bad people, nor are people who *are* Catholic necessarily good," she stated.

This was a direct contradiction to what my religion teacher had implied. The idea that I could be taught something by a teacher that wasn't positively accurate was enormous to my seven-year-old self. Since my mother was still listening, I decided to be bold. "Mom," I asked, "how do we know for sure our religion is the *right* one?"

I thought she might get angry, but instead she replied, "*All* religions are the "right" religion, if they're right for the person following them. They all teach basically the same things: to love one another, be the best people we can be, to never deliberately harm someone else."

"Then why are there different ones?"

She thought for a moment. "The best way I can describe it is that it's like decorating a house. Some have furniture that might seem strange to *you*, but the people who live there are happy with it."

81

This was more to digest. Only once did I witness my mother get truly furious over what had been discussed in my religion class. This time the subject of what I'd learned came up after dinner and my father was with us.

"Today my teacher told Alice Wilson her mother wasn't going to heaven. She said that only Catholics can go to heaven when they die."

"*What?*" said my mother. "Are you sure that's what she said?"

"Yes, because when she said it, Alice started to cry. And when the teacher saw Alice crying, she said, 'I'm sorry, honey, but that's the way it is.' "

My father stared at me. Then he turned to my mother, whose mouth was hanging open.

It was fun getting that kind of reaction, so I continued, "She made Alice cry *twice*. She always asks us who we want to say a prayer for before we leave. Alice said she wanted to say a prayer for her dog, because he just died. But the teacher told her we couldn't pray for dogs, because dogs have no souls and don't go to heaven, either."

My mother stubbed out her cigarette and pointed at me. "Patricia, you better not be making this up, because if I find out you are, you're going to get a beating that you'll never forget."

"I'm not making it up!" I cried. "That's what the teacher said! I know because I raised my hand and asked how she knew dogs don't have souls."

"What did she say?" demanded my mother.

"She said that we should, 'Look in the book.' "

"What's she talking about? Let me see your religion book." My father paged through my book, while my mother stood up and lit another cigarette. "I don't see anything in here about dogs," he said.

"Who does that woman think she is?" My mother railed. "Jesus Christ's cousin, maybe?"

My father tried for diplomacy. "Well, maybe she's had training. Don't you have to have training to teach those classes?"

"*Hah!*" my mother shot back. "Do you know who it is they've got teaching?" With her newly-lit cigarette, she stabbed the air in the direction of our neighbor's house. "It's Eileen Perotta from down the block. The Irish princess with the four wild kids and that husband with the *guinea* mentality."

"Nancy!" my father chided, glancing over at me anxiously.

But my mother was all worked up now. "I don't care! Let her hear me. It's the truth," she continued, defiantly. "Yesterday, those brats were playing

82

hockey in the street. They knocked over every trash pail on the block, and she didn't say *a word*. Then *he* came out and said, 'For *chrissakes*, woman, can't you control your kids?' "

My mother continued to rant, smoke, and sneer. "Can you imagine? '*Woman*'. 'Her' kids. Like *he* had nothing to do with it. The 'retired' fireman at 35 years old. When everybody knows there's *not a thing* wrong with his back." *Puff-puff-puff.* "*My* tax dollars. Boy, she'd better worry about who's going to heaven or not at her *own* house."

My father, observing my fascinated reaction, said, "Nancy, I think you're getting a little too upset."

"I'm *very* upset. Who does she think she *is*? How does *she* know who's going to go to heaven and who's not? You know they asked every one of the mothers if we'd volunteer."

"Who? For what?" my father asked.

"The *church*, Joe. Are you paying attention? They asked us if we'd volunteer to teach. Said all we had to do was read from the book. I said, 'no' because I didn't think I was qualified, but Eileen said 'yes' and she's no more qualified than I am."

My father smiled. "They would have gotten more than they'd bargained for if you were teaching the classes."

My mother glared at him. "This isn't *funny*, Joe. She's no more qualified than I am," she said again, "and she's no more 'Catholic', either." She paced back and forth across the kitchen. "I went to Catholic school, church every Sunday, I took all the sacraments, memorized all the prayers and sins. Because if you didn't, the nuns used to slap you across your palms with a ruler that stung so much it made your eyes water. *That's* how Catholic I am."

My father and I sat mutely, watching her.

She turned to me, pointing again for emphasis, "And because I am, I'm telling you this, you go tell your little friend, Mary Alice—"

"—It's just 'Alice', Mom."

"*Whatever*. You tell little what's-her-name that *your* mother is just as Catholic as Mrs. Perotta and she says that Mrs. Perotta is *wrong*. The very next time you see that poor little girl you *tell* her that *your* mother says her mother *is* going to heaven, do you *understand* me?"

"Yes, Mom."

"And if her dog was a good dog and he didn't bite people, if she wants to see him again when she gets to heaven, Jesus will let her. Jesus can do that whether the dog has a soul or not, if He's the one who made the dog in the first place. That just makes sense, doesn't it?"

I figured it did. Jesus should have the ability to let a dog into heaven if He wished, despite what the church thought of it. "Yes, Mom."

"Okay, then." She flicked ashes into an ashtray. "One more thing." She leaned down and looked me straight in the eye. Then she waved her finger up and down with every word she spoke. "From now on, I want to know *every sentence* that woman speaks in that class. You tell me all of it, because everything she said today… it's all just *crap*. You got that?"

"Yes."

"Good. Go get ready for bed."

As I walked off, there wasn't a doubt in my mind that Alice Wilson's mother was going to heaven, because my mother would make *sure* of it. And her little dog, too.

There'd been a tightness in my stomach when I came home from the church. It was gone now, dispelled by my mother's righteous fury. I hadn't felt afraid while she'd been fuming. I'd felt relieved.

It wasn't until I was grown that I recognized what an extraordinary stance she'd taken. A proletarian housewife, in 1963, of Sicilian-born parents, who defied the stringent guidelines of her Catholic upbringing by proclaiming them, "crap." Her approach to the religious tutoring of her offspring was unprecedented, compared with other Roman-Catholics of the same socio-economic class and era. It helped me to reflect on God and the hereafter as I liked, without guilt or fear.

By the time I met Gregori, my divine beliefs were solidly like my mother's. It's true that religion, money and sex, are "the big three" that can cause serious rifts in a marriage. And the dividing of the household chores, of course. Any of us who've been there would advise the newly-engaged to get it *all* in writing, including who takes out the trash.

Gregori didn't mind taking out trash, but I could tell he was concerned about what theological suppositions I'd pass on to our future children. As in every other difference of opinion with my fiancé, I chose to believe the best of him. I assumed that his firm stance on the divine was the reason that even though he was willing to marry a non-Greek, he was adamant our marriage take place in a Greek-Orthodox church and our children be raised Greek-Orthodox. I remember a conversation we had early on. I'd made the comment that it didn't matter to me whether Jesus was the Son of God or not:

He: (worriedly) What do you mean?

Me: (reasonably) Well, we could be right about that, or wrong. It's not worth killing each other. That's the *last* thing Jesus would want. *That's* what's important, what He stood for, who He was.

He: (adamantly) *Exactly,* it's important who He was. He was, *is,* the *Son* of God!

Me: (soothingly) Maybe you're right. Maybe the Jews are.

He: (aghast) How can you call yourself a Christian if you don't believe that Jesus is the Son of God?

Me: (calmly, but icily) I can call myself a Christian because I believe in the *values* that Jesus Christ taught. I'd follow those teachings whether or *not* Jesus was the Son of God. Even atheists can be Christians, if they agree with the basic principles of Christianity.

He: (confused and shouting) You're not making any sense! You're talking *sacrilege!*

Me: (disdainfully and raising my voice now, too) Do you know *anything* about Jesus and what He preached? The Sermon on the Mount? His parables?

He: (wildly, now) I *know* that I go to church, that I *wear* my Cross. I know that I do these things because I'm a *Christian* who believes that Jesus is the *Son of God!* (Banging fist on table) *That's* what I know!

Me: Oh, calm down. We're just having a conversation.

As you might guess by our theistic ideology, neither my parents nor I had any real objection to a Greek Orthodox Church instead of a Catholic one. (My father was still holding fast to his opposition to the specific *groom,* so it didn't matter to him *where* the dirty deed took place.) I wasn't keen on ultimatums, but if Gregori was more *devout* in his practice of the Greek-Orthodox faith than I was in the practice of Catholicism, it seemed unloving not to agree. So I did, with a condition of my own — should we have children, I'd raise them as my parents had raised me. Anything our children were taught at church that I thought was out of place with our principles, I'd have the right to dispute. Gregori didn't seem to care about provisos, as long as his children would be going to *his* church.

I then wanted to learn more about what I'd be promoting, so I set out to have religious instruction all over again, this time on the teachings of Orthodoxy. That's how I finally learned the history of two churches, centuries at battle with one another — Gregori's and mine.

Goats on the Left

> *"Every day, people are straying away from the church and going back to God."*
> **–Lenny Bruce**

The Eastern Orthodox Church and The Roman Catholic Church are like two feuding branches of a big Italian or Greek family, who can hold an eons-long grudge against each other over... *not much.*

One cause behind their schism was dispute over papal authority. Many years ago, there were *three* Popes. The Pope in Rome claimed he held supremacy over the eastern patriarchs, while the eastern patriarchs claimed that the pre-eminence of the Patriarch in Rome was voluntary. The Pope in Rome demanded his position as, "first among equals." (I have no idea how *that* phrase can possibly make any sense, but it did to the Pope in Rome.) That verbiage annoyed the other two Popes, but what really stuck in the craw of the feuding papacy was a Roman Pope's insertion of a few extra words into The Nicene Creed, the prayer that every practicing Catholic, Orthodox, and Protestant learns at the onset of their religious instruction. It's their assertion of belief not only in their church, but in the Holy Trinity — "The Father, The Son, and The Holy Spirit."

That creed starts like this:

> *"We believe in one God,*
> *the Father, the Almighty,*
> *maker of heaven and earth . . ."*

...and goes on.

The biggest spat between the Roman and Orthodox churches started when a certain passage was added to that prayer, called "the *filioque* clause," a word which comes from the Latin "son," referring to "Jesus Christ." The *filioque* clause is inclusive of these three words: "and the Son." In the Orthodox tradition, the line in question reads, "We believe in the Holy Spirit . . . who proceeds from the Father," while in the Catholic tradition, it reads, "We believe in the Holy Spirit . . . who proceeds from the Father *and the Son.*"

The paramount debate then, between the two churches is, "*Who is where* at God's table?" So, to paraphrase Bugs Bunny, it's "just a little preposition trouble." A difference of opinion in semantics that caused the two factions of 'holy' men to slaughter each other wholesale and demolish each other's places of worship.

As a result of the violence, a convocation from the highest-held positions in the hierarchy of churches parleyed. Did they meet to contemplate solutions to the systematic annihilation of various ethnic groups, starving orphans, or any other number of topics one would think might concern those who've dedicated their lives to God's work? No, they sat around for thousands of years debating the inclusion or exclusion of *three words* in a prayer.

In addition to the prayer squabbling, the Roman Catholic Church and the Greek Orthodox Church follow different holy calendars. That's why, except for leap years, they each celebrate the Resurrection of Christ (Easter) on different Sundays. Orthodox Easter always falls later than Roman Catholic Easter. (Or, as my Catholic family and friends would say, "The Greek Easter" and "the *real* Easter.")

The disparity in the dates our two families celebrated Easter had some perks for Gregori and me. Apart from once every four years, we never had to worry about which set of in-laws we were going to offend by not spending the holiday with them. Second, all the Easter goodies were marked down fifty percent the day after Roman Catholic Easter, so we got a bargain on our chocolate bunnies. One year, I even ran into Angie Poulos buying marked down Easter items. I hadn't seen her in years. She was amazed when I told her I was marrying a Greek who'd been born overseas.

The theologian also taught me that Orthodox priests can marry. Some Catholics were aghast when I mentioned this. I guess priests having sex with grown, consenting women was more outrageous to them than what some Catholic priests got caught doing.

There were also distinctions between the way the Greek Orthodox and the Catholic receive Baptism and Holy Communion. Holy Communion is the sacrament that celebrates accepting Christ's goodness into one's soul. Catholics receive Holy Communion for the first time when we're seven years old. Don't worry if you witness bunches of seven-year-old girls and boys dressed like brides and grooms on a Sunday in the spring. It's nothing to do with polygamist sects. It's just us Catholics.

During my First Holy Communion rehearsal, one of the nuns cautioned us severely that we were never to *chew* the wafer which represented the 'Body of Christ', saying this, "No one who loves Our Lord and Savior would chew His *Body*, that's for sure!"

According to the Catholic Church, a more seemly way of letting the metaphorical Body of Christ wafer enter our digestive systems was to let it *melt* in our mouths. I have to be frank — it's unrealistic assigning this mission to a seven-year-old. That wafer doesn't melt. It just gets gooey. Then it plasters itself to the concave roof of the mouth. At First Holy Communion as I remember it, we young ones sat, stiff and itchy through the lengthy service, in deference to our newly-elevated rank at God's table. Our mini-bride veils and bowties were by now askew, our small legs numb and our empty tummies growling from the required "fast" before receiving the Sacrament. But the worst was watching everyone's eyes bug, jaws contort and tongues roll back, in our vain attempts to dissolve a paste lump that clung tenaciously to our upper back molars.

In contrast, practicing Orthodox can receive First Holy Communion right after they've been baptized. An Orthodox baptism takes place usually when children are over the age of six months, because a baptism in an Orthodox church requires the full dunking of the youngster in Holy Water. The other reason Orthodox parents wait six months is because it takes at least that long to book a catering hall for the baptism celebration that offers bouzouki players, a belly dancer and the special soup Greeks like, made from egg, lemon and I think, liquid wallpaper paste. Only certain catering halls in The United States offer that soup, so you really have to book ahead.

Sometimes Orthodox parents wait until their children are old enough to walk before they're baptized. This creates problems. If they can walk, they might jump out of the font and run off. It's not an attempt to flee their spiritual destiny; it's only that the church budget doesn't provide for heated water. The other obstacle is that calling a baby by his Christian name before he's been baptized will bring 'the evil eye' on him. So everyone calls the baby by the generic, "baby", like this: "Did you know Baby said her first words today?" That's why some children cry if their parents wait a year to baptize them. Suddenly, instead of being called by what they *thought* was their name, they're being called something alarming like, "Ha-rah-lah-beh," or "Steel-yah-nee."

In the Orthodox Church, people don't have to swallow a wafer at Holy Communion. They get wine-soaked bread, instead. The priest dips a spoon into a chalice that contains the bread-wine mixture and places a portion of the mixture into each parishioner's mouth. Instructions on how to partake of this sacrament state, "Chew, if needed." I winced the first few times I saw people chomping down on bread in church. That nun had her effect on me, for sure. Apart from that, the only other reservation I had about communion in an Orthodox church was that the wine and bread mixture was placed into everyone's mouths from the *same* spoon. When I asked Gregori's mother if she worried about getting sick from this, she got miffed, "*Certainly* not! Everything is *blessed!*"

More lessons in Orthodoxy included the memorization of observance days, fasting policies, and the all-important creed, in *Greek*. Committing these to memory had as much of a purifying affect on my psyche as going for my yearly mammogram and made me thankful that I'd been raised with my parents' approach to religion. Other Catholics I'd known had had spiritual educations that were like deep moles in their skin. They were impossible to remove and could go bad at any moment.

And now, twenty years after Alice Wilson and I sat in one church classroom, she crying because her mom was going to hell, I moved on to another church classroom, where I studied every tiresome bit I've recited here. My secret hope had been that the Greek Orthodox Church would be more munificent in its criterions than the Roman Catholic Church. As you can tell, I was disappointed.

My disillusionments weren't over. Now that I was indoctrinated into the Orthodox fold, there were new church protocols I also had to learn. Upon being apprised of what would make a proper impression on other churchgoers, I thought of my mother again and her assessment of those who proclaimed themselves to be 'good Christians'.

In the Greek-Orthodox churches in Queens, New York, women wore expensive designer suits, shoes, and handbags to Sunday services. In winter, they wore their full-length minks. They looked like they were dressed for a party, but you knew they were going to church because they also wore large, 18kt-gold crucifixes embedded with diamonds or birthstones.

I've always wondered — why an image of *death* as the chosen symbol of Christianity? If by some chance Jesus had been executed by guillotine, would we wear those around our necks?

The grandiosity was fine by the clerics. I learned *that* the first time we stood as a family on the line to the altar to receive communion. Next up was a teenage girl wearing a chic, dark-blue pantsuit, low heels and little makeup, what I thought was attire appropriate for worship.

The priest disagreed. Pointing to her outfit, he exclaimed, "You're wearing *trousers* in *my* church? Get out!"

Turning from the altar, a stricken looked on her face, the girl ran out of the church.

I whispered to Gregori, "I don't want this priest to give us communion. Can we leave?"

In a gesture that was going to become very familiar, Gregori put his finger to his lips. I was becoming quite aware of how much other people's opinions of us meant to him. "You're right, but my parents and brother are here. We don't want to make a scene."

Did I want to make a scene in church, in front of future in-laws? Truthfully, I didn't. So, I let that awful priest give me Holy Communion. It didn't taste right.

After that incident, I took no chances. I wore longish skirts to church, matching suit jackets, low heels, and minimal makeup. These didn't help me avoid censure.

One summer Sunday, my future mother-in-law and I went alone to receive Communion. As we stood on the usual long line, the temperature in the church became oppressive, so I took off my suit jacket. A fellow parishioner standing behind us leaned over, hissed something in Greek and slapped me on the upper arm! I stared at him in disbelief. Before I could ask what was going on, it was our turn to get Communion. After we got home, Gregori's mother tried to brush it off, but I wanted to know what'd happened. What had that man said? Then that slap, out of nowhere. Demetra admitted reluctantly to Gregori and me that the man had taken offense because I was wearing a short-sleeved blouse under my jacket and had exposed my bare arms.

"That backwards son-of-a-bitch," Gregori fumed. "It's a good thing I wasn't there. I would have punched him in the face."

I was surprised that Gregori got so angry. I was already used to him chastising me for my "non-Greek" ways. But when he said, "It's a good thing I wasn't there," I suddenly noted he hardly ever was. He'd told me how essential his church was to him, yet he was only present at his church once a year on Easter Saturday. He'd dress up, appear two hours into the six-hour ceremony, make a quick Sign-of-the-Cross, (Orthodox-style) light a candle in the foyer and kiss the nearest icon. Then he'd stand outside the church, holding another unlit candle, chatting to everyone he knew. At midnight, when the Ascension of Christ was announced, someone would set off fire crackers, everyone would light their candles and the priests and procession would go back inside the church, where the most devoted Orthodox would remain for another three hours. But much of the congregation would leave, the fun parts of the ceremony over. These included Gregori and his group. His total 'worship' time had been about an hour. Why was it so important that we be married in an Orthodox Church and our children be raised Orthodox — just so the children and I would be at church with him a few hours every year? I'd learned as much as I could about Gregori's faith, because it was something that meant a lot to him, I thought. But what did it mean, *exactly*?

That bore scrutiny. However, counting down the months until my wedding, it was the last thing on my mind. I was excited about our engagement, looking forward to the celebrations surrounding our upcoming marriage and our lovely wedding ceremony.

If we managed to get that far.

Chapter Six: My Tastefully Sized, Elegant, Greek Wedding

"My toughest fight was with my first wife."
–Mohammed Ali

The Maid of Dishonor

There's nothing like planning the foolish, all-encompassing particulars of nuptials to distract from the more necessary contemplation of whether the bride and groom are suited to be life partners in the first place. My wedding to Gregori was no exception. But it also had lurid complications, like the one my maid-of-honor threw at me.

My cousins, Marie, Marietta, and Josephine, were going to be my bridesmaids. I loved them all equally and I couldn't choose one over the other to be my maid-of-honor. For that reason, I thought it'd be a nice gesture to ask Thoulah, Gregori's sister-in-law. This didn't turn out to be one of my better decisions. I never imagined I'd obtain a starring role in her divorce, but that's what happened.

Thoulah rang me to say she wanted to meet, "just the two of us." It was "*very* important," but she couldn't tell me over the phone. We arranged to meet in a café a few hours before our dress-fitting appointment with the bridesmaids. The moment we sat down, she made me swear that I wouldn't tell anyone what she was about to say. Once I did, she confessed that her husband, Gerry, was having an affair.

I felt dreadful. "Oh, Thoulah! Are you sure?" I asked.

She was, because her husband's lover had come to their home while he was at work and introduced herself! An action, Thoulah bewailed, that was intended to get her to divorce Gerry, something she didn't want to do. After these declarations, Thoulah sat dejectedly, blinking at tears.

I had no idea what to say. This certainly explained a lot of her behavior over the past few months: the snide comments on my engagement ring, ("That doesn't look lost on your hand at all") and the setting my hair on fire at church during a candle lighting ceremony. (Well... she did say *that* was an accident.) Now I understood that Thoulah felt resentful in the face

92

of my happiness. Her marriage was falling apart.

"Oh, you poor thing." I patted her arm. "No wonder you've been out-of-sorts lately. When did you find out?"

She snorted limply. "Two months ago."

"You've known this for *two months,* Thoulah? How've you been handling it all this time?"

Very quietly, she replied, "I've been handling it by getting him back. I've been sleeping with... Bruno."

I stared at her. "You're not serious."

"Of course I'm serious. Did you think I was going let that bastard get away with this?"

I was confused. "But, Thoulah... you said you didn't want your marriage to end, so how does this *help?* Bruno and Gerry have been best friends for *years.*"

She spread her hands wide and shrugged her shoulders. "It just happened, Patricia. It was terrible finding out about Gerry's affair. I was upset, I phoned Bruno, asked him to come over. One thing led to another."

There might be some who'd say, "Good for her. He deserves it, the pig." But she was only rolling around in the muck with him by doing this. I just didn't get it.

Then the ramifications of my being privy to her affair seeped through. "Thoulah... why are you telling me?"

"I needed someone to talk to and I knew I could trust *you,*" she said, weepy-voiced.

"But don't you see the position this puts me in? You don't want me to tell, yet now that I know, you're asking me to keep it a secret from Gregori and it involves his *brother.*"

Her manner changed instantly. "Oh, for *godssakes,* Patricia, you're *so* naïve. You honestly think Gregori doesn't know what Gerry's been up to?"

"Yes! He'd *never* condone such a thing."

Thoulah snorted again, loudly this time.

"The point is," I continued, trying to gain back some control, "You've put me in this and now expect me to pretend *I don't know?*"

She looked at me, smugly. "Sure. Who'd believe it, anyway?"

I gazed at her in bafflement as she sat, calmly sipping her coffee. Why had she tangled me up in this mess? "I've got a lot of thinking to do," I finally said. "In the meantime, tell Bruno he won't be receiving an invitation to his 'best friend's' brother's wedding."

"We'll see. Listen, Patricia, whether you want to believe me or not, Gregori *knows*. He's no better than his brother. Your marriage will be *no better than mine*." Her voice hitched on that last, but then she composed herself. "Coffee's on me. I'm not going to be able to make it to the fitting. I've... got other plans."

My knees were shaking as I walked out. I couldn't think and I was running late. I'd have to phone my cousins.

*** ***

Thoulah knew I wouldn't feel right about keeping her and Bruno's affair from Gregori and that when he found out, he'd tell Gerry. That had been her purpose in involving me. She wanted Gerry to find out, but she suspected the news would be more devastating for him if he heard it from his brother, rather than from the wife on whom he was cheating. Perhaps a part of Thoulah also wanted to warn me about what could be in store for me down the road. I didn't figure any of this out right away. That day, I just recounted the sordid details to my cousins and three pairs of big, brown, Italian, distressed-filled eyes focused on me.

Marietta spoke first. "Tell Gregori," she said. "He'll be upset if he finds out you knew and *she'll* tell him that when this comes out, *believe* me."

Marie chimed in. "But, if she tells him before the wedding, it'll spoil it for him. He won't dare tell his brother until after the wedding, anyway. Who knows what'll happen, if he does?"

Marietta looked unconvinced. "How can she keep a secret like this?"

"I don't think she should *forever*, I'm only saying... till after the wedding," countered Marie.

Feeling miserable, I looked at Jo. She hadn't given an opinion. "What do you think?"

Jo stared at me with her lips clasped together, as though by keeping them clamped, she could will herself not to reply. Then she sighed, "I *really* don't want to say this. But... I can't lie. I think... you should call the whole thing off."

Marie interjected, "No! *Come on*, it's not Gregori's fault. Why should she break it off?"

Jo said, anxiously, "How do we know he doesn't know?"

Marietta emphasized, "That's why I think she should *tell* him... to see what he says."

I looked at them all. "I'm *sure* he doesn't know... don't you think?" That came out as a plea. Only a short ways away from a wedding I wanted *very* much, I was eager for anything that could put a positive spin on this nightmare.

Marie studied me keenly. She knew what I wanted to hear. So, she advised, "Pretend you don't know just for *now*. Tell him when you're back from your honeymoon. This way, he can enjoy the wedding and, if he thinks it's the right thing to do, tell his brother *afterward*."

I was so grateful for this. "*Thank you*, Marie. That makes sense. That's what I'll do." I smiled at her and glanced at the other two. Josephine was still clamping down on her lips and Marietta still looked grim.

*** ***

When I got home, a message from Gregori said that we'd been invited to his parents for dinner and to finish writing wedding invitations. When I arrived, my stomach did a flip when I saw Gerry and Thoulah were there, too. Keeping in mind Marie's guidance, I pretended I had only invitations on my mind. Thoulah had another scenario worked out for the evening. She and Demetra were sitting at the kitchen table, *tête-à-tête*. They looked up from their talk, Gregori's mom with an indecipherable look on her face.

"Patricia," she said, "Thoulah's just told me that you're not inviting Bruno to the wedding. Why not?"

Speechless, I looked at Thoulah. She had a furtive, but edgy look in her eye. *What was she doing?*

Demetra's question got Gregori's attention. He looked up from his newspaper, "We're not inviting Bruno?"

Still staring at Thoulah, I thought, *I have no clue what game you're playing, but I guess I'll find out.* Then I smiled at Gregori. "It's your decision. I thought we were trying to keep the numbers down."

Gregori's mother was still peering at me strangely, so along with other questions I had, I wondered what Thoulah had told her, exactly. "You have to ask Bruno," Demetra said to Gregori. "He's like part of the family."

I said nothing, but as far as I was concerned, I wasn't going to let my wedding day be the trade-fair for my brother-in-law's humiliation, with me as an accessory. Concluding that Gregori wouldn't have excused his married brother's affair, I stuck with the plan to tell Gregori after the honeymoon. I still had an unwanted wedding guest with whom to contend, though.

So the next day, I rang up Bruno, that scoundrel, and told him to expect an invitation he'd better *decline*, if he knew what was good for him. The last thing I expected was that he'd be genteel about it. He apologized

95

("I never imagined she'd tell you and so close to your wedding day. Don't let this spoil that for you…") and as per my request, returned his invitation with "regrets."

I told Gregori about his sister-in-law's affair after our honeymoon. He was stunned. Within the week, he'd informed his brother. We never saw Bruno again. Gerry and Thoulah separated shortly thereafter. Gregori and I were in agreement that her conduct was deplorable, but I now see we had different reasons. To me, there was something off-kilter about her believing an affair with Bruno was the way to get her self-respect back. But there were lots of things off-kilter about the family that I still was blind to, more secrets, more lies, more betrayals to come. Gerry and Thoulah's notions of "love, honor and cherish," were diametrically opposed to mine. I hadn't put it together yet, that Gregori's were, too.

The Best-Behaved Man

> *"If I were two-faced, would I be wearing this one?"*
> **–Abraham Lincoln**

I'd had the astounding lesson that my brother-in-law and sister-in-law's marriage was a sham, but more tutorials were coming with the next round of wedding business. First I'd discover that Gregori and I were not nearly as good at wedding subterfuge as Margie and Sean had been. Next, I'd be wishing desperately for a bridal registry which we weren't allowed to have. And third, I'd come to realize that the illustrious Louie had acquiesced way too easily regarding our impending marriage and his role in it as best man.

At this juncture, Gregori and I had to choose what the Greeks and Italians call, "*boubounieras,*" which are, "wedding favors," token gifts given to each wedding guest as a remembrance of the occasion. These gifts are usually a romantic porcelain figurine, such as two swans entwined, with the bride and groom's names and date of wedding painted on it. As near as I can tell, we're supposed to immortalize the favors in a curio cabinet filled with these bric-a-bracs, accumulated from every wedding to which we've ever been. Once a month, we should open the sideboard, dust all the *boubounieres* off and then put them back.

In the Greek-Orthodox tradition, the wedding favors are purchased by the "*koumbaro*", which is the "best man". The best man also provides the "*stefania*", which are the wedding crowns worn by the bride and groom during the marriage rites and the "*lambadas,*" the freestanding, white candles that are placed on either side of the altar specifically for the ceremony. The best man considers it a hallowed duty that his contributions be considered 'outstanding'. He'll spare no expense to achieve this. Retail shops that provide these falderals are aware of the mania and charge accordingly.

Louie was no exception in wanting our *boubounieres, stefanias,* and *lambadas* to be spectacular. Our quandary was that Louie's motto in fashion, décor and art, seemed to be "when in doubt, ask a drag queen."

His first choice for *lambadas* were six-foot high tapers, a foot-wide apiece, each dressed in more white silk fabric than was used for my entire wedding gown. When Gregori saw the colossal altar candles Louie had chosen, he said, "The only way anyone's going to be able to tell which is the bride and which are the candles is that Patricia's going to be the shortest of the three."

Louie had the best intentions. Each of those candles would have cost him half a month's wages had Gregori sanctioned them. But, how to tell him we didn't like his taste, without hurting his feelings?

Since his lies had been so successful at the cheese dinner, ("Cheese? No — *no* cheese") Gregori lied again, "Louie, those candles are nice, but on the island of Rhodes where I come from, it's a tradition to use much smaller, simpler ones."

Yes, it was a lame excuse, but, fortunately, Louie bought it. He returned the giant, puffy *lambadas* and selected daintier ones. It wasn't necessary to be dishonest when it came to our wedding favor, because Louie picked out a half dozen and invited us to go along with him to make the final selection. One of the six was a white porcelain music box portraying a dancing couple, delicately embellished with 14-karat gold. Though it wasn't exactly Gregori's and my taste, it didn't offend our sensibilities like the other five. It was only after it'd been ordered, that we noticed the tunes tinkling out of it were, "Jesus Loves Me," followed by "Feelings." After the 'close calls' with the *lambadas* and *boubounieres*, Gregori was bracing himself for what kind of *stefanias* we'd have to wear, but since they'd only be on our heads for a short time during the ceremony, it wouldn't be so bad.

This same sticky situation came up with wedding gifts. Back when Gregori and I were getting married, the older folks from Italy and Greece weren't familiar with bridal registries. They had every intention of presenting the couple with a gift, but a 'bridal registry' appeared too specific and greedy to them. How much money was spent on gifts always left an impression, both good and bad, with these two particular crowds. Therefore, to those who were counting their pennies, giving a gift from the bridal registry was embarrassing because then the newlyweds would *know* what they'd paid.

As a result, my generation of Greek and Italian brides spent the early weeks of our marriages guessing what shop our seventh coffee pot had come from and then returning it to get something else we desperately needed. Playing "guess the shop" was hard. Don't forget that *figura* was important, even in gift giving. Some presented their wedding gifts in boxes that had come from... let's say, *Saks*, when the item in that box had actually been purchased at *Woolworth's*. Since making a good impression on the newlyweds by wedding guests meant resorting to trickery, we newlyweds employed the same:

Visiting Relative: What a lovely little apartment you and Gregori have, Patricia. Is it yours?

Patricia: No, we're renting for now.

Visiting Relative: Oh, too bad. My daughter and her new husband bought their own. By the way, where's the kitchen clock *we* gave you, the one with the red plastic lobster and ears of yellow corn on it?

Patricia: Oh, we *loved* that one. Funny thing, though. Its electric cord was missing. They didn't have any more at the shop with lobsters and corn on it, so I got this one, instead.

Visiting Relative: But the lobster clock was battery-operated.

Patricia: *Oops...* silly me.

Many people have been to weddings where sending a gift a week ahead of the wedding ceremony to the future bride's home is the only correct thing to do. However, at many Greek and Italian weddings, guests put checks or cash in greeting cards, bring them to the reception, and hand them to the bride. This was what was expected, and anything *else* was bad form. When guests bring cards with cash in them to a Greek or Italian wedding reception, the bride places them in a 'money purse', which is made from the same material and lace as her wedding gown. When guests stop at the dais to say "congratulations" to the newlyweds, they hand the couple their gift card and the bride slips it into her money purse.

Since our wedding reception ended at 7 P.M., there'd be a small family celebration afterward at my in-laws' place. We were leaving on our honeymoon very early the next day, so we weren't expected to attend. But we were instructed by Gregori's parents that we *had* to open our cards on our wedding night and write down the amount each person on their side of the family had given.

Gregori's mother explained, "We've given so much money at so many weddings, I want to make sure *every one* of our relatives is giving back their fair share to my son!"

That was the plan for after our wedding reception. We had our money purse ready, we had our *lambadas*, *boubounieres*, and *stefanias*. Louie had been so gallant throughout the selections process, I started to think I'd misjudged him.

Then it happened. The night of Gregori's bachelor party, Louie rang me.

"Are you worried about Gregori misbehaving tonight?" he asked.

"No, I trust him," I smiled into the phone, "And I've got you to watch him for me, too," I teased.

"That's not all the best man is supposed to do," his voice deepened seductively, "The best man is also supposed to get a chance to sleep with the bride before the wedding."

"Really," I said. I was surprised, but not shocked. *Yet.* I thought he was joking, though he had never made a comment of this kind before.

"Yes," Louie crooned, in that same low tone. "So, how 'bout it?"

Now I was shocked. He couldn't be drunk. I'd never seen him drunk and the bachelor party hadn't started yet. In fact, Gregori was still here, walking toward me. *Thank God.*

"Who's that on the phone?" he asked.

"It's Louie. He wants to talk to you," I handed Gregori the phone and ran out of there.

I never told Gregori what Louie said in that phone conversation. I still can't decide if Louie was serious and if so, even creepier than I'd thought. On the other hand, it could have been that, in his mind, he was devising some sort of a "foreign woman trap." Maybe he was hoping I'd take him up on his offer, so he could run and tell Gregori, thereby rescuing him from marrying me. Or maybe it was just a joke.

But... still. *Yuck.*

The Two Grandmothers

"My mother buried three husbands.
And two of them were just napping."
–Rita Rudner

While these performances wreaked havoc, there was one last wedding bit that needed to be tackled: an in-law dinner before the wedding. Gregori assured me this dinner should go much better than that first, because we'd be at a restaurant, so everyone could order whatever they liked. In addition, there'd be so many of us this time, that our parents would have no opportunity to say more than a few words to one another.

A number of Gregori's relatives from overseas were flying in for the wedding. Gregori was pleased that his father's brother, Elias, a priest from Crete, had agreed to travel to the States to marry us. Accompanying him would be his wife. (A Greek priest is called a "*papas*" or "*papa*", and a Greek priest's wife is called a "*papadia*.") Another happy surprise was that Gregori's paternal grandmother, who lived in Crete with the priest and *papadia*, would also come. It would be at this formal dinner that my grandmother and Gregori's would meet for the first time.

Like Gregori and me, our two grandmothers shared some commonalities. Both had spiritual, feminine names. Gregori's grandmother was *Ourania*, derived from the Greek word for "Heavenly." My grandmother was *Graziella*, taken from the Italian, meaning, "One filled with grace." Both our grandmothers had been beautiful in their prime. Ourania was light-haired and petite, with bright green eyes and a riveting smile. Graziella was strikingly dark-haired and dark-eyed, statuesque for her day. Both could laugh as easily as they could cry, the gladness and sadness in each evoked by shifting circumstances in their children and grandchildren's lives. Both, as you might have presumed, were outstanding cooks. Both had lived through war, poverty, illnesses, and death of loved ones. That they'd endured was marked by the strength in their backs, straight still, despite their years. I'd seen Ourania grab the nearest heavy thing she could find — a large cookbook — and slam it down on a mouse that'd had the temerity to run across her kitchen. And my own grandmother had once put down the newspaper she'd been reading and took off her shoe to kill a scorpion. Without a shiver, she cleaned the mess, put her shoe back on, and picked up her paper again.

In every other aspect, however, the lives of Ourania and Graziella were wholly divergent.

My grandmother 'Grace' was Graziella Zarcone, Citrone, Buonaguro, Livoti, Picataggi. The first surname was her maiden surname, the last four the surnames of four successive husbands. With the exception of the first, who was my real grandfather and the one true love of her life, she met all her husbands at a "senior citizen club" in Brooklyn, New York. They'd all had been besotted with her and each bought her a diamond engagement ring at least a carat in weight.

My grandmother believed in the institute of marriage as a way of maintaining a preferred social status and financial position. She believed it was infinitely better to marry for companionship and security, rather than rely on her grown children for those. And she made a good wife, by her definition. Her husbands ate well and lived in cared-for homes. They also got clean clothing, altered to their perfect fit, since Nonnie was a seamstress by trade.

When I was young, my grandmother seemed indomitable. I thought that if death *could* happen to her, it'd have to be as eventful as she was. Maybe she'd die heroically, like jumping from a helicopter on a reconnaissance mission, her parachute failing to open. In my wicked moments, I'd think, maybe if I splashed some water on her, she'd shrivel up and disappear.

One thing I admired about Nonnie was that she afraid of nothing. She'd survived an earthquake in Sicily when she was two years old. She loved to tell us how her father heard her crying from under the rubble and frantically pushed aside rocks until he reached her. When repeating this story for Gregori, she said proudly, "I still have a scar — see?" Much to his mortification, she lifted up her dress and bared her upper thigh to him.

I was accustomed to seeing my grandmother dress cheerfully and I had no idea she was the pioneer of bright-colored clothing for the middle-class, senior woman. She made her clothing herself, which explained how she got the shades she wanted. She wore matching accessories, too. If she had a red jacket, white blouse and a white skirt, she wanted red enamel earrings, red shoes and a red handbag. When she couldn't find red shoes at the 'old lady shoe shops' she frequented on 86th Street in Bensonhurst, Brooklyn, she'd buy white ones and dye them. My grandmother refused to confine herself to the fashion limitations our youth-oriented culture had consigned her. To enhance her ensembles, every week, she had her hair 'done'. 'Done' meant the salon would tease up her pure white hair, smooth it back down and spray it from a bottle labeled, *Old-Biddy Hair Gum*, until the hair was literally unbendable. What they did next was ambiguous. They called it, "toning," so that the stiff whiteness on her head tinged blue or purple. When they were finished, Nonnie's hair looked and felt like blueberry-flavor cotton candy.

The first time Gregori met my grandmother, he stared at her so long, he was practically ogling. "I've never seen a woman that age dress like that," he said.

"Dress like what?" I asked him.

When I met his grandmother, I understood. Gregori's grandmother dressed only in black, top to toe. It wasn't because black is slimming and chic or because she was 'into Goth or Metal'. *Yiayia* wore black because she was a widow and black symbolizes 'in mourning'. Her husband had been dead for more than twenty years, but no matter. Ourania wore black from that day forward, for as long as she lived. 'Black forever' for widows is common in the Italian culture, too, within certain groups. My grandmother kept some traditions, but she didn't buckle under this one, and I'm glad.

After meeting my grandmother, Gregori asked me, "If I died before you, would you wear black?"

"At your funeral, I would," I answered.

That troubled him. "You'd only wear black for me at my funeral, but after that, you'd... dress like your grandmother dresses?"

I squinted at him. "Did you just insult my grandmother?"

"I just meant, why does she dress so bright?"

"Why *not* so bright?" Before he could answer, I jumped in. "Gregori, if your father passed away tomorrow — *God forbid* — would you want to see your mother only in black for the rest of her life?"

The question hit a nerve, still he had to continue, "But I'm saying, when I die —"

"—Save it, Gregori," I cut him off again. "I'm sure *I'll* die before you do, anyway."

My opinion on this subject didn't affect my feelings for *Yiayia* Ourania. Though she was more old-fashioned regarding women's place in society, I liked and respected her. And one could argue that wearing decades of black for the one man in your life, the man who'd fathered your ten children, was an impressive statement, too. Listening to her tales of her husband and their life in Crete, I did sometimes wonder, what if I'd borne ten children with my one love and then, like Ourania's husband, he fell asleep in his chair never to wake and smile at me again? If I had to look at that empty chair every day, as our grandchildren grew and he wasn't there with me to experience it all, maybe... just *maybe*, I'd wear black forever for him, too.

Yiayia Ourania adored Gregori, and he her. I loved to watch them together, the way she fussed over him, the way he'd tease her, making her laugh. Of course, food was a great part of the way she expressed her love. The moment Gregori walked into the kitchen, she'd prepare him Greek coffee just the way he liked it. Knowing it would please her, he'd make a show of inhaling its aroma, sipping, and savoring. "Yiayia, nobody makes this like you do. It's the *best*."

Yiayia was familiar with the foods and sweets Gregori liked, too. That's why, when coming from Crete for our wedding, she smuggled in two of his favorites, Cretan honey, which is prized for its fantastic texture and color, and Cretan *graviera* cheese. When her son, the priest, translated what she was asked at customs, "Are you bringing in any foods?" she'd stated without compunction, "Certainly not." Then, at Gregori's parents' home, she opened her cases, revealing wheels of cheese and jars of honey. She'd kept them from breakage and the eyes of customs agents by wrapping them in her dark dresses and tights.

Seeing this, the priest admonished, "*Mama*, why did you lie?"

Unabashed, *Yiayia* asserted, "I didn't lie, son. You said they asked if I had '*food*'. 'Food' is food, 'honey' is honey, and 'cheese' is cheese!"

*** ***

The pre-wedding dinner took place and Yiayia Ourania and Nonnie were introduced formally. Grace stood majestic in a salmon-colored sheath, a beige silk jacket, matching shoes, pearl earrings and, of course, diamond rings. Ourania sat regally, draped in luxurious black, her silvery-hair tied in a chignon at her neck, her only adornments her plain, gold wedding band and delicate, gold cross. They couldn't communicate, as one spoke Italian and English and the other only Greek, but their royal nods to one another made them look like a flamingo bobbing crowns with a wren.

Afterward, as I escorted my grandmother back to her chair, she whispered something to me that made me laugh. And Gregori's grandmother said something to him that made him chuckle, too. Here's what our grandmothers had to say about each other:

"*Poh poh poh* — how can she wear those *colors*?"

103

"Pee-ew — her dress smells like cheese."

Ah, well. My 'Nonnie' and Gregori's *'Yiayia'.* They'd never be "best friends forever," I supposed.

Kala Stefana (Greek Wedding Salutation)

"I always cry at weddings. Especially my own."
–Humphrey Bogart

We'd managed to slog through my father's peccadilloes, the matron-of-honor's duplicities and the best man's tackiness. Nothing else was left to conquer, save the wedding day itself. I promised myself I'd enjoy it, whatever else happened.

If weather was any indication of how the marriage would go, our life stood to be superb. We had sunshine, but not too much heat, considering it was a New York July. The church was cool, but the sun sparkled on the exquisite stained glass windows and mosaic tiles that make Saint Paul's Church so magnificent. Oh, you should have seen it — the flowers and the bridesmaids were beautiful, the men looked stylish, and everyone was smiling.

The Greek Orthodox wedding ritual has three parts, the betrothal, the crowning and the common cup.

In the 'betrothal', the *koumbaro* places the rings on the bride and groom's fingers and exchanges the rings on their fingers three times, which symbolizes the three stations of the Cross. The 'crowning' is the focal point of the ceremony. The two wedding crowns (*stefania*) are connected by a ribbon that represents the unity of the couple with Christ. The officiating priest (in our case, it was Gregori's uncle, Elias) holds the two connected crowns, blesses them and places them on the bride and groom's heads. The best man steps behind the bride and the groom and interchanges the crowns also three times. In remembrance of Christ's miracle of changing water into wine at the wedding in Cana, the priest gives wine to the couple, chanting, "From this moment on, this couple's joys will be doubled and sorrows halved, because they will be shared."

To complete the wedding ceremony, sugared almonds are placed on a special tray with the couple's wedding crowns and passed around to the church guests. *Papa* Elias explained the religious significance of them:

"The egg shape represents fertility and the new married life. The almond's hardness represents the endurance of marriage and the sugar coating the sweetness of their future. There are always an odd number of almonds. An odd number is indivisible, just as the bride and groom shall remain undivided."

The ceremony was moving for both of us, with our family and friends there to share it. The setting for the reception at *The Swan Club* was glorious, the food and the music spectacular. Despite the rocky start, it all went off without a hitch.

Okay, there might have been... one or two tiny ones.

The first transpired as my father and I were about to walk down the aisle. Dad's gaze went to the altar where Gregori and the rest of the bridal party waited. He sighed deeply. Then he looked at me and said softly, "Patricia, this is our *last* chance. Say the word and I'll take you out of here *right* now." He had his hand on my arm in a tight grasp, like a pet owner gripping an untrained puppy's leash.

I smiled. "Dad, don't be silly. I don't want to leave."

He persisted, "Is it because we've already hired the caterers? Because the guests are already here? To *hell* with all *that*. We can still go."

"Dad," I admonished, "you're swearing. We're in church."

He shook his head adamantly. "We're not in *yet.*" He enunciated this last in a stage whisper, "We. Can. Still. Go."

His persistence was starting to wear on my nerves. And it certainly wasn't the time to confess I'd been having a doubt or two, myself.

"Dad," I whispered exasperatedly, "the wedding march has started! *That's* our cue."

He said nothing more. And walking slowly, choking back sobs, like Agamemnon forced to sacrifice his daughter, Iphigenia, my father brought me down the aisle to my future husband.

That wasn't the end of my trials. After my father lifted my veil, kissed my cheek, and shuffled away hopelessly, my maid-of-dishonor turned to me and pulled my veil back down over my face. From the corner of my eye, I could see the photographer smack his forehead.

"Thoulah," I murmured agitatedly, "my veil's supposed to be off my face for the ceremony."

"No, it's not," she whispered back.

I was stymied. The priest was *waiting* to start the ceremony. The photographer was playing "Charades" at me, putting his hands on his face and sweeping them back over his head. Short of setting my bouquet down on the ground and pulling the veil back off my face myself, I didn't know what to do.

Marie came to my rescue. She handed her own bouquet to Josephine and, gracefully stepping around Thoulah, she smoothed my veil into place and even adjusted my train. Then she stepped back to the other bridesmaids and Jo handed her back her flowers. The photographer gave them both a "thumbs up." With that, *Papa* Elias started the ceremony.

*** ***

I hadn't seen my grandmother at church. When we made our way to the restaurant, I discovered why. She was there, sitting on the front steps, her head in her hands, crying. The sun glinted off the sapphire tinge of her 'just-done' hair, nicely accentuating her peacock-blue gown. Grandpa Sal II was patting her back, soothingly.

My mother and my aunt reached her first. "What *happened?*" they asked.

Nonnie cried. "Sadie and Frank couldn't find the church, so they brought us here instead! I never saw a Greek wedding before and now I missed the whole thing!"

"I told you *we* would come and get you!" my aunt said.

"It's *too far* for you to come all the way to Brooklyn. I said Frank and Sadie would take me! And *they* got lost!" my grandmother wailed.

"All right, forget it now. You're here now," my aunt tried to calm her.

Gregori on my arm, bridesmaids in tow, I sailed over, leaned down, and kissed her. "Hi, Nonnie."

She looked at me through drama-drenched eyes. "I missed your wedding," she repeated.

"How are you, *signora?*" all three of my cousins chorused.

My grandmother had cataracts that she refused to have removed. She squinted up at my cousins. "Who are you?" she asked.

My mother was losing her patience. "It's Marie, Marietta and Josephine, from Joe's side. Can you *get up* off the steps now, please, and come inside?"

My grandmother stood, still focused on my cousins. Grandpa Sal II brushed off the back of her gown as she spoke.

"My God," my grandmother declared to Josephine. "You look just like your mother in that dress, God rest her soul." Then, loudly to Sal, slapping his hand, *"Lascilo!"* ("Leave my dress alone!")

"Let's go *in*," my mother repeated.

106

As we walked toward the garden where cocktails were being served, I heard someone ask Gregori's mother in Greek, "Who was that woman with the blue hair crying on the steps?"

"That was Patricia's grandmother," Demetra replied.

"Dressed like *that*?" came the response.

*** ***

The final impediment to an otherwise 'perfect' wedding day was that my new husband went missing. After the reception, we headed back to our apartment. I had a silk sack filled with cards that my in-laws wanted counted straight away, before we were even out of our wedding clothes. Then I realized Gregori's parents needed to deposit the gifts into our bank account, since we'd be gone for five days.

"I'll take them over to their place," Gregori said.

"Why not just wait till they take us to the airport in the morning?"

"I'll do it now, so we don't forget." Before I could say another word, he was out the door.

Oh, well. I thought. *While he's gone, I'll change out of my gown.*

Except I couldn't. I'd forgotten about the dozens of pearl buttons that ran down the back from the neck to the waist. There was no way I could get to them without help. I'd have to wait for Gregori.

An hour and a half later, hot and uncomfortable by now, I was still waiting. I'd taken off my shoes and headpiece, but was stuck in that gown. *Where* was he?

Then I knew. His parents were having the after-party. Oh, *please* don't tell me he'd decided to join the festivities there, without me. It'd be too mortifying to phone at my in-laws and ask for him. *What to do?*

I heard noise outside and ran to open the door. My new neighbor, Colleen, was standing on her front porch. She greeted me with a big smile. "Hi, there, pretty bride!" she exclaimed. "How did it go?"

I smiled back. "Just… great," I replied. "Listen, would you mind helping me out of this damn dress? It's got buttons down the back I can't reach."

"*Um…* where's your husband?"

I rolled my eyes and sighed, "At his mother's."

With no more questions asked, Colleen stepped inside and helped me out of my wedding gown. It was the beginning of a beautiful friendship.

After she left, I settled back and waited for Gregori. He'd come home, eventually. Because… for better or worse, we were now husband and wife.

Chapter Seven: The Honeymoon is Over

"I knew nothing about sex
because I was always married."
–Zsa Zsa Gabor

A Leisurely Repentance

My marriage to Gregori, just like my first trip to Greece with him, was not going at all the way I'd imagined.

It started right from our honeymoon. We didn't have a honeymoon in Greece as Gregori wished we had. Instead, we honeymooned in Puerto Rico to save money. It was gorgeous there, absolutely. Even Gregori said, "It's almost as beautiful as Greece."

I didn't compare Puerto Rico to Greece. I took pleasure in being there, not only because it was so lovely, but because Gregori and I were finally alone. Our honeymoon would be the ideal opportunity to bring up something that'd been niggling at me. It had to do with... lovemaking. I'd been making excuses to myself... we *still needed to get to know one another... we were nervous because of all the wedding preparations,* etc. Now that we were married, I thought I could address it, delicately.

Big mistake.

"Are you saying that I'm not a good lover?" Gregori asked, offended.

"No! I'm not saying that *at all.* I'm only saying that... now that we're *married...* on our honeymoon... isn't it the perfect time to explore... alternatives?"

"What do you mean, 'alternatives'?" asked Gregori, suspiciously.

"Different... things that you might like better and... that I... might like better," I finished lamely.

Gregori was insulted. *Very.* "Let me tell you something," he finally said, "if you don't like the way I make love, *you're* the one with the problem. Other women have never complained!"

And that pretty much summed up our sex life. I tried hard to 'get it right', doing everything I could think of to increase my own pleasure. I also noticed that, strangely enough, now that we were married, Gregori didn't seem very motivated to make love with me. I'd thought that once we slept in the same bed every night that would make things easier.

I didn't have much sexual experience. Kurt and I had only been together for a very short while and though that had been nice, it wasn't the earth-shattering encounter some other women, like Sharon, for instance, had described. I'd been with one other man before Kurt, and that had turned out to be so devastatingly awful, that I told no one the details of that period in my life, except my cousin, Marie. She was five years older and already married. She assured me the trouble had nothing to do with me, but with identity issues the particular man I'd chosen was having. I believed her then, but now, I wasn't so sure. Because here I was, married to a man I loved and who loved me, and there was still a problem. I couldn't figure out what it was. I hadn't gained weight, I didn't look any different than when we were dating, and though Gregori was still driving the taxi, which he complained was hard work, it wasn't as though he was working any more hours than he ever had.

Six months into my marriage, I decided to confide in Margie. She was so happy with Sean that she was nearly delirious with it. I figured she'd have some insight. But I didn't want to have this conversation on the phone. It would have to wait until we could meet. We always tried to meet at a restaurant halfway between our two residences. She remained on Long Island, was now working part-time, and was a class mother at Jared's kindergarten. Gregori and I lived two blocks from his parents in Astoria and I had my first job teaching English at a private high school there. That meant Margie and I couldn't manage a meeting more than about once every two months. So, we looked forward to speaking face-to-face with no interruptions from the husbands or the little one, drinking Peach Bellinis and sharing a fattening dessert.

It was after my second Bellini that I divulged my dilemma. Just as I'd expected, Margie blushed.

"You mean, you've never...?" she hesitated.

"No. I mean, *yes*, I... have. It's just so much *work!* And Gregori says it takes me too long," I said. "I think there's something wrong with me. I must be built wrong or... something."

"There's *nothing* wrong with you. You're perfect," Margie declared, loyally.

"Then why has my husband lost interest in me?" I asked, despondently.

Clearly at a loss, Margie patted the back of my hand. "Don't be silly. He hasn't, I'm sure. It's just that sometimes... men... if they have work issues or worries on their mind, they can get distracted. They might need a little extra... stimulation."

I watched her carefully. "What do you mean?"

Her face shined like a tomato now. Nevertheless, as my friend, she persevered. I experienced *déjà vu* as she leaned in to whisper sexual confessions, "Well... let me tell you about *Cosmopolitan* magazine..."

And so, after that conversation with Margie, I bought my first copy of *Cosmo* and introduced into our bedroom reinforcements designed to "extra stimulate" my husband. In alphabetical order they were: fruit, g-strings, ice, ice cream, lace-up corsets, silk scarves, striptease, video camera, and whipped topping with chocolate sauce. All recommended in one issue, I might add.

My husband was titillated for a while. But for all my efforts, I just got more of the same. He'd put his full weight on top of me and the session would end as it always had — with my feelings of failure as a woman and aches from the usual two bruises on each of my inner thighs where his hip bones had ground into me. It wasn't that he lacked skill as much as he lacked caring. I felt like I meant no more to him than any attractive woman he might find in his bed, wearing provocative underwear. We'd do the deed, he'd say "good night," and fall sleep. And I'd do my best to make sure he didn't hear me crying.

In the end, I concluded Gregori was right. It was my fault. So when Margie asked me how 'things' were going, I lied.

About a year into our marriage, Gregori brought two other Greek taxi drivers over for drinks, new friends I hadn't yet met. They were polite to me, but had come to visit Gregori, so I left the three of them alone in the living room. Immediately, they started speaking in Greek. I could hear them from the kitchen. My Greek was still poor, but this I understood:

"Pretty wife, Gregori," said one, "but a wife's still a wife, eh?"

"Boy, that's the truth," said the other. "Whether I touch my wife's ass or my own, it feels the same."

They all laughed at that, including Gregori.

As if my husband's perspective on married sex wasn't disheartening enough, there was the deteriorating relationship with my parents to cope with, too. It turned out that Kurt was right. A power struggle was taking place between them and my husband:

"Why did you get an apartment in Astoria? Why not here?" was what my mother asked, when I'd phoned to tell her Gregori and I had found a place to rent.

"It's only twenty minutes to Manhattan, Mom. Brooklyn takes over an hour. Gregori works the taxi in the city," I pointed out what she already knew.

"You had to move *two* blocks away from *his* parents' place?" she went on.

"Their apartment has a garage and ours doesn't. Gregori uses their garage to keep the taxi in at nights, or else it'll get broken into."

"Yeah. *Sure*," my mother replied, sarcastically.

And, a later phone conversation:

"What do you mean you're not coming for Christmas?"

"We were at your place *last* year for Christmas, Mom. It's Gregori's parents' turn. They invited you and Dad, too," I tried.

"I don't want to spend Christmas with those people," my mother groused. "That man is obnoxious and I do *not* trust that woman. She's sneaky."

"I understand, but to be fair, I *have* to go. It's their turn," I said, as firmly as I could. "I'll tell you what—why don't we drive over Christmas Eve and exchange gifts then?"

"If you don't come for Christmas Day, don't bother coming, *period.*"

And then she hung up on me. Neither one of my parents spoke to me again, until the following February, as penalty. When we did see them, they were barely civil to Gregori, who remained unfailingly polite, but carped about it endlessly to me afterward. And that's the way it went. One or both my parents would make a demand, while at the same time expressing their contempt for Gregori, his family and my choices. I'd try to placate and convince. When that didn't work, I'd get angry and tell them off. Then they'd stop speaking to me, sometimes for days, sometimes for months. I made the decision to hold firm and not let them rule my life or insult my husband. But it was gut-twisting and instead of appreciating how that felt for me and respecting that I'd marshaled the maturity to stand up for myself and him, Gregori threw the situation in my face.

"*Poh, poh, poh,*" he'd say. "Your father is so spiteful and your mother has such a big mouth."

At the same time this made me seethe, it made me ashamed, because I knew he was right. I began to see my parents much less and confided in them hardly at all. We spent more time with Gregori's family, who included

111

his parents, his *Thia* Marina and *Thio* Sotiri, who also lived in Astoria, and his brother Gerry and Gerry's girlfriend, Doosie.

Gerry and Doosie could be fun, but there was something off about Doosie. She was Gerry's fiancée now, but before that, she'd been the mistress who'd turned up at Thoulah's door. She liked to brag about that, as well as about the fact that she and Bruno, with Gerry's knowledge, had actually discussed her coming to Gregori's and my wedding, as Bruno's *date*, just to rub Thoulah's nose in it. And Bruno had *already* been sleeping with Thoulah at the time. This information was odious, to say the least. In fact, Doosie's general line of conversation was often odious, such as the time she expressed her revulsion that my best friend was Jewish and a Christian had married her. How hypocritical can you get? Needless to say, she was not one of my favorite in-laws, but I ignored her as much as I could, because she and Gerry came as a set. Then there was the aunt and uncle, Marina and Sotiri. Sotiri was Demetra's older brother and it was this couple that Gregori and his parents had stayed with when they'd first moved to the States. There was some hard history between Demetra and Marina. I didn't know what had gone on between the sisters-in-law, exactly, only that they spoke civilly, but weren't close.

Just as Gregori had said, Marina was quite a character. When she was first introduced to me, thinking I wouldn't understand her Greek, she announced loudly to everyone, "*Wow* — she's got a set of big ones."

Marina, like my grandmother, dressed imaginatively and wore lots of expensive jewelry. She also wore a wig, because her hair had fallen out due to illness. Sadly, despite her Mae West attitude, Marina was not a well woman. She was a heart patient and a diabetic who enjoyed sweets vicariously by forcing them on her guests. My first visit, she piled my plate with Greek sweets, filled with custard and nuts and doused with honey. On the same plate, she placed three pieces of fudge and two scoops of ice cream.

"Eat it," she ordered and sat back to watch, envy in her eyes.

Just looking at that pile of sweets was sending me into my own sugar shock. I waited for an opportunity to sneak my plate into the kitchen. But Marina came back into the dining room, with my dessert in her hand and glared at me. "Is there something *wrong* with this?"

"*No*," I stammered, "I just couldn't finish it all."

Offended, she plopped the plate back down in front of me, melting ice cream and all. "Eat it a bit at a time, then," she sniffed. "You have *all* evening."

Gregori found this hilarious, but I was mortified that I'd made a bad impression and nauseated, too, by being forced to eat *dessert*.

With Gregori's parents, there were language issues. I was still learning Greek by rote repetition. This had disastrous results occasionally, like the time Gregori thought it would be amusing to teach me, *"Na klanees o lee tee nikta."* He told me it was an expression that meant "pleasant dreams."

I didn't know *klanees* is the second-person singular of the verb, "to fart." So one evening, when I thought I'd offered my father-in-law "pleasant dreams," I'd in fact told him I wished he'd pass gas all night. He didn't have much of a sense of humor about it, unfortunately.

But that language lesson was minor compared to the fiasco that followed. This one involved mixing up one word with another, very similar-sounding word, *psomi,* which is the Greek word for "bread." The other word differed by only *one* consonant sound variation — an "L" instead of an "M," a *"lee"* instead of a *"me."* You'd think it wouldn't make very much of a difference, right? *Wrong.*

There I was, describing for Gregori's aunt and his mother, my special garlic bread recipe:

"Well, I usually get the longest loaf of bread the bakery has. I split the bread in half lengthwise, and place lightly salted butter on each half. Then I sprinkle the bread with granulated garlic, place it in the broiler, and cook on the highest setting until it browns slightly and the butter melts. After I take the bread out of the oven, I scatter bits of chopped parsley on top to give it some color."

That's what I *thought* I was saying. But read the description of how to make garlic bread again, this time, replacing the words "bread," with an utterly crude slang term for "penis." *That's* the difference one change of consonant made in this particular instance.

Gregori's mother almost choked to death with laughter when, after I'd finished reciting my 'recipe', Marina commented, *"Hmmm* — 'butter'? Maybe. 'Garlic'? Never — the taste is already too bitter. 'Slice it in half and broil it in the oven?' I hope you wait until you catch him cheating on you before you attempt *that."*

So, Niko, Demetra and I first tried communicating in Italian exclusively. But my Italian was no better than my Greek, really, and this also frustrated my father-in-law. He'd say, *"Why* didn't your father teach you to speak Italian? It sounds nothing like Italian. What is it — Armenian?"

113

After hearing this several times, I surprised everyone by showing some spunk. "What about *you*?" I said. "You've been in the States for *20 years*. Your English teacher should be shot."

To my surprise, that comeback got a big laugh from everyone, this time including my father-in-law.

Sometimes my father-in-law, mother-in-law, and I would pool all our languages into one sentence:

"Patricia, *theleis na* make *salata oggi?*"

(English-Greek-Greek-English-Greek-Italian, for "Patricia, do you want to make a salad today?")

This was so much easier it became our very own language. Professional linguists call this a "pidgin." Listeners who weren't linguists, however, thought we were mad.

For the most part, I got along with my parents-in-law. Though I have to admit, they could get intrusive too:

"Gregori, your mother stopped by *again* today, without phoning first. I was grading papers, I didn't have time to sit and chat. Do you think you could talk to her?" I lamented.

"What am I going to say? That's the way Greeks do things. She would be insulted if you asked her to call first," he argued.

And:

"Why do we have to eat at your parents' *every* Sunday, Gregori? Colleen and Brian invited us to a barbecue."

"And what am I supposed to tell them? I don't want to hurt their feelings!"

I said something then that I never thought I'd say, "*Holy cow* — where is it written that bowing to our parents' wishes is compulsory no matter how old we get?"

There were some bright spots, though. We were making a nice group of friends through our workplaces and we socialized with our new neighbors, Colleen, and her husband, Brian. Every Friday night, Gregori went out with his taxi driver friends, but Saturdays was reserved for the two of us and our crowd. Also, though I seldom saw Donna and Sharon because they were still single and on fast-track careers, we still kept in touch, and as for Margie, the day wasn't complete for either of us unless we talked at least once on the phone.

Marie, Josephine, and Marietta were spread out far and wide, as well. Josephine was also a single career woman, living in Bayridge, a very nice part of Brooklyn. On the few occasions I did see my parents and grandmother now, I'd take a detour over to Jo's place when she was available. Marietta, her husband and two little girls lived on Staten Island, and Marie, her husband and two young sons lived even further out on Long Island than Margie did. Even so, we'd have cousins' get-togethers at least six times a year for birthdays or barbecues, and even an occasional, dressed-to-the-nines New Year's Eve gala, when sitters could be found. My cousins were fun and they went out of their way to please Gregori, always making sure there was something for him to eat besides the tomato sauce and pasta we loved and he hated.

I also liked my work at the private high school. I cared for my teenage pupils very much, and their struggles to discover who they were resonated within me. Most were also very supportive of my efforts to present a good lesson. I was pitifully inexperienced and didn't feel any more competent as a teacher yet, than I did as a daughter or wife. That's why, at school, I did my utmost to learn from colleagues who were older. So, work, family, and friends were keeping Gregori and me occupied. We were also saving for our own house.

One day Gregori sat me down and said, "Look, my father's going to retire soon. They want to buy an apartment on Rhodes. My brother and I want to help them pay for it. Then it would belong to all of us. Can you stay in this apartment a little longer? You're not unhappy here, are you? I'm making some investments and I think we should do well with them. My parents are getting older and my father really wants to go back to Greece."

How could I say no if he put it that way? I sighed, "All right, Gregori."

He kissed me. "Good girl."

And that was my life as a newlywed.

Greece and the Priests

> *"Find a priest who understands English*
> *and doesn't look like Rasputin."*
> **–Aristotle Onassis**

Generally, I spent the first three years of my marriage worried about our love life, the behavior of both sets of parents, whether or not we'd ever get a house, and why my husband seemed so unhappy. He didn't like living in New York. He didn't like his job. He wanted to go back to Greece. That's why a trip there in the summers was so important to him. But he also said it wasn't *worth* going to Greece, unless he could take at least one month off.

The average working person in Greece has two paid months of holidays, which include an additional month's holiday pay as a bonus. Therefore, most Greeks, unless they're self-employed, work *ten* months, but are paid for *thirteen*. We were coming from two contradictory perspectives regarding work expectations, clearly. This was illustrated also when I talked about teaching. I was working very hard to become skilled at it.

My supervisor said, "You know, it takes five years to make a good teacher. You seem determined to do it in two. Good for you!"

I came home thrilled with this assessment, but Gregori's estimation was, "So what? Are they paying you any more for that? You're killing yourself for nothing. It's just a job."

We were more different than I'd thought. But building strain between us eased up a bit, when, to my husband's delight, we managed a one-month trip to Greece the third year we were married. This holiday in Greece was much more fun than our first. To start, Gregori and I were married, so it was okay to stay in the same room — expected, actually — because everyone was hoping for a new addition to the family. To help in this endeavor, relatives went out of their way to insure our privacy when we stayed with them. Which we had to, of course.

Another thing about this holiday I relished was that we didn't go only to Rhodes and Athens, but spent time in The Peloponnese and Crete. The Peloponnese is an area of Greece, and no words I can think up describe the splendor of its ancient sites. These include Corinth, The Theatre of Epidavrus, "The Lions Gate" at Mycenae, the Byzantium castle of Mystras, the ancient Temple of Apollo in Sparta, the giant fallen columns from the Temple of Zeus, and the ancient stadium of Olympia, where the Olympics first began. We also passed through Delphi, the site of the famous "Oracle", before going on through the Peloponnese. I'd dreamed of visiting these places since I was a little girl. The experience surpassed my greatest hopes. Even someone with just a slight fancy to walk through these sites, can't do so without being keenly responsive to the sustained aura of the men and women who created its magnificence, who make themselves known to every future generation, through the beauty of their art that remains. They worked, worshipped, loved, and died there. Their presence lingers in the surrounding air.

We made our way from place to place, round one stomach-churning curve after another, in our miniscule hired car. The car had no air conditioning, but we wouldn't have dared use it if it had. Its engine ground fiercely whenever Gregori switched gears and forced the meager little thing to work its way upward. We traveled on treacherous mountain roads that had no safety rails, in that tiny mini-cauldron of a car. From Athens up to Delphi, back down to Corinth, from there to Nafplion to Spetses and back again down to Sparta. We passed groves of olive, orange and lemon trees and great chiseled rocks jutting from gem-colored seas. Gregori's left arm blistered from sun-exposure and his face was tanned more on the left than the right. I kept my head covered with a hideous straw hat and slathered sunscreen on my face and arms. We drank endless bottles of water. I had guidebooks and even my notes from my archaeology and mythology classes. I read them aloud to Gregori as we drove.

In between visits to sites, we sat outdoors and sipped wine, ate fabulous Greek food, met locals as warm as the days themselves, laughed, and chatted. We spent our time in the Peloponnese enraptured by every experience. At last, I was in the civilization I felt I'd been born to see.

And Gregori had taken me there.

*** ***

Our next stop was Crete. I noticed right off that Crete was not like Rhodes. It had its own singular beauty. Called "Kree-tee" in Greek, it's an historical treasure trove, home to the site of Knossos, where sits the remains of the Palace of King Minos. The colorful palace is known for, among other things, the myth of the "Minotaur". Crete's economy doesn't rely strictly on tourism, as do many of the other Greek islands. It's known for the quality of its agricultural products. Sheep and goats are raised for their milk, wool and meat. (And, of course, Cretan cheeses and honey are so good, they're worth smuggling.) In Crete, we'd stay with Gregori's uncle, the priest who had married us.

I didn't get to spend much time with *Papa* Elias and his wife, Popi, when they'd come over for the wedding. Though Gregori assured me that his uncle and aunt were not at all like what one might expect a priest and his wife to be, my nervousness only increased when, upon our arrival at their home, an assemblage of four very formidable-looking priests were standing outside. Not one was smiling. All wore long, black robes with tight sleeves. Three had white beards down to their waists and because they were out in the blinding sun, all wore dark sunglasses.

Were they priests, or *ZZ Top*?

Then *Papa* Elias boomed from the balcony, "*EER-THAH-NEH!*" ("They're here!")

En masse, the priests and *Papa* Elias rushed toward us, robes flapping. They engulfed us in a tight, black circle, as Gregori's uncle kissed him on both cheeks and began thumping him on the upper arms.

"How are you, my child, are you well?" *Papa* Elias bellowed in Greek. "Has your voyage been a good one?"

Before Gregori could reply, Elias boomed again, in Greek, "Here's your new wife! Come here!" Now it was my turn to be thumped, kissed, and shouted at with joy.

While Gregori and I were still gasping from that, *Papa* Elias pushed us toward the other priests, whom he introduced as his "friends." They were *Papa* Stavros, *Papa* Kostas, *Papa* Christos, and *Papa* Vangelis. Still grim-faced, they shook our hands vigorously, welcoming us to Crete.

"*Lee-pone.* Patricia, *pez,* '*Hah-ree-kah*,'" instructed *Papa* Elias. He pointed from me to the four priests and repeated, "*Pez 'hah-ree-kah*.'"

I was being asked to say formally in Greek, "Nice to meet you." I hesitated, then made the attempt, "*Hah-ree-kah*", and nodded to the priests.

At this, the change in their demeanor was nothing short of... *miraculous.* They laughed uproariously and *Papa* Elias beamed, "*Brah-voh, kore-ee-tsah-kee-moo.*" ("Good job, my daughter.")

Then *Papa* Elias' wife, *Thia* Popi, came out, along with her mother-in-law, *Yiayia* Ourania and the kissing and laughter began again.

The priests were invited to have dinner with us that night. Despite their momentary cheerfulness, Gregori and I anticipated this would be a staid affair. I saw how wrong we were when dinner was ready. We barely had time to get up behind our chairs before *Papa* Elias was standing, leading us through what sounded like a very rushed prayer.

He explained his haste. "We'll do an 'express' prayer tonight. I can hear Father Vangelis' stomach growling from here."

Father Vangelis was the oldest and hard of hearing, but that remark he caught. "*My* stomach? That's not me, that's Stavros!"

*** ***

We spent a lot of time with the priests and learned that they didn't expect to be treated like demigods. They had failings like everyone else.

"Father Vangelis and his sons haven't spoken for years," *Thia* Popi confided to Gregori and me one day. "He believed his children had to present a good example to his parish and was very strict with them. Now that his sons are grown, they want nothing to do with their father."

"What a shame," Gregori commented.

"Worse than you might think," Popi added, sadly. "Vangelis is sick. He wants to mend fences before it's too late, but he doesn't know how. We're afraid the situation is making Vangelis more ill than he already is."

Then there was Father Kostas. He'd decided to become a priest without discussing this first with his fiancée. Though she'd gone ahead with the marriage, three years and one child later, she hated the stringencies required of a priest's wife. Divorce was out of the question, so Father Kostas was now agonizing over the possibility of leaving the priesthood.

It appeared the clergy grappled with the same family dynamics as did their congregations, with the added torment that it was their vocation oftentimes at the root of their household turmoil. The longer we stayed in Crete with *Papa* Elias and his family, the more we saw the complications his chosen life produced for himself and his family. The simplest things needed to be carefully considered, such as what beach would be secluded enough for the family to swim, because it was inappropriate for a priest to be seen wearing a bathing costume.

Even eating out could be a trial. No one wants their priest to observe them smoking and drinking at a *taverna*. What if he gave them the 'fish-eye' at the next Sunday's services? And what would the members of his congregation think if they saw the priest or his wife having wine themselves, with dinner? Pulling off the precepts for a priest and his family in Hellenic society required an exceptional family group, with a strong bond and plenty of fortitude. *Papa* Elias and his family managed it better than most.

Though we learned of their struggles, their faith was demonstrated unmistakably the evening Father Stavros showed us his prized possession, a chunk of wood believed to be a piece of the Cross on which Jesus Christ had been crucified.

"Is it authentic?" Gregori asked his uncle.

"We believe so," replied *Papa* Elias, "It's been known to make miracles here."

Papa Stavros eagerly showed us the wedge of wood. "It's been in my family for centuries," he said.

We examined it. Nothing made it appear to be anything more than an ordinary chunk of wood. Nor did it look centuries old. Still... you never know.

Then Father Stavros asked Gregori a curious thing. "How are you feeling lately, Gregori?"

That startled Gregori. "Um... fine."

Gregori did seem restless since we'd gotten to his uncle's house, but I was surprised that a priest who hardly knew him had noticed that.

Father Stavros smiled. "It's the Cross. It picks up feelings and then, somehow, I can sense them, too."

Gregori was reluctant to be the center of attention. But he divulged, "Well... I have a little tightness, I guess, in my chest."

Father Stavros stood up. "Then come with me." And he left the room, with Gregori following.

"Where are they going?" I asked *Thia* Popi.

"To *Papa* Elias' office. Gregori will tell you why when they come out."

After a while they returned, Gregori with a look of astonishment on his face.

"What happened?" I asked, as Popi and Elias walked with Stavros to his car.

"I'll tell you later," he said. "It's amazing."

Staying in Papa Elias' Room

> *"I know God will not give me anything I can't handle.*
> *I just wish He didn't trust me so much."*
> **–Mother Teresa**

After Gregori and I were in bed, he told me what Father Stavros had done:

"He said a prayer over the piece of wood. Then he placed it on my upper chest and my shoulders, you know... moving it around." He paused a minute. "When he moved it over my heart, Patricia, I could feel it vibrate. The piece of wood, I mean."

"You don't think you were just getting caught up in the moment?"

"No," he shook his head. "Because it wasn't a little bit. It... felt like a buzzer, like an electric razor kind of a buzzer."

"Wow," I said.

"Yes," Gregori concurred. "Then he asked me if I'd ever had my heart checked."

120

I sat up straight. "Why?"

Gregori shrugged. "I don't know. He also asked if my father has a heart condition. I told him he doesn't." Gregori thought for a moment. "His brothers do. My Uncle Sarantis in Australia died from a heart attack. And *Papa* Elias has a slight heart condition. Nothing serious but he has to watch what he eats — that sort of thing."

"You're lucky to have such a nice aunt and uncle. They're good people."

"I know," Gregori sighed. "I know."

I looked at him. "Gregori, what is it? Father Stavros was right. You seem very anxious."

"I don't know." He slumped down in the bed. "I mean, I *do* know, but... I feel bad about it."

I waited.

All at once, he burst out, "It's this *room!*" He gestured, wildly. "*Why* did they put us in this *room?*"

"What's wrong with it?"

He jumped up out of bed, "Come here!" He pulled me up and dragged me into the adjacent office. He moved his arms around, "Every where you look, there's an icon. Or a Cross. Or an altar. Or a candle *on* an altar — a *lit* candle!"

He had a point. It was rather like sleeping in a church rectory. I wasn't bothered by it, but for some reason, it disturbed Gregori. A lot. He grabbed my shoulders and held. "Do you know what happened the first night we were here? There was a lit candle on the altar in here. It was shining into the bedroom. I couldn't sleep. So I got up and... I blew it out!"

"You... blew it out?" Clearly, the man didn't know much about lit candles on altars.

He nodded frantically. "*Yes!* You know what happened the next morning? *Thia* Popi came in and she said—" he swallowed hard — "she said, '*Poh poh poh.* How did this candle go out? Your uncle has kept it lit since his father died.'"

Gregori was practically in tears as he reiterated, "I blew out a candle that my uncle had lit since my *grandfather* died more than *twenty years* ago."

I opened my mouth, then closed it. What could I say?

In torment, he went on, "We should have *insisted* they put us on the pull-out bed."

"We *did*. They wouldn't take 'no' for an answer. They're just trying to be sweet. They wanted us to have our privacy—"

"—But it's *their* room," Gregori said, yet again. "We have *ten* more days here. I can't sleep in this room. I can't make love in this room…"

"Why can't you make love in this room?"

He looked at me as though I were mad. "You could? In *here?*" Once again, there were those gesticulations, "with the Cross? All the saints?"

Oh, here we go. Gregori and his proprieties again. I couldn't stop myself from responding, "And where do you think *they* do it, Gregori? On the kitchen floor?"

He made a sound as though hot water had been thrown in his face. "*How* can you say that? They're my aunt and uncle! He's a *priest!*"

"*Uh huh*. And their three children got here by divine messenger."

He fell back on the bed and covered his head with his pillow.

Now that I knew what was ailing him, my worry was gone. "Let's try to get some sleep," I sighed.

Lifting his head from under his pillow, he continued, "But I *can't*… I told you."

I lay under the sheets. "Well, I don't know about you, but I'm going to sleep. *Thia* Popi said we had to get up early tomorrow."

That got his attention. "Why?"

"Don't you remember? It's your uncle's name day."

Once again, Gregori covered his face with his pillow and groaned.

Papa Elias' Name Day

"Kronia Polla" ("May you live many years.")
–Greek Name Day Salutation

Popi was an extraordinary woman, I observed. She was quick to laugh and her sense of humor converted many events which could have caused stress in her day-to-day life, into entertainment for her and her family. It was an approach I promised myself I'd adopt. Her attitude served her well in her role as head priest's wife. This was never more evident than when she had to prepare for her husband's name day.

A 'name day' is a specific day of the year associated with every person's religious first name. For most Greeks, a name day is more important than a birthday. While friends might not know your birth date, they'll certainly know your name day, if you're named after a saint, because there's a festival every year on that day, celebrating the saint who shares your first name. The church festival for Prophet Elias is unique, because it's held at a monastery on the highest point of a region, usually a small mountain. People climb up the mountain to the Prophet Elias monastery, just to light a candle in his honor and in honor of every 'Elias' they love.

Name days are ordinarily simple affairs, unless you happen to be a priest in the capital of Crete. In that case, all your parishioners want to wish you "many years", all of them want to bring you flowers and treats and all of them want to sit with you for a while in your home. And since your parishioners can number in the hundreds, your name day celebration requires the precision implementation of a military course of action.

Two days before Papa Elias' name day, an announcement appeared in the local newspaper:

> *"On Sunday, July 20, 1986, Papa Elias of Saint Titos' Church, Heraklion, Crete, will be welcoming visitors to his home for his name day celebration, anytime after Sunday services."*

Popi and Elias had a daughter, Lenia, who was studying in Athens. She'd returned home to see Gregori and me and to help her mother with the name day preparations. The morning of the celebration, Lenia marched into the kitchen where I'd been sitting with *Thia* Popi. "I took the four chairs and the bench from *Yiayia's*. Gregori went to *Thia* Sofia's to get six more chairs. We have another bench and four more chairs from the table outside on the patio, two from the small kitchen table and six from the dining room."

Thia Popi was counting to herself as her daughter recited. "We need more."

Lenia was thinking, too. "Oh!" she exclaimed, suddenly remembering. "We have six folding ones in the storage! They'll need to be cleaned. Patricia and I will do it. You don't mind, do you, Patricia?" Lenia asked.

"Of course not. I'm glad to help." Still unaware of the magnitude of their project, I asked, "How many guests are you expecting?"

They both laughed.

"A few," answered Popi.

By the time we'd finished, there was seating in the small drawing room and back patio for about fifty people. Seats had to be arranged so that the guests in the one room could face each other. Everyone would be there to visit Papa Elias, so everyone would want to actually *see* him. He'd divide his time. When he was with the one group in the drawing room, his wife or his mother had to sit with the others on the patio. As Ourania and Popi sat with the guests, Lenia and I would work the kitchen. Being male, Gregori wasn't expected to help serve refreshments, but he'd do his part by standing against a wall most of the evening, freeing up an extra chair.

Well-wishers were estimated to arrive in shifts of approximately forty people at a time, starting from as soon as Papa Elias finished services in the late morning, until well into the night. Now that we had somewhere to contain them, I was coached on how we'd feed them. Lenia pantomimed the action from the front door to the drawing room. "The guest arrives and sits down. We come in and say, 'Hello.' My father or my mother will introduce you and Gregori and you say, in Greek, 'nice to meet you.' "

I interrupted, "I'm not sure how—"

"—I'll tell you. Don't worry about *that* part. *This* part is more important," coached Lenia.

"Now," she ticked off items on her fingers, "First they get a coffee. After they drink it, we take the cups, bring them in the kitchen and come back out with sweets. After they eat the sweets, we go back to each guest, take their napkin and plate, bring them to the kitchen and come back out with a liqueur."

"Coffee, sweet, liqueur," I recited. "Check."

"Good," said Lenia. "After they get the liqueur, they'll get up to leave. We go out to the foyer and I'll wish them 'good bye'. *You* say, 'Nice to have met you,' in Greek."

"How do you know they'll leave after we give them the liqueur?"

"They know the liqueur is the signal that it's time for them to go, so we can make room for more visitors. Shall I write this all down for you?"

I smiled. "I think I can handle it. Let's just practice the Greek."

"All right," she agreed. "So, 'nice to meet you,' is *'her-ete'.*"

I repeated, "*Hair-ah-tay*", and she burst out laughing.

"What's so funny?" I asked.

"Nothing," she said, smiling, "That's good enough. Now, 'Nice to *have met* you,' is, '*Harikah*'."

Ah. That one I'd practiced with *Papa* Elias and the other priests. "*Hah-ree-kah*," I repeated as carefully as I could.

This time, she swallowed her giggles. "Good."

I repeated, "So it's, '*Hah-ree-kah*' and '*Hair-reh-tay*'."

"No!" she exclaimed. "The other way around. First, '*her-ete*', then, '*harikah*'."

"*Okay*," I said. "*Hair-reh-tay, hah-ree-kah*, coffee, sweet, liqueur. Got it, general. *Geez.*"

From the kitchen, Popi heard us and chortled.

*** ***

Reciting the order of the greetings and the food while I was getting dressed, I wondered where all the sweets would come from. Then I realized that if the guests followed tradition, they'd be bringing them. However, when I went into the kitchen, *Thia* Popi, Lenia and *Yiayia* were arranging trays of sweets. And they were all quite formally dressed.

"*Uh oh*," I said aloud. "Should I be wearing a skirt, instead of trousers?"

Lenia looked me up and down. "Have you got one?"

"Sure," I said.

"There's no rush. We're just putting the trays out for the first set of visitors. The other trays are stacked over there," she pointed, "for when everyone else comes."

That's when I remembered that it isn't proper in Greece for guests to be served anything they'd bought for the hosts. So sweets had been purchased for the first group of visitors, but the second group of guests would be served what the first group had brought and so on. A logical plan, but one that required vigilance. We'd have to keep track of who brought what sweets and which sweets to serve when. In that effort, it helped knowing for sure when each guest would be leaving. That would be, I reminded myself, right after the liqueur, which Popi had in the cupboard.

"I'll go change," I said.

Yiayia leaned over and murmured something to Lenia in Greek.

Lenia sighed and with a look that pleaded for my patience, she translated, "*Yiayia* asked if you would put your hair up and... a little less lipstick?"

*** ***

125

We were in a fix almost immediately. The bottles of liqueur required a corkscrew and we couldn't find one.

Popi said, "I'll send Gregori to Sofia's for one. We'll stall the first set of guests. We'll give them two coffees straightaway."

"We *can't* do that!" said Lenia. "If the second group finds out, they'll be offended that the first got two and they didn't. Besides, we won't have enough clean cups for the second group!"

Popi pinched her lips together. She picked up one of the bottles and started to knock it against the stucco wall. It made a "*thump-thump*" noise, but nothing happened. She grinned broadly. "It was worth a try. My father once got a cork out of a bottle that way. Well, I'm out of ideas. Any of you have a thought?"

I didn't know if my idea was a good one, but I offered it. "Look, it's eleven o'clock in the morning. Nobody really wants a liqueur now. Let's give them a coffee, a sweet and then a coffee *again*, instead. *Yiayia* can mention that the priest thinks it's too early to drink. Who's going to argue with *him*? Gregori can go out and get the corkscrew in the meantime. I'll stay in the kitchen and wash the cups for the second go-round of coffees. You can introduce me to the second group *after* the sweet, instead of before the coffee."

It seemed the only solution. "All right, let's do it that way," Popi decided. "Tell Gregori he has to go to Sofia's again."

Then it was time for action.

The doorbell rang. Popi and *Yiayia* greeted the arrivals. Popi took whatever treat the guests presented to the kitchen and labeled the box to indicate who'd brought it. Sometimes the guest handed her flowers instead of a sweet. These were taken away and placed in the bathtub. *Yiayia* ushered the newcomers into the drawing room where Papa Elias sat. After unloading the parcels, Popi went in, too. Chitchat ensued for a moment or two, until the doorbell rang next. Up would jump Popi and *Yiayia* again and... repeat process until four new guests had arrived. *Four* new guests were the signal for Lenia and me to bring out cups and the special silver coffee pot, filled with Greek coffee. These were presented on trays faced with white lace doilies. We'd set the trays down and Gregori and I would be introduced to the new guests. I'd say my one word, "*Hair-reh-tay.*" After all four guests had their coffees, Lenia and I would go back to the kitchen and exchange the empty, soiled trays for two clean ones holding sweets, this time. Coffees were drunk quickly, so we had to be back out in a flash. And then, as the guests left, I got to say one more word, "*Hah-ree-kah.*"

The scene repeated itself with a few variations, depending on which calamity we were addressing at the time. It had a nice rhythm:

Coffee.

"*Herete.*"

Tray.

One, two, three…

"*Harikah.*"

"Oh, *shit!*" Lenia swore.

It was now seven in the evening. Eight hours down and only about… four more to go. We had a bathtub overflowing with flowers and a trash bin filled with coffee grinds. My feet hurt and my head was muzzy from trying to decipher endless streams of Greek. Apart from that, I thought things had been going well.

"It's *Kyria* Kourapaki!" said Lenia. "She's come back with her brother, but she was here this morning *already!* This is *bad*, because we were going to serve the sweets she brought this morning *now!* I don't have anything else to serve."

Lenia was frazzled and then her mother came into the kitchen looking almost as frantic as she. "*Kyria* Kourapaki…" began Popi.

"*I know!*" said Lenia to her mother. "She *always* does this and she *knows* better. *Poh-reh gah-moh-toh.*" (I won't translate.)

"*Lenia!*" Popi admonished. "*Meen vree-zees!*" ("Don't swear.")

Lenia wasn't having it. She was worn out, more so than I, as she'd actually been having to make conversation, non-stop, with a pageant of people since morning. "What am I going to serve? What am I going to serve?" she repeated over and over again.

Popi handed her a glass of water. "Get a hold of yourself, *koh-pel-yiah-moo*. (Cretan lingo for 'daughter') Let's *think*. Did we eat the *baklava* that Gregori and Patricia brought?"

"It's down at *Yiayia's*, but it'll be stale by now."

"Stale or not, it will have to do," said Popi.

"I'll go get it," I volunteered.

"You can't go," Popi declared. "You have to stay and distract *Kyria* Kourapaki. The baklava isn't enough for everybody. We have to divide the sweets into two sets. We'll give *Kyria* Kourapaki's sweets to the people sitting *outside* and we'll give the baklava to the people sitting *inside*, where Kyria Kourapaki is. But Patricia, you have to keep her occupied, so she doesn't *see* us go out with *her* sweets. She speaks English well and works at the Heraklion Museum. I told her you're interested in Greek art. Go in there and ask her questions and keep her facing *away* from the kitchen."

Popi turned to her daughter, "Lenia, wait until you see Patricia go out to talk to *Kyria* Kourapaki and then hurry past them to the patio with other sweets. Okay?"

Lenia and I both nodded, in awe of Popi's composure. The woman wasn't easy to fluster.

But she did look a bit disconcerted when I asked, "Which one is *Kyria* 'Koo-roo-pah-kee?'"

Not _That_ Papa Elias

"On a deaf man's door, you can knock forever!"
–Anthony Quinn, *in the film, Zorba the Greek*

Gregori wanted to spend the next day with his grandmother, since we'd be leaving in two days. She was getting on in years, so who knew if they'd see each other again? *Papa* Elias would be at church all morning, as he was every day and *Thia* Popi and Lenia had elected to have a lie-in. (Who could blame them?) I needed a break, too. But not sleep. A walk alone was just what I needed.

"You'll get lost," Gregori laughed.

"I will *not*," I said crossly.

"Make sure you have the house number and change for the phone, just in case!" he laughed after me.

How dare he say I'd get lost? I wouldn't.

I did.

I turned a corner behind the house, onto a long, wandering dirt path, which was lined with olive, lemon, and orange trees. The olive trees shined like silver and the lemon and orange leaves perfumed the air. I walked for at least an hour, so wrapped up in the nature surrounding me that now, nothing looked familiar.

Oh, this is just what I needed. They'd be expecting me for lunch. It'd be rude to keep them waiting. It appeared I had no way out but to ring the house and take the ribbing from my husband I knew he'd gleefully give me.

Unless…

128

What if I walked to the main road and asked someone in one of the shops for directions? With all the locals who knew *Papa* Elias, I was sure to meet up with someone who could direct me back to the house. The small hitch in my plan was the communication barrier. I sat down on a large rock, to consider. Two weeks in Crete had been total language immersion.

Think, Patricia! I could say, in Greek, "*Sig-noh-mee. Kseh-reh-tay... poo eenay... toh spee-tee... toos... Papa Elias... ah-poh... Ay-ohs... Tee-tohs... klee-see-ah?*"

That meant, I was almost sure, "Excuse me, do you know where the house is, of *Papa* Elias, of Saint Tito's church?"

I sat for a while longer, practicing until I felt confident enough to give it a go.

I came upon a small fruit stand first. The woman working there squinted her eyes in concentration as she tried to decipher my question. People responded to my difficulty speaking their language with reactions that ranged from scorn to effusive sympathy. This fruit seller sincerely tried to help. But in the end, she made a *"tch"* sound and moved her head up, then down, in the Greek gesture that looks like "yes," but means the opposite. "*Oh-hee. Then-tohk-seh-roh. Sig-noh-mee.*" ("No. I don't know. I'm sorry.")

I thanked her and moved on to a kiosk that sold newspapers and chocolates. It was manned by two teenage boys who laughed at me. I could hear them ridiculing my accent as I left. Discouraged and annoyed, I tried the next place, a petrol station.

Bingo.

The middle-aged man who ran the shop said happily, "*Papa* Elias? Yes, young lady! I know him very well."

He asked me who I was and I remembered the words in Greek, "I'm his niece."

Thrilled with this news, he shouted for his wife. Out she came, wiping her hands on a rag, and the husband introduced me as though he were introducing a princess. "This is *Papa* Elias' niece," he told her.

She looked at me with delight. "How *nice* to meet you!" she exclaimed, as she shook my hand enthusiastically.

"Where are you from?" they asked me.

When I told them, they said, "We had no idea *Papa* Elias had a niece who lived in New York."

I began to think something wasn't right, when the wife asked, "How is it that we didn't meet you at the name day celebration last night?"

So *that's* what was wrong. "I'm so sorry. I guess we must have missed being introduced." We were all silent for a moment, reviewing the events of the previous evening. I still couldn't make out how that'd happened.

After a few minutes, I said, "I hope you'll excuse me, but I should go. *Papa* Elias and everyone else is expecting me for lunch."

"I'm happy to take you back to *Papa* Elias' house whenever you like, but if you wait a bit longer," suggested the man, "the *papadia* should be here soon. She comes every morning to have coffee with us."

"The *papadia* is coming *here*?" I asked. *Thia* Popi hadn't mentioned she spent time every morning at a petrol station.

The wife looked at the husband and speculated, "You know, with having all those people last night, maybe she isn't coming today. You should just take Patricia now."

I said "good-bye" to the wife and made my way to the main road with the husband. By now, my paltry store of Greek had been used up, so we smiled at each other now and again, but said nothing more, as we walked up a hill.

Up a hill? …*Papa* Elias did not live up a hill. Even though I was lost, I knew he didn't live on this side of the main road, either. Could this be a shortcut? I said nothing until we reached an apartment building. Not a house.

The man gestured, "Here you go. *Papa* Elias' place."

Oh, boy. Well, we most certainly weren't at *Papa* Elias' place, but I knew only one word that might suit to explain that, "*Lah-thohs.*" ("Mistake.")

My host, who'd been charmed by me until that moment, now looked as though I'd deliberately offended him. "*Lah-thohs?*" he repeated. "*Then eenay 'lah-thos.' *" ("It's not a mistake.")

And to prove it, he rang the bell.

From the top floor window, a very old, thin priest, with a shock of white hair and another long white beard, stuck his head out, looked down and hollered, "HELLO? WHO IS IT?"

In addition to being elderly, the priest must have been hard of hearing, because the man from the petrol station bellowed up to him, "YOUR NIECE IS DOWN HERE, FATHER ELIAS!"

I tried to intervene, but the old priest was shouting too loudly for either he or the man from the petrol station to hear me.

"MY *NIECE*? WHICH NIECE?" And he moved his head back and forth, looking for someone he recognized below.

I turned to the man who'd brought me there, frantically trying to come up with words that would help. "Not him," I finally managed in Greek, "another *Papa* Elias."

Now my escort looked at me with actual misgiving. "*Eh?* What do you mean, 'another *Papa* Elias'? There *is* no other *Papa* Elias at Saint Constantinos Church!"

"Oh, no!" I covered my mouth with my hands. Then said abashedly, "Not Saint *Constantine* Church, Saint *Tito* Church!"

The man from the petrol station made a sound of complete exasperation then and said unsympathetically, "I can't help you, in that case! I have no idea where *he* lives!" And off he strode, back to his shop.

I scurried after him. Now I *had* to phone.

*** ***

When the right *Papa* Elias picked up, he didn't even bother to say, "Hello." He just said, "Yes, Patricia. Where are you, my daughter?"

"*Thio,*" I began apologetically, "I'm sorry. I got lost."

"Yes, we figured that out." In the background I could hear Gregori laughing and *Thia* Popi, too, naturally. "Why didn't you ring us sooner?"

I sighed. There was no point in trying to save face now. "I wanted to find my way back on my own. I ended up at the other *Papa* Elia's, the one from Saint Constantine's."

"Really? I know that old priest. He's very deaf. Well, are you having lunch with him or us?" More laughter in the background at this.

I smiled wearily into the phone. "I'd rather have lunch with you, thank you. I'm at the petrol station next to the kiosk on the main road. Do you know the people who own the station, by the way?" I asked him.

"No, but I guess we'll meet them now," was his reply.

*** ***

Everyone got a kick out of hearing about my expedition. When I got to the part where I'd been told that the *papadia* was expected for coffee over at the petrol station and I wondered why *Thia* had never mentioned that to us, Popi laughed and slapped her leg so hard, I thought she'd leave marks on herself. I could see I was forgiven for holding up lunch. At the end, it wasn't so terrible being the *Amerikanaki* this time around.

Two days later, we left, knowing we'd miss Crete and everyone there. We'd had such a wonderful holiday and I felt it had been good for our marriage. Little did we know how soon we'd be returning to Crete and for another reason altogether.

131

Chapter Eight: November 17th

Death Biscuits

On November 17, 1986, three months after we returned to The United States, something dreadful happened that brought me closer to Gregori for a while. With no prior warning, Gregori's father died. Niko's wife and sons only *thought* he'd escaped the family predisposition for heart disease. He complained of a stomachache one evening, a bad one, Demetra told us, that lasted all night. Neither she nor Niko suspected he was having a heart attack, but he still felt so ill the next morning, that they went to his doctor, who promptly sent him to the local emergency room. Doosie and Gerry had been with them the night before when Niko got sick, and when they checked in the next day to see how Niko was feeling, Demetra was frantic. It was Doosie who phoned me at my school with the news. I left work straightaway and hurried to the hospital, then was desperate to locate Gregori, who was still in Manhattan driving his taxi. There was no way to get in touch with him back then, except to hope he had his CB radio on to Channel Eight, the station on which all the Greek taxi drivers communicated. I called Louie, Aleko, every taxi driver we knew, hoping to find one at home, who could then track Gregori by radio. I'll never forget the expression on Gregori's face when he ran into that hospital. He made it in time to say "good-bye."

For a while, we clung to the hope Niko would come through, but it didn't happen and the shock was indescribable. Niko was only 62. One moment he'd been vibrant and vocal, sitting in his chair, exclaiming over what he was reading in his paper, shouting over the background din of the television his wife kept on as constant company. And the next, he was dead in a hospital bed, his family in tears, surrounding him.

And at only 57, Gregori's mother was now a widow. She and her husband had been so happy about moving back to Rhodes into their own apartment, which was still being constructed. Instead, Gregori and his brother, so devastated themselves, tried to comfort their mother, as she stood, crushed and disbelieving, "But, he didn't even get to see our new place!"

Gerry sobbed openly in his mother's arms, but Gregori was too shell-shocked to take it in. All at once, he slumped defeated in a waiting room chair, silent tears streaming, hands stiff in his lap, as I smoothed my hand over his beautiful head of hair in mute powerlessness. It'd all happened so fast. That shuffle home without Niko, the silent consciousness that we were leaving him behind for good, were dreamlike. How could it be that there was nothing left to do for him, except plan his funeral?

And those plans would be maddening. The bereavement obligations Niko's family felt they needed to adhere to were as exacting as the decorum we'd followed on *Papa* Elias' name day. Those had been taxing, but in their own way, fun. However, the requirements for this circumstance meant we'd only be allowed to truly grieve *after* every trifling remembrance specification had been satisfied.

The first order of business was where to have the wake, of course. But before Niko's body could even been transported from the hospital to the undertaker's, black clothing had to be purchased for Demetra, because, when people came to pay their respects, it would be "indecent" if she accepted them while not dressed in proper mourning.

Then Gerry mentioned that he had a client who owned a funeral home. If we took Niko there for the viewing, they'd do their utmost for us.

I don't know how Demetra found the composure to muse dully, "Yes, but it's farther than the one in town. Last time we held a wake there, *Thia* Eleni complained because she had to take the train two extra stops."

Gregori said pretty much what I was thinking. "We have to worry about what an old lady thinks, when she's still alive at her age and can take the subway, but our father is dead? Let one of her great-grandchildren drive her."

The item that struck me as the most important was the one we talked about last — where Niko would be buried. He wasn't my father, so the decision wasn't mine, but I knew that he'd hoped desperately to go back to Greece. I had the dismal image of his hated New York rain falling down on him for all eternity if we buried him here. Yet, transporting a body from the United States to be interred in Greece was complicated and costly. I kept silent while Gregori and his brother discussed the practical aspects of the nearby cemetery as compared to the expense and difficulty of sending his body to Crete, where Niko's family had its own mausoleum.

"What about *Yiayia?* His own mother should be able to visit his grave..." trailed off Gregori woefully. My whole body compressed with pity for him.

We still have some savings left, I thought. *Perhaps...*

Then Gregori turned to me and asked, "What do you think?"

Since he'd asked, I didn't hesitate. "I think we should all chip in to bury him in Greece." I could see by the looks on everyone's faces that, for once, my suggestion was well received.

We phoned Gerry's undertaker client with our decision to transport the body overseas. I told Demetra I'd pick her up early the next morning, so we could shop for what she needed. Afterward, we'd telephone everyone and break the news.

Then, she said wearily, "Somebody has to go to the *zah-ha-roh-plas-tee-oh* to order the *biscotti* for when visitors come."

"I have *biscotti* at home, "I offered.

Again that '*tch*' sound. "Not *Italian* biscotti," my mother-in-law said. "We need the kind the Greek pastry shops make when somebody dies."

This was too much. I stared at her. "We have to have *specific* biscotti to serve just for this occasion?"

Gregori interjected resignedly, "We have to serve something, but it can't be too festive, obviously. These biscuits are very plain."

Plain was an understatement. When I saw them, they looked like lumps of dried clay and biting into one was like crunching on a bone. What was the bloody *point*? The answer was the same as always, "That's the way we do things."

That we felt shattered excused us from no expectations. We were compelled to spend the next several days dressed in restrictive clothing, greeting mourners, making *them* comfortable, serving endless pots of coffee and plates of death biscuits.

There was also a one-day viewing at the funeral parlor. My parents came from Brooklyn for that, though they stayed only briefly, but Marie and her husband, Mike, drove the long way in from Long Island and stayed with me for several hours, as did Margie. Colleen and Brian stopped in, and Donna, Josephine, and Marietta sent cards and flowers. All of Gregori's friends were there. Even Thoulah showed up to pay her respects, much to Doosie's displeasure. In addition to waiting on visitors, we had to *fast*, as if not eating meat might generate some Lazarus-like effect on my poor father-in-law. After a week of switching off the same two black suits, hosting for hours in heels and eating nothing but boiled pasta, I'd had it.

Gerry voiced it first. "That's it. I'm going out for a quiet meal. Nothing we're doing is going to bring my father back. We have to travel to Greece soon and do this all over again. I need a break. Who's coming with me?"

All of us followed him out door.

My Father is Going to Be Late

I thought the days of people coming by Gregori's parents' home would never end. I wanted just one moment of solitude with my poor husband. But once the paperwork to transport my father-in-law's body was complete and the stateside memorial was over, the five of us got on a plane, headed to Athens, where we'd switch planes to go on to Crete. Niko's coffin was placed in the hold of the plane, while we sat in coach, huddled together for the long flight, a dark mass of worn-out misery. We were barely able to stand by the time we arrived in Athens. When we did, there was more bad news.

I was waiting for Demetra, who'd gone off toward the toilets, while the others went to find out when the coffin could be transferred to the smaller plane that would take us to Crete.

Doosie returned, white-faced. "They won't let the coffin onto the second plane."

"What! Why *not?*"

She shook her head. "I don't know. It's something to do with some paperwork, I think."

"Oh, this is just *great,*" I said. "We've got dozens of people waiting for us in Crete."

"Gregori and Gerry are trying to sort it out." She looked behind me. "Somebody's got to tell *her*, though."

I turned around and saw my mother-in-law heading toward us.

"Oh, *crap*," I said.

*** ***

When I told Demetra, she took it well. Leaning her head back against her chair, she chuckled wanly and said, "I'm not surprised. This *is* Greece."

Greece's federal and city agencies thrive on complicated paperwork. *Olympic Airways* is the Greek national airline. Before Greece became part of the European Union and other airlines won bids to fly to the mainland of Greece and the Greek islands, *Olympic* had the only flights in and out of Greece. As a result of their monopoly, they had nothing to lose by delaying us. The airline personnel were dispassionate when they informed us that until the paperwork was corrected, my father-in-law was stuck in Athens.

"How long will this take?" Gregori asked one.

The apathetic fellow shrugged. "You'll have to ask in the back." He pointed us in the direction of another office and walked off.

When we got there, we explained what was happening to another disinterested clerk, who picked up an interoffice phone and relayed our dilemma in a monotone voice, to someone else again.

"*Kyria* Papadopoulou will be out soon. She's in her office." The clerk motioned dully to a door behind her.

We waited.

"What time does the flight to Crete leave?" asked Gregori.

"In one hour," said his brother.

Abruptly, Gregori's patience shattered. "This is *bullshit!*" Stepping behind the counter he charged at the door that the clerk had pointed out. Frightened, I ran after him, his brother following, the clerk doing nothing to stop us.

Behind the door, a woman in her twenties sat behind a desk, chatting on the phone. We could hear she was engaged in a personal conversation.

Gregori was murderous by now. "Are you *Kyria* Papadopoulou?" he barked.

Not recognizing the danger, the girl on the phone nodded "Yes," held up her index finger to indicate we should wait and went on blithely with her conversation. I clutched my brother-in-law's arm and recoiled, as, with a snarl, Gregori pulled the phone away from her ear, and slammed it down. She jumped and cried out in fright.

Then, leaning over the desk, practically nose to nose with her, Gregori shouted, "I WANT MY FATHER ON THE PLANE TO CRETE! HIS MOTHER IS WAITING TO BURY HER SON! *GODDAMMIT!* DO YOU UNDERSTAND ME?"

This conduct would have landed my husband in jail had he attempted it in the States. At the airport in Greece, it had an effect I wouldn't have dreamed possible.

"Okay, I understand," the girl said, holding up her hands in front of her. "I can't do anything about it tonight. He'll be on the first flight to Crete tomorrow morning. I promise you."

This calmed Gregori somewhat, but still he glared at her. "My brother and I will stay in Athens tonight to make sure of it. God help you if you're not telling the truth. I'll tear this place apart tomorrow."

Gerry and I stared at Gregori, both repelled and awed by what he'd done. Who'd have thought that getting what you want in Greece is not accomplished by logic? Yell hard. Threaten. You won't be arrested; you'll just get you what you need at that point, when they should've helped you in the first place. Now that I'd witnessed this inclination, I hoped I'd never see it again.

Gregori looked down at me grimly. "Gerry and I will find a hotel. You get on the plane with my mother and Doosie. I'll call Crete and let them know..." he paused for a moment to collect himself, "...that my father can't get there tonight."

"Oh Tee-Thelee-Oh-Theh-ohs"

It was just us women then, who made it to *Papa* Elias' house that evening. Once again, there was the battalion of priests. It looked as though every priest who knew Papa Elias had come into town for the funeral. Though they appeared as daunting as ever, I recognized many of them now, and felt comforted by seeing them again.

Gregori and his brother arrived the next day with their father's body. The woman in the Athens airport had kept her word. *Thia* Popi organized a hearse and driver to pick them up at Heraklion airport. The hearse was quite old, but spotlessly clean. Gregori, his brother, and four of the younger priests, brought the coffin into the house and placed it on a table in the drawing room. When Father Stavros opened the lid, *Yiayia* Ourania sagged against *Papa* Elias. Then she straightened and held onto his arm as he led her to the coffin, where she leaned in and touched her son's face.

"*Toh Niko-laki moo, kai-men-oh,*" she cried softly. ("My poor little Niko.")

She gripped her hands together, willing her tears to stop, then stood back as dignified as ever. Stoically she prayed, as priest after priest crossed her son's body and blessed him.

Shortly thereafter, the priests and the others left, saying they'd see us at the funeral the next day. For the first time in over a week, there was no one to attend to besides ourselves. My father-in-law would be spending the night in the drawing room as we slept upstairs.

In the middle of the night, I woke and saw Gregori wasn't in bed. I went down the stairs to look for him and heard whispers and tears coming from the drawing room. There sat Gregori, holding his grandmother, as they looked across at where his father lay.

Quietly, I went back upstairs.

*** ***

137

It occurred to me that my father-in-law had died on the same date the Greek students had been slain by soldiers after they'd protested the dictatorship. November 17 was a national remembrance day now in Greece and Niko would've appreciated his life having ended on that particular date.

Now it was late November, but the day of the funeral in Crete was resplendently sunny and warm, just the weather my father-in-law had loved. "The weather is *always* like this in Greece," he'd have said.

His coffin was put back into the hearse that had brought him to his brother's house the day before. The funeral mass was not being held at *Papa* Elias' church, but at a smaller one near the family tomb. At the end of services, my father-in-law would be put to rest in the mausoleum, where his father already lay. After the coffin was loaded into the hearse, we were all instructed to follow behind on foot. The procession was a graceful homage, as the hearse edged slowly along the small dirt road that led us to the monastery.

Apart from a few whispers now and again, the walk was quiet, as those who stayed behind the hearse were solemn and no one else was about. Everyone in the area knew there was a funeral that day. Flyers had been posted throughout the vicinity. Those who knew the priest and his family would meet us up at the little church. Those who didn't kept their dogs and other animals, even their children, hushed, as we went by. We passed the back of the priest's house, where I could see *Yiayia's* tiny cottage. Then the road zigzagged around the gardens of the neighbors, where the branches of their fruit trees were heavy with colorful fruit. I was seeing flowers I'd never see in November in New York. Abruptly, the dirt road widened and straightened into a direct line, parallel the graveyard, where the chapel waited, looking gentle and sweet. It was jammed with people. They stepped back so we could make our way into the foyer and up to the altar. They let the pallbearers pass to carry the coffin up.

Papa Elias wouldn't be conducting the mass. That was being done for him by his friends. Patiently, the priests stood while the men set the coffin down. The pallbearers stepped back so the priests could open it for the final time. Demetra crumbled into tears. These were the last hours she'd see her husband's face. The family stood in clusters, Gregori, his brother and mother, weeping, holding tightly to each other, Doosie and I, standing behind them. *Yiayia* Ourania, the priest, his wife and daughter, on the opposite side of my father-in-law's coffin, with *Yiayia* clutched onto *Papa*

138

Elias and Lenia holding her mother's hand. We stood like that as the priests gave the mass their poignant all. The chanting reverberated, as they sang and prayed and we prayed and cried.

When it was over, we stood side-by-side at the church entrance. As the mourners passed through to speak soothingly to us, I saw that the most heartfelt compassion was expressed to *Yiayia* Ourania. Everyone empathized profoundly with her particular loss. *Yiayia* thanked every person who spoke with her, and to reiterate her convictions, more for herself, I think, than for them, we heard her repeat over and again, "*Oh tee thel-lee Oh Theh-ohs.*"

"Whatever God wants, we accept."

Yet, only short weeks later, Ourania, who'd still been robust for her age, followed her son in death.

*** ***

Though Demetra remained in Crete for a time, Gregori, Gerry, Doosie and I returned home, sorrowful, depleted, but knowing that we'd done our best for him.

Chapter Nine: The Quiet One Sets the Village on Fire

"Resentment is like drinking poison and waiting for the other person to die."
    —Carrie Fisher

Why a Donkey?

After we got back that November, I made the classic error. I believed having a child would put some happiness back into my husband's life. He was more morose than ever now that his father was gone. We'd planned to hold off becoming parents until we bought our own house. But with the purchase of the apartment on Rhodes and the unexpected death, our savings were depleted. I was thirty. I thought we shouldn't delay any longer. I also felt elated that I could do *something* to take Gregori's mind off his grief. I'd have our baby, then go back to school at night to finish my Master's degree and pursue a writing career. This was what we'd planned before we married and Gregori was on board with my being a stay-at-home-mother. As much as I loved teaching and strived for excellence at it, I'd always planned to leave it when we had children. We'd agreed that Gregori would handle the bills as I raised our children and built up my writing portfolio. The only change now was that we'd do these things before we owned a home, but if we were frugal, we'd get one eventually.

Late January 1987, only two months after the funeral, I was pregnant. Gregori and I were thrilled.

I wanted to share our joy with my parents and grandmother. As we drove to Brooklyn, the long ride made me feel ill and anxious, because I was already experiencing morning sickness and mood swings. I went downhill from 'ill and anxious' after we got to my parents':

Nonnie: (to me and Gregori) Well, congratulations. *Huh.* I didn't think you wanted a baby.
Me: (guardedly) Why would you say that?

140

Gregori: (easily) Of course we want a baby.

Nonnie: (to me, with accusation) Then why'd you wait so long? That means you don't want one. (To Gregori, with certainty) And if *you* want one, *you* only wanta boy. That's all they like in the old country — boys.

Me: (defensively) That's not true.

Nonnie: (to me) I hope not. Because I dreamt you were having a girl.

Gregori: (to Nonnie, easily, again) I dreamt we were having a boy.

Nonnie: (to me, smugly) *See?* What did I tell you?

Dad: (to me, gratingly) Where *the hell* are you gonna put a crib in that tiny apartment?

Me: (heart thumping wildly now) There's plenty of room.

Mom: (to me, changing the subject) So, have you picked out names yet?

Me: (cautiously) Well... if we do have a boy, naturally we'll name him 'Nicholas'.

Mom: (to me, eyebrows raised) '*Naturally*'? Does that mean if it's a girl, you'll name her 'Demetra'?

Me: (defensively again) Of course not.

Gregori: (firmly) Of course.

Me: (to Gregori, alarmed) We never said *that!*

Nonnie: (laughingly) *Holy shit...* here we go.

Dad: (to Gregori, even more gratingly) How come you don't have a house yet?

Me: (to Dad and Nonnie, with frustration) Will you *stop* it — both of you?

Mom: (to me, angrily) Don't talk to your grandmother and your father like that!

Me: (to Gregori, desperately) I feel sick. I want to go home.

*** ***

The argument in the car going back was brutal.

"Why did you have to say that to them? You just made everything worse!" I bawled.

"To *hell* with what they think! I want a daughter named after my mother. That's *it!*" Gregori shouted.

I fought back hard. "No! I *never* agreed to that. I'm happy to name our son Nicholas, because your father's gone, but I don't like the name, 'Demetra'!"

"Oh, so you're going to be like your mother, now?" Gregori taunted, his voice drenched with scorn. "You want to be a troublemaker, like *her*?"

"*YES!*"

The word roared out of me. I astounded myself and Gregori. He almost hit the car parked ahead as he maneuvered into a space near our apartment. But I wasn't finished. The minute he switched off the engine, I fumbled in my handbag, pulled out my car key, then jabbed it so close to his eyes, he recoiled instinctively. "Say one more word about my mother, and I'll *blind* you with this; I swear!"

Heaving, face flooded with tears, I got out of the car, crashed the door shut, and stomped to where my Toyota was parked.

"You shouldn't be driving in your condition, if you're upset," he called to me nervously.

"*Now* you're worried about my condition?" I screamed. "You... you... *kolo-tree-peeda!*"

I hadn't forgotten that word since Helen had expressed it so emphatically. Speechless, Gregori watched me as I zoomed off.

Fuck him. Fuck them all, I thought as I drove.

There was traffic. It took over two hours to get to Margie's. She was thunderstruck to see me on her front porch. My in-laws' habits were rubbing off. I hadn't phoned first and could tell by the smells coming from her kitchen that she was cooking dinner. All she did was say my name and I started crying again. She pulled me into the front room, where little Jared was watching *Mary Poppins*. He saw my tears and ran off, yelling, "Daddy! Aunty Patricia has a boo-boo!"

Sean came hurrying in, looking worried. Assessing the situation as I sobbed in his wife's arms, he told Jared, "Son, get your coat — we're going out for pizza!"

*** ***

"I know you're upset, but they're your parents."

That was the first thing Margie said, after I calmed down enough to tell her what'd happened. I knew she was trying to be helpful. If I'd driven to Marie's, instead, she'd have said the same thing.

I sighed, leaning my head back on her couch. "Margie, you and I have lived by that canon since we were kids. And you know what? I can think of at least two students who, when they confided their terrors to me, if I'd said *that* to them, instead of contacting the authorities, I would've been sending them home to their deaths."

Margie nodded sympathetically. "What are you going to do, then, about... everything?"

142

"I don't know yet, but things have to change."

The phone rang and Margie got up to answer it.

"I'll bet that's Sean, wondering if it's safe to bring Jared home," I joked feebly.

Margie came back in. "It's Gregori."

*** ***

Gregori didn't apologize when I got home, but he never mentioned naming our baby after his mother again.

The next day, my mother phoned to berate me, her 30-year-old, pregnant daughter, "I don't care *what* they said to you or *how* they said it — you're not going to talk like that to them in front of *me*."

This time I was ready. "But it's acceptable for them to talk 'like that' to *me?*"

And *this* time, when she hung up on me, I didn't phone back. I loved them, but enough was enough. I didn't hear from my parents or grandmother again for my entire pregnancy.

As hard as these two battles had been with my parents and my husband, they were only skirmishes compared to what lay ahead.

Demetra was still at the priest's in Crete, so we phoned there with our happy news. Popi and *Papa* Elias exclaimed joyously, but Demetra told Gregori sadly, "I wish it'd happened while your father was still alive."

Of course, I understood Demetra's pleasure over our announcement was hampered by Niko's death. Nevertheless, I wasn't prepared for how altered she'd be by becoming a widow and by my becoming a mother. Our interactions were about to change drastically.

Gregori and his mother had always shared a close bond. I thought they'd both appreciate my also wanting to have a close bond with Demetra. I thought this'd be especially true since Demetra had no daughters of her own. Unfortunately, of all the thoughts I entertained about what my relationships with both my husband and his mother would be, *those* were my most erroneous. The reality was, I didn't know what Demetra's estimation of being a "mother" and "mother-in-law" was, nor did I know that I was up against a whole cultural perception of these.

Let's see — how can I best put this across? The Bible states that a man should leave his mother and "cleave unto his wife." Many Hellenes disregard this advice from their good book. Instead, they follow the sentiments of a popular Greek love song, the main lyrics of which are, "You remind me of my mother. That's why I'm in love with you." I guess it's no wonder then, that theirs is the country that came up with the Oedipus myth. Gregori would be one of those Hellenes who'd take what he perceived to be his obligations toward his mother to an extreme.

In Greece, grown children often build apartments directly above their parents' apartment. There are logical reasons for this. Land is at a premium and living on land already owned by parents is a more cost-effective option for newlyweds. When the couple has children, the grandparents are able to look after them while the younger couple works. Both sets of couples have a higher standard of living by pooling their resources. And when the time comes that the older couple's health begins to fail, grown children are nearby to help. With this proximity, the generations interact regularly and mother plays a major role in her grown children's lives right up until her death. This can be helpful to everyone, but the downside can be that when the adult child needs to have a life somewhat separate from mother, their close bond might impede it.

I was about to experience this firsthand. Added to Demetra's cultural expectations was the cruel fact that, with the death of her husband, her entire everyday purpose had changed for the worse. The drab clothing in her wardrobe was confirmation of that. Although she was still relatively young, a 'second chance at love' was unthinkable to her *and* her sons. She had no outside interests, no sense of self, other than as caretaker to her family. But Niko was dead and Gregori and Gerry were married to other women who were caring for them. And now one of those women was further usurping Demetra's position in the family by becoming a mother herself.

Demetra's buried resentment about what she'd been taught was her place in this life was about to become unleashed. But it wasn't a furious unleashing. It was slow and quiet. That's why it caught me off guard. Her girlish voice and unassuming ways had me characterize her as tolerant and uncomplicated. I'd only been on the lookout for loud, overbearing women to cause vexation. My grandmother and mother, specifically. They were like hurricanes. When they blew my way, I knew I had to run for cover, jump, *anything* to avoid being caught in their eye. But I was wholly unacquainted with termites. And, oh, *boy*... those can be so much more damaging to a home than a hurricane. You might see a hurricane coming in enough time to buttress the doors and shutter the windows. But you can't evade a termite, because *you never even suspect that it's there.* It eats, silently and ceaselessly at your foundation, until before you know what's happening, the whole of your life crumbles around you.

Just like with every aspect of my association with Gregori and his family, there were clues I hadn't picked up on, tiny piles of sawdust, if you will, that indicated that I'd tagged Demetra *'apli'* just as erroneously as Gregori had tagged me. My first inkling that she wasn't the humble woman I thought she was should've been when she discounted my concerns and made her cheese dish. The second indication that I'd underestimated Demetra should've been when her brother, *Thio* Sotiri, asked me this canny question shortly after Gregori and I married, "So how do you get on with your mother-in-law?"

And when I responded, "Fine," *Thia* Marina sniggered.

And when I added, "What's not to get along? She's very quiet," all three of them laughed outright: Gregori, his uncle and his aunt.

After he stopped laughing, *Thio* Sotiri looked at me somberly and said, "It's true she's quiet, but remember this — *she can make a donkey die.*"

I'd never heard this Greek saying, so it went over my *Amerikanaki* head. I've learned it now, far too late to do me any good. For that reason, I'll pass my enlightenment on to you, should you happen to come across any prospective mothers-in-law to whom it might apply:

Some small Greek villages have mountain roads that are too narrow for automobiles. Locals use donkeys to traverse them, because they're resilient, sturdy animals. Their strong traits make them so obstinate, however, that if one donkey on the way *down* from one of these mountain roads, meets another on its way *up*, there's a chance that both will refuse to let the other pass. Then the villagers can be stuck up there for hours because one donkey *has* to give way. No amount of shoving, cajoling, even beating of the animal, will make it budge until it's damn ready.

Therefore, the saying, "can make a donkey die," when applied to a person, means that said person (mother-in-law) is so stubborn she'll *never* capitulate. The donkey she's facing off with will drop dead from thirst and she'll step over the poor beast's body, go on ahead and *never* look back.

I *wish* I'd asked Gregori's uncle to explain this expression when he first brought it up. My difficulties with Demetra started the same way as with those donkeys, when what each of us expected from the other was not what we were prepared to give.

After Gregori and I married, apart from the expectation that we eat at their place every Sunday, when I did cook for Gregori, she'd insist that I use only the products *she* used. ("Greek, not Italian, because that's what Gregori likes.") She'd even order our meats for us. (Have I mentioned my father was a butcher?)

I'd come home from work to discover she and Gregori had gone shopping to purchase a new piece of furniture — for *our* place. Or that she'd rewashed the clean cups in my cupboards because, "They had an odd smell."

At first I tried to regard her as one of those mothers-in-law in the TV 'sitcoms' — annoying, but humorous and well-meaning. Our program, however, became more like a cop show, where the star (me) gets a weekly thump on the head from the same thief who keeps stealing her handbag.

I didn't know how to get it back from her. I didn't know how to say, "Stop," or "Go away." The last thing I wanted was to argue with my *husband's mother*. So I made my first mistake — I let it go on far too long. And when I couldn't bear her meddling any longer, I complained about it to my husband. And that was my second mistake. As I voiced each frustration with Demetra to Gregori, his reactions started at 'not so good' and went to 'awful'.

I now know with the utmost conviction that when confronted with this type of mother-in-law, you've only two options: Set her straight, yourself, without saying *one* word about it to your spouse — *ever*. And you have to do this the *very first time* she does or says anything that gets your knickers in a twist. Changing in mid-marriage from compliant to defiant, won't work. You must start as you mean to continue. If this doesn't work, your second option is this: *Run like hell*, fast and far.

I'd yet to guess that my mother-in-law deemed she should have top rank in her sons' lives, always. She went about claiming this station in such a subtle, dainty way, that it was hard to explain to my husband what unnerved me about it. To apply another Greek saying, "it's always the quiet one who set the village afire."

Demetra's invasive proclivities took a lot away from us as a couple. And after her husband died and her grandson was born — *God help me*.

He's Probably Hungry

> *"The temptation to postpone a baby's sleep so that*
> *he may be admired by some relative or friend who*
> *is late in arriving . . . must be strongly resisted."*
> *–Marc Weissbluth, M.D.*

Though I was thirty-one years old when our son was born, it's obvious to me now, I still wasn't an adult. It was lucky, not just for him, but for both of us, that his appearance transformed me instantly into one. In point of fact, it was the "preview" of him, in my third month of pregnancy that accomplished this.

I was lying on an exam table waiting for my first sonogram, thinking that if I got one more repulsive, enormous pimple on my face, I'd smash all the mirrors in our apartment. Every part of my body felt swelled to an impossible degree, each and every one of my toes, right up to my nose and back down to my breasts. *Those* were so ridiculously engorged that I was already wearing nursing bras with cups so large that when I stopped having to wear them, I could fill them up with soil and use them as sapling planters. I was also thinking that there was an unidentifiable but disgusting smell in the room, and it was going to make me puke any minute.

Then the technician came in. She squirted ice-cold slime on my bare stomach, took something that looked like an upside-down microphone, slid it around my gooey belly, and then stopped.

"There's your baby," she said.

Sure enough, I was looking at a grainy black and white image of my child, who was wiggling what looked like teensy, incompletely formed legs.

"See?" she continued. "He's moving his legs because he doesn't like the sound waves."

"Then *get them off!*"

Where had it come from, that overpowering surge of protectiveness that howled its way through me then and hasn't left me for a moment since?

It's no longer about you, or Gregori, or your parents, kiddo, I told myself as I stared at that screen. *You're going to be a* mother. *So whatever's wrong with your psyche, you'd darn well better fix it and quick!*

After that sonogram, I was fully resolved to be the best mother I could. I had no inkling that my husband and all our relatives were fully resolved to do their best to stop me.

*** ***

I started out strong. When our son was born, Nonnie called me at the hospital and started up all over again.

"So — your husband got the boy."

"Yes, he did."

"And he's gonna be a little king in that house."

"Yes, he is."

"And you named him 'Nicholas'."

"You bet."

"Well, we're not coming to see him."

"Your loss."

Sadly, that was the last conversation I'd ever have with my grandmother and the last I'd hear from any of them for another four years. My parents were hanging tough that they were right. I wouldn't give in to their emotional blackmail this time, but I understood more than ever why Margie and Sean chose the path they did when their son had been born. It was just so much less painful.

That phone call from my grandmother was even more taxing because I'd just been in labor for 84 hours. (But who's counting?) The doctor at last decided I needed a caesarean. The day they performed it happened to be the same date as my mother-in-law and father-in-law's wedding anniversary. Nicholas even looked like his grandfather — male of Mediterranean ancestry, very short, with a loud voice, receding hairline, and a penchant for screeching suddenly when you were trying to watch TV.

Were these extraordinary facts of his birth mere coincidence? Demetra thought *not*. To her, they were compelling signs from God that she was going to *truly* raise her grandson and I would just stand in to wet nurse. And I'd *truly* thought that breastfeeding would be a bonding experience for my baby and me. Instead, she and Gregori both made it harrowing:

She: How do you know he's getting enough milk?

Me: He eats when he's hungry.

She: Why is he fussing, then?

Me: Babies fuss occasionally.

She: He's unhappy. You're doing something wrong. You should check with the doctor. You're not eating enough. You don't have enough milk.

Me: I have plenty of milk and the books say to drink more fluids, not eat more food.

She: No, *no*. These American books, these American ways, they're *wrong*. You're worried about your waistline at a time like this. The baby needs nourishment. You should be eating *twice as much*, because you're feeding *two* people.

Me: I'm not feeding two *adult* people and he's getting *plenty* of milk!

148

Demetra left and met up with Gregori outside as he was coming in from work. I could hear her jabbering away in Greek. The word, *"gah-lah,"* ("milk") came through loud and clear.

Gregori came into the bedroom. "What's going on?"

I was changing the baby. "She's obsessed with how much milk I have. She thinks I don't have enough."

Nicky chose that ill-timed moment to start crying. Gregori looked at him, then at me. "How do you know she's not right? He does cry a *lot*."

I was feeling more stressed by the minute. "And I feed him, *every time* he cries. He certainly doesn't look underweight."

"That's true," agreed Gregori. "But, couldn't you at least ask the doctor?"

I sighed. What if I were wrong? Suppose I *was* starving him? "He has his ten-day check-up on Wednesday. I'll ask the doctor then."

When I brought our son in for his ten-day check-up, he'd gained back all the ounces he was expected to lose after birth and had put on an additional pound.

Naturally, the doctor asked the provocative question then, "How do you know when he's hungry?"

I leveled with him. "Look, I *don't* know. I just feed him when I *think* he's hungry. My mother-in-law is driving me crazy. She thinks I don't have enough milk and he's crying because he's hungry."

The pediatrician laughed. "Are you kidding? You're carrying around enough milk in there for quadruplets. Look at the size of this baby. Does he look like he's going without? From now on, go with your instincts. Most mothers can tell what their babies need."

"Why is he crying, then?"

"How many times does he nap?"

"I think... just once."

The doctor smiled. "There's your problem. He's overtired. The more babies sleep, the better off they are, in most cases. He's not sleeping as much as he'd like and he's cranky, that's all."

He'd armed me with more confidence. I was ready to face my mother-in-law.

That hope withered quickly. The next day was Saturday and Gregori would be home from work, which meant that Demetra would come over early for coffee and stay too long. Apart from my frustration with her in general, I was worn-out from all the night feedings, trying to catch up on sleep whenever I could. That wasn't often possible with a husband who didn't understand that I needed rest and a mother-in-law who came by whenever she wished.

In fact, here was Demetra *now* — right at the foot of my bed. Even though I'd had the bedroom door closed, she came right in as I was breastfeeding Nicky.

"Hello," she said, smiling. Then loudly, "*There's* my grandson."

Nicky, who'd been about to fall asleep, opened his eyes.

I whispered. "I'm *feeding* the baby. It's time for him to go to sleep and I want to take a nap, too."

"*Mmmm,*" she said.

I burped Nicky and shifted him over to the other breast. Demetra watched, a peculiar smile on her face. Suddenly, she stooped in a half-crouch and slinked closer to us, until she was directly at my elbow. Then the weird smile turned into a creepy grin, as she leaned in and kissed the baby.

While he was *still* attached to my nipple.

She kissed and *kissed* him, noisily and with gusto. Nicky startled awake and began to wail. I could only stare at her, because... truthfully? She'd *scared* me. I put the baby on my shoulder and soothed him as she straightened up, smiled again less maniacally this time, said, *"Yiah-soo,"* and left the room. I heard her say laughingly to Gregori, "I think Patricia's upset. I woke the baby up!"

After she'd gone, Gregori came in. I was trying to soothe Nicky, but my whole body was shaking. With gritted teeth I said, "I don't want her near me *ever* again when the baby and I are in here with the door closed!"

Gregori raised his eyebrows. "Just because she woke him up, accidentally?"

"*Never* again! I mean it."

*** ***

Demetra didn't come in my bedroom anymore because I kept the door *locked*, not because Gregori looked out for me. In fact, apart from changing a diaper or two, which impressed his family no end, he was giving me no support at all. He didn't prevent his family and friends from visiting, even if our son and I were both exhausted. My feelings were so conflicted over this. On the one hand, it was wonderful to see so much excitement generated over the baby, since my own parents had put their interests before any they might have in their new grandson. Plus, I loved seeing Gregori smile. That had been the idea, after all. I even identified with Demetra's perspective to a degree. This was her first grandchild. She'd just lost her husband. On the other hand, I was so dead worn-out, I could scarcely function.

I said dozens of times in the first three months, "Gregori, I'm tired. Please... I'm *so* tired."

He'd reluctantly tell everyone to leave, in a tone that conveyed what a killjoy I was. They'd all shuffle out, Gerry and Sotiri the only two with neutral expressions, but Marina's looks were dark as she grumbled, "*kalee-neek-ta*" ("good night") and Demetra's were wounded. Those reactions only increased my feelings of culpability.

When I did manage to catch some sleep, Gregori would wake me by snapping on lights, jiggling the mattress, watching television while he chuckled and cracked pumpkin seeds in bed right next to me. His self-absorbed habits were galling when I was teaching and had to get up early; now the lack of rest was taking its toll on my health.

When Nicky was three months old, I caught a fever. The doctor told me I had to stop breastfeeding until the fever went down. "It won't harm the baby to get formula for a few days. Just express your milk and it won't dry up," he instructed.

I followed the instructions on the breast pump I bought, but no milk came out. I looked at the instructions again. This was a 'hand pump', not an 'electric'. Hard pressure on the breast was required. I tried again, forcing my breast into the cone of the pump, pulling hard on the handle. My breast suctioned further into the plastic tube, contorted into a cylindrical shape, then snapped back out. *Ouch.* No fun at *all* and still no milk. The ache was getting worse because my milk glands were engorged, popping up like boils under my skin. That milk had to come out. *What now?*

Oh, wait... I could ask Gregori to help. He was probably still at his mother's.

Gregori had breakfast every morning with Demetra. Since he kept his taxi parked in his mother's garage, he'd drive her car home to our place every night and bring it back when he retrieved the taxi in the morning. Since he was there *already*, "They might as well have coffee together," he'd said.

"*Hello?*" Demetra answered the phone.

"Hello, *Mama*. It's Patricia. How are you?" I asked politely.

"*Fine.*"

I waited a moment for her to reciprocate the courtesy, but she said nothing.

"Is Gregori there?"

"He's in the toy-lettah."

"Uh… well, would you please have him ring me back, when he… gets out? It's *very* important."

"What's it about?"

There was no way I was going to tell her. "Please tell him to phone," was all I said.

"Mmmm," was all she said.

Gregori rang me back, about ten minutes later. *"What is it? I'm late for work."*

"I need you home for something important. I can't explain it over the phone."

He swore. Then he hung up on me. Which meant he was coming home.

I was sitting on our bed, breast pump at the ready, when he came in, looking cross. When I told him what the problem was and what he needed to do, he barked impatiently, "Are you kidding me? How long is this going to take?"

I'd had it with him. "Oh, be quiet!" I snapped. "You have a *taxi*. You can drive it whenever you want. You're having coffee there for more than *two* hours and now that *I* need you, you *have* to go to work? Do you know how my breasts *feel*? No and you don't care, do you? This milk has to come *out* and *you* have to help me."

My heart was pounding from this exchange and I could feel the fever had risen a bit. There was no chance I'd be able to do what the instructions suggested and "relax." I put my breast carefully back in the plastic cone of the pump. Even just doing that, it felt sore.

"Okay, go ahead," I instructed Gregori. Pressing his lips together, he pumped.

A few drops of milk trickled out. I sighed, "Oh, *thank God*, it's working. Try again."

More milk dribbled into the glass container, but not the flow that I badly needed to get relief. Sweat beaded on his face and he swore loudly in Greek, as he pumped with frenzy. I ignored his swearing, focused on the pain and the task. Anyone who walked in at that moment (his mother, maybe?) would think we were two perverts with a very twisted fetish.

Just when I thought I'd get some relief, Gregori looked up abruptly, fury on his face. In the same way he'd done with the hapless *Olympic Airways* worker, he screamed at me, nose-to-nose, "I CAN'T DO THIS! IT'S TOO HARD! I HAVE TO GO TO WORK! DO YOU UNDERSTAND ME?"

Just as the worker had, I jumped back with a screech. The pump pulled away from my breast and fell on the bed, its meager contents of breast milk spilling on the sheets.

Gregori had to justify himself. "This is *your* fault. If you weren't so stubborn and ignorant, you'd ask my mother to come and help you! Why do *I* have to do this kind of shit?"

As we looked across at each other, both fuming, the baby woke up and started to cry.

I hated Gregori then, with every degree of the fever that was burning through me. "You make me sick," I said.

Swearing in Greek, he slammed out of the apartment.

This was the point, in my mind, where Gregori and I were no longer a team. It was he and his mother against me.

Now, I had no one but myself.

The Insanity Clause

"Your mother is crazy. And she never leaves you alone."
- Mikis Theodorakis Lyrics

I gave up on breastfeeding shortly after that. Nicky was fine on formula, thank goodness. At almost six months old, he was a calm, healthy, happy baby.

Yet, if you'd listened to Demetra, you'd have been sure his well-being had nothing to do with me. I dressed him in the wrong clothing, I let him cry too long and sleep too much and worse, I didn't protect him from those external evil forces.

Her litany had started from the day we brought him home: "Pin a blue eye to his clothes; Don't take him outside for forty days; Don't cut his nails for forty days."

Why "forty days"? In Scripture, the number signifies a time of penitential preparation or punishment sent from God. I knew which it felt like for me. *My* sent afflictions lasted *far* longer than forty days.

153

Nicky was like a play doll to Gregori and his relatives. Gregori and Demetra wanted him dressed in 'adorable' outfits always, "in case" family dropped by to see him. When family inevitably did, they'd jiggle things in his face, car keys, Greek 'worry beads', anything to stimulate him to gurgle and amuse them the *entire* time they were with him. When they dropped by, they wanted me to wake him up and then, just like in the song, they wanted him to "stay up all night."

When he'd fret from all the raucous hilarity and their ceaseless booming, "Look, Nicky!" "Here, Nicky!" Demetra would pick him up and keen, "*MAH-NAH-MAH-NAH-MAH-NAH!*" in a high-pitched caw. He'd just cry more loudly at that. So she'd 'soothe' him, by bobbling him up and down vigorously, until he spat up. Then she'd say, "Oops!" and hand him back over to me.

At which point, he would lay his little head on my shoulder and collapse into sleep. At least, I hoped it was sleep. I hoped he wasn't blacking out from trauma.

Sometimes when Demetra was handling him this way, he'd even twist around to focus on me, with a look that seemed to plead, *"Pick me up. I've had enough."*

It felt like I'd been spending every night since his birth supervising at a party for a bunch of six-year-olds who'd been drinking too much soda:

"Don't give him *that*. That's not for babies to eat."

"You know, his neck will snap off if you keep shaking him like that."

And then when I couldn't bear any more, "Okay, let's put the toys away. Time for everyone to go home."

That technique didn't work on my in-laws anymore than it does on children. Though the men in the family just pretended I was invisible when I voiced my concerns, Demetra and *Thia* Marina criticized my nurturing skills. Ordinarily those two weren't allies, but as a combined force in a campaign to prove I was a deplorable mother, their methods were varied and creative.

Such as Marina asking me questions that were not questions, but accusations framed as questions: "Why aren't you putting any sugar in the baby's milk? Don't you know that sugar is good for the baby's *bones*?"

Or Demetra stating her measure of my inadequacies directly to her baby grandson: "*Poh poh poh.* You let your mother dress you in *this* foolish outfit? You'll be freezing. What is going *on* in *this* house, eh, Nicky?"

If I offered them my ideas about child rearing, they'd nod condescendingly and then exchange amused looks, as if to say, "Let the *Amerikanaki* talk. She's pathetic, but harmless."

After another afternoon spent with 'The Weird Sisters', I made this observation to Gregori, "Your mother and aunt never criticize Gerry's wife. Why not? She's American, too."

Gerry and Doosie had gotten married just around the time Nicky turned three months old.

Gregori explained, "They don't criticize Doosie to her face because she's *really* American. She's so foreign to them she might as well be crazy. So they close their eyes to the things she does. You, on the other hand, are *Italian*-American, which is more 'European'. That makes you like a *real* daughter-in-law. By pointing out what you're doing wrong, they're letting you know they see you as one of us."

I observed that my 'crazy' American sister-in-law got to live her life free of in-law officiousness and I wasn't so sure I wanted to be considered "one of them" anymore.

In this instance, Gregori tried to explain the reasons for his mother's behavior, but other times, he got defensive. Even if he did agree with my standpoint, he wouldn't back me up, because he didn't want to hurt her feelings.

"She *just* lost her husband," he'd say, reproachfully. "She's so happy that she has her grandson. Can't you be a *little* patient with her?"

That speech had magic, malevolent power. I felt both guilt and hatred, every time he said it. And those terrible feelings made me cry.

"Now you're *crying!*" Gregori would shout. "I can't *stand* being in the middle of this! I've got problems of my own! I'll *tell* her, okay? Will that satisfy you?"

Gregori never broke that promise when he made it, which was why he didn't unless pushed. He was like a fly stuck in a web between a house spider and a black widow. Either way spelled danger, but one looked a whole lot scarier. If he came home without speaking to his mother, he'd hear whining about it from me. If he went to his mother with my objections, she'd moan to him, too.

Aha — but, you see — that's *not* what she would do. Her technique was much more effective. If Gregori spoke to his mother as promised, he'd come home looking ill.

"What'd she say?" I'd ask, anxiously.

155

He'd dither, "Well... she didn't say much when I talked to her this morning. Then when I brought the car back, I went up to see her again and she was lying down. She said she felt like she had that 'bleeding thing' again that she got when I was seeing... that woman she didn't like."

Suspiciously, I asked, "You mean her hysterectomy?"

He nodded glumly.

Ah. The hysterectomy for which Gregori held himself responsible, because he'd been dating Thoulah's sister. Greek Orthodox Church dogma frowns upon "two brothers marrying two sisters." I won't bother explaining why. Gerry was already engaged to Thoulah when Gregori started seeing her sister. Despite his mother's condemnation of this, Gregori did what *he* wished, for once. Then Demetra got sick, and he blamed himself. With Demetra's help, of course.

I looked at him levelly. "You do know she couldn't possibly need *two* hysterectomies, right? Unless she has *two* uteruses?"

"I *know*," he snapped. "I just don't want her to get sick again, okay?" And he stamped away, leaving me stymied.

She's... mind-boggling, I thought. Something else went through my head, too. *Poor Gregori. He believes her.*

"Poor Gregori" was how I'd been describing my husband a lot. As if the problems with Demetra weren't enough, I was feeling powerless in other areas of our life, too. Gregori was unhappy with everything — his job, his weight, our finances, the city in which he worked, the country in which we lived. He said he loved me and yet, our sex life, never the best, was now practically non-existent. He was always tired and disinterested. Even Nicky, a delight to Gregori, could only distract him from his melancholy temporarily.

I worried he was still depressed over his father's death. I worried that maybe, at 32, he hadn't been ready to be a father. Maybe he needed a change in career, or a financial advisor. Or more *Gucci* socks, or even a 'shrink'. I didn't know. All I knew was that my husband looked happy *only* when he was getting ready to go out with his friends. "Boys' night," was still every Friday night.

And every Friday night, while he was out, after I put the baby to sleep, I'd call Marie, Josephine or Marietta, to lament over my week's dealings with Gregori and the rest of the lot. Sometimes I'd even sit at Colleen's and complain. Every week, they'd listen sympathetically and stoically. Margie got to hear it every *day*. Then I'd always ask, "What should I do?"

They did what they could to shore me up, but there was nothing for them to advise because they all knew I didn't want to hear their one blunt suggestion. (Of course, if I'd been speaking to my parents, they wouldn't have hesitated. Just one more reason never to phone them.)

I didn't want a divorce. I wanted my husband to be happy and my mother-in-law to leave me in peace. I had to think of *something* to accomplish these things.

Thia Marina's False Teeth

> *"I'm really sorry for everything that's happened.*
> *And I hate Linda Tripp."*
> **–Monica Lewinsky**

Three years later I still hadn't thought of anything. I had suggested counseling, but Gregori said, "Greeks don't believe in that." The only difference now was that Gregori had had some unsuccessful business ventures, so, on top of everything else, we were broke. This didn't improve Gregori's disposition any. He went from being morose to blatantly nasty.

By divine intervention, our son had the total opposite disposition. Cheerful with everyone, he was my one source of family happiness. I loved him dearly, loved being his mother. We had such fun together and it kept me centered to observe how much he enjoyed life.

But he was four years old. That meant four years of living with an unhappy husband and letting his mother push me around. She'd outwitted me at every turn, prying relentlessly, while my husband made it known through word and deed that her wishes were more important to him than mine. I'd stuffed down these hurts, not felt in control of my life, for more than *four years*. I'd put up with all this, thinking I'd win my husband's and mother-in-law's approval. It hadn't worked. The fact that I was so easy to manipulate (something I hadn't known about myself) was probably what Gregori and Demetra had liked about me in the first place. Other women I knew could manage difficult in-laws and impatient husbands, but *I* couldn't. Let's face it; I was a wimp. Louie would've been impressed by my servility. He'd worried for nothing.

157

My dreams were falling apart. Feeling this way, there were times when I wanted to grab Nicky and run. Then he'd smile at me and I knew I couldn't do that to him. I'd made a promise when I'd walked out of that sonogram five years before that I'd be a good mother. That pledge included having my son raised in a home with a father in it. I didn't want Nicky to sense my troubles. So as he and I played and laughed together, little did my son know that I was often thinking:

"Nicky, would you be frightened of me if I beat your father with a shovel until he promised to change his obnoxious behavior? What if I murdered your grandmother and buried her body under your sandbox in the garden?"

Yep, I was 'losing it'. Something had to give.

And several things did. The first was that Marie and Josephine's Aunt Ester, on their mother's side, died of breast cancer. Though I hadn't known Ester very well, I knew she was Marie's favorite. I wanted to support her as she and Mike had supported me when Gregori's father died. Gregori stayed home with Nicky so I could attend the wake. I was astonished to see my parents there. My father had three surviving brothers and he wasn't speaking to a one of them. There was a long history behind this and clearly, it was my parents' practice to sustain pride and rancor above all else. From their perspective, anyone connected to my father's brothers, including my cousins, was tainted by association and had to be avoided, too. Actually, this was another thing they held against me — that I'd kept close ties with relatives they didn't.

Nonetheless, they were there. I've always wondered if they knew I was going to be there and that was why they'd come. I have to admit, it was good to see them. It'd been over four years. I was startled by how much older they looked. As intolerable as they could be, I'd missed them. There'd been many times during that four years I'd wanted to phone. I wanted my father to know I'd finished my master's degree and that my pieces were being accepted for publication. I knew he'd be proud. I wanted my mother to know Nicholas, to see how adorable he was. Nicky would enjoy having her as a grandmother, too, because she could be so much fun. One of my best childhood memories was of my mother lying on my bed next to me, reading *Dr. Seuss* stories. I'd snuggle up to her, she smelled of tobacco and soap and she'd laugh at every line as she read. As good as I was at reading aloud to Nicky, I knew she'd be better. I wanted that for him. And dealing with Demetra, being married to Gregori all this time, made me see my mother in a different light.

158

What was it like for her, growing up with Nonnie as her mom? Nonnie was inimitably entertaining as a grandmother, but as a mother, she couldn't have been easy. Though my mother was devoted to Nonnie, they'd always had a thorny relationship, too. I realized it was only natural that my mother would have some control issues. Then, there was my father. Growing up, I'd always felt sorry for him, because my mother seemed so bossy. Now I saw that she made every decision in their lives and he took responsibility for nothing. Perhaps that was the way she wanted it. I couldn't know. I only knew that she'd been just twenty when she'd married my father, twenty-two when she was pregnant with me. As a mother myself now, I was able to see how young she'd been.

On the other hand, they'd let four years go by to prove a point. Four years of their grandson's life. Four years of mine. I thought of all the things I'd been going through, when I could have used their help instead of their judgments. And at the same time I was glad to see them, I was still so angry at them.

I walked out of the funeral parlor to get some air. I didn't see my father follow me out. He called my name. I turned and watched him as he walked over.

"Nonnie's dying. She has cancer," was the first thing he said to me.

"I'm sorry to hear that," I said. And I was.

"Your mother doesn't realize she's dying yet. Your grandmother's fighting it. She didn't want to go to the hospital." He shook his head. "We had to drag her there. She curses all of us for that every time we visit her. She accused your mother of being glad she was sick."

My poor mother. "That sounds like Nonnie, all right."

But this was not the most heartrending bombshell of the evening. My mother stepped outside now, as well.

"I want to talk to you," she said to me.

She marched over, then stopped in front of me with a look on her face like a general facing a firing squad. And what she said next blindsided me.

"I want you to know this whole thing is my fault." Her face crumpled. "*Oh God* — I *fucked* up my *whole life!* Give me another chance." She clenched her hands together and held them out in front of her, like a prayer. "I'll be such a good grandmother, I *promise* you."

I didn't know what she meant by "fucking up her whole life." Maybe I was afraid to ask. But it was the bravest speech I'd ever heard. Because I believed it, I accepted it. I hugged her fiercely and she hugged me back. I hugged my father, too.

159

Marginally at first, my mother and father came back into our lives. Their introduction to Nicky was timely, because he'd coincidentally asked me about them for the first time a few weeks before:

"What about your parents, *Mama*? What are their names? How come I never met them?"

I made the excuse that they lived far away and that seemed to satisfy him. But I fretted about it afterward. Now that I'd introduced them to him, he was almost blasé about having a new set of grandparents drop into his life. He had just one concern:

"*Baba* (Dad) always makes me kiss people and I hate it," he said.

Once he was reassured that they didn't expect kisses, the three of them got on well.

My parents were also making a prodigious effort with Gregori and that was a real quirk of fate, considering the state of our marriage as they reentered our lives. As for Gregori, he accepted them, too, simply because, to quote Margie, "they were my parents."

It was only a few weeks later that Nonnie died. I attended her funeral because my mother asked me to, but it was hard. Looking at my plucky grandmother lying stone still in a box, I wished her spunk and eternally youthful outlook hadn't been the only things I could admire about her. Plus, I was returning from a four-year exile from my mother's side of the family. They hadn't stayed out of the messy business between my parents and me. They chosen sides and some had done so with glee. They reveled in malicious gossip, which is why I preferred my father's side to most family members on my mother's. Just as I'd expected, my presence drew attention from the purpose of the gathering. As I walked up the church steps, heads turned toward me, then away, then drew together in whispered speculation. After that, those same people went into the church for the mass and prayed. Their perception of *figura*. I couldn't wait to get out of there.

And so, the first significant development that took place was my parents back in my life and the burgeoning of new perspectives regarding certain concepts I'd believed in, as a result. The next change was more external, though equally noteworthy. It concerned Doosie. Always considered a madwoman by her in-laws, she 'snapped' for real.

Gregori's brother came home from work early one day and caught her swimming nude with a young man who'd been hired to tile their master bath. 'Tile boy' was — *ahem* — 'barely' legal age. Her excuse was that

160

she'd been drinking. Investigations revealed that drinking and taking drugs had been her main occupations for some time, along with fixating on *Guns n' Roses* videos and convincing herself that she was an undiscovered supermodel with whom the actor, Don Johnson, would fall in love.

My brother-in-law did his husbandly duty by placing her in the best facility money could buy and then turned to other women for consolation. The rehab counselors told Doosie that Gerry was "an emotional void for her" and likely at the root of her problems. That's why after she dried out, she dumped him. Luckily, they had no children.

Personally, *I* don't think her mental instability had anything to do with her being a 'WASP'. Still, this episode was all the reaffirmation Gregori's family needed that American women were weak-minded and unsuited for marriage to a Greek. However, they still had one American wife left in the family — me. They held their collective breath that since I wasn't *as* American as Doosie was, more like 'American-*ish*', I might be able to hold it together.

On the heels of that, came the third adventure. The escapades of Marina and Demetra had never included jeopardizing Nicky's life. That is, until they, along with Sotiri, took him on an outing. I was gardening when they returned in the car. Imagine my surprise, to put it mildly, that Nicky wasn't in a safety harness. Marina had him on her lap in the front passenger seat.

The whole block heard me screech.

My mother-in-law giggled. "Don't lose your shirt. It was just one time."

The world turned red. They'd endangered my child on a whim.

Sotiri finished parking and Nick ran over to me. "Hi, *Mama! Yiayia* said it was okay to sit in the front."

I knelt to him. "Yes, but it's *not* okay, Nicky. You *know* that. Now go inside for a moment, so I can explain it privately to *Yiayia*."

When he'd gone, I turned on the three. "If you *ever* take my son for a car ride again with him not wearing a harness, *so help me God,* I'll call the police. And you'll have to pay a fine."

Thia looked genuinely confused. "But why, Patricia? I had him tight in my arms. He was *safe*."

I ignored her. "If you do it again and something happens to him, I'll *sue* you. I'll make sure you *all* end up in *jail.* On your lives, you'd better believe me!"

"Okay, Patricia," soothed *Thio* Sotiri, who for some reason, found this more comical than threatening. "We won't do it again."

As I stomped back into the house and left them there, I heard Marina say, "*My God.* She's crazy, too. We'd better not upset her again. We don't want to lose another one."

*** ***

Two weeks later, Sotiri and Marina were in a car accident. Marina was sitting in the front passenger seat and as usual, wasn't wearing a harness. Fortunately, the accident was a minor one and *Thio* had been driving on the side streets slowly. Even so, he'd had to slam on the car brake. Marina hurtled forward into the windshield, cutting a gash over her eye and dislocating her jaw. After she recovered, she was a changed woman, bless her heart.

"I went *flying!*" she told us in astonishment. "The first thing I thought about was Patricia."

Uh oh. Was I about to be blamed for giving her 'the evil eye'?

She turned to me with an unabashed look of veneration on her face. "*How* did you know how hard we could hit? Sotiri wasn't even going fast! Imagine if it'd happened while I was holding Nicky, on the *highway*? He'd have gone through the window!"

"*Mmmm,*" said my mother-in-law. "Thank God it didn't happen."

Marina felt her duty to make reparation wasn't yet complete. Nicky was playing in his room, but came out when she called him. She looked at him soberly. "Niko*laki,* remember that day I told you to sit on my lap in the car?"

Nicky nodded.

Thia held her index finger up. "*Poh-tay.* (Never.) *Never* again, sit in a car with no seatbelt. *Thia* was in a car accident and she wasn't wearing one. And look—"

Thia took out her false teeth.

Nick reared back. "Wow!" he gasped. His eyes fixed on *Thia's* open mouth.

Thia popped her teeth back in. "See what happened because I didn't listen to your mother? My face hit the car window and *allll* my teeth fell out, because I had *no seatbelt,*" she exaggerated for her great-nephew's benefit.

Nick opened his own mouth and felt around his teeth. "Wow!" said Nick, again.

162

"Remember — *seat belt*. Okay?" finished *Thia*.

Nick nodded emphatically. Then off he ran.

I had no objection to *Thia*'s quirky illustration of her lesson well-learned. But I could tell, Demetra was *not* amused.

The Queen is Deposed

> *"Anybody can become angry—that is easy. But to be angry with the right person to the right degree, at the right time, for the right purpose, and in the right way, that isn't within everyone's power and is not easy."*
> **–Aristotle**

After Marina showed Nicky her false teeth, the team spirit between her and Demetra collapsed. Having come to the dubious conclusion that I was a *wunderkind*, Marina began asking me for advice on a multitude of subjects.

When my mother-in-law huffed, "She doesn't know *everything*, you know!" Marina laughed at her. Demetra came by to see us less often when she knew Sotiri and Marina would be there, making the excuse that she had to care for her "Poor Gerry," who'd "just lost his wife and was all alone."

When she did visit, I was more assertive. It wasn't because I had Marina's backing. Something altered inside me the day I'd demanded my little son's safety. Saying, "no", always slammed up against what I'd been taught — respect for my elders and *figura*. This exacerbated all my uncertainties. But my in-laws had given me a perilous choice: I could remain deferential and hold the blame for any resulting harm to Nicky, or I could take charge of him when they were wrong. I'd chosen the latter, and found that saying, "no", though it still felt unnatural, could be a magnificent tool. With practice, I had less trouble with it.

It didn't all go smoothly from then on, because when I said "no", to my husband and relatives, they only accepted it sometimes. Other times, all hell broke loose. I can think of one incident in particular:

Demetra had sustained a steady snit since the car-seat incident. And because he'd sided with me on that, for the first time in all the years since he'd dated a girl she despised, Demetra was demonstrating dissatisfaction with Gregori.

163

As always, Gregori would go to his mother's for morning coffee, but when he tried to make conversation, she'd only say, "*Mmmm*". When coming over to see Nicky, she sat the entire time, reading the paper, directing her sole conversation to her grandson, and ignoring Gregori and me. Gregori was guilt-ridden and I was incensed, but neither of us discussed Demetra's performance nor the cause of it, knowing that it'd only lead to another quarrel.

However, one day, she stopped by. "Gerry wants to take his nephew to lunch."

It was a queenly command. Nevertheless, I smiled at her. "That'll be fine," I said, as though she'd asked my permission. "He's got a haircut this afternoon, though, at three."

I called to Nicky, "Nick! Would you like to have lunch with *Yiayia* and *Thio* Gerry?"

"Yeah!" he rang out joyfully from the other room.

Turning to my mother-in-law, I held my smile, but reiterated, "Remember, *three* o'clock. I'll be waiting when you get back."

She only glared at me, said, "*Elah, Nicky*," grabbed his hand and off they went, with Nicky waving "good bye."

The real fun hadn't begun. Demetra didn't tell Gerry that Nicky had a haircut appointment at three. When she sashayed up the steps at four-ten, with my son, I watched calmly, but inside, I was seething. I'd had enough. Entrenched donkeys can be shot between the eyes and tossed over the mountainside, if passage is that crucial. She had no idea what was coming in the next few moments.

And neither did I.

I smiled at Nick, "Did you have fun?"

He nodded gleefully. "We had *carbonara!*"

"*Ooo*, your favorite!" I said.

"Okay, I'm leaving!" announced my mother-in-law from the entranceway. "*Yiah-soo, Nikolaki!*" She thought she'd make her getaway, assuming I wouldn't make a scene in front of Nicky. If it'd been only one day before, that would've been an accurate assumption.

"Not so fast," I said, my smile fixed firmly in place. "I want to talk to you."

She was smiling, too. "Can't. Left my handbag in the car. The door is unlocked. Sorry."

"Oh, you will be, if you don't come in," I purred, "because I *will* say what I have to say, right here, where all the neighbors will hear."

Her smile froze. *Got* her.

Know why? *Figura,* that's why. She didn't want the neighbors to get a bad impression. And since when had Patricia stopped honoring *figura?* She hadn't planned for *that.* Now she was left with two thorny choices — stay where she was and have a public argument with her daughter-in-law, or come into the apartment and take her lumps in private. Nick was already in his bedroom playing music cassettes with the door closed. Good. He wouldn't hear us, no matter where we argued. Demetra made her selection. She chose 'in'.

Did I say "argue?" I should have said "brawl." With the exclusion of fisticuffs, what followed was nothing short of a drag-her-by-the-hair, brassy brawl, to which the two of us gave our shrill, boorish best.

"Oh, *yeah?* You have something to say?" she sneered as she came into my foyer. "You think because you're a *teacher,*" she spat the word, "you're going to teach *me* something?"

As shaken as I was by the change in her demeanor — she looked like a completely different woman — I held my own.

"You bet!" I jeered back. I held my index finger up an inch from her nose, "Lesson number one!" I used the same finger to point toward the room where Nick was listening to *Raffi* cassettes, oblivious to our squabble, "That child in there," the same finger again, this time toward my heart, "he's *my* son; *not* yours."

With undiluted loathing, she taunted, "Don't you *dare* shout at me. This is not *Brooklyn.*"

Pow! Direct verbal cuff to the face. Brooklyn, area celebrated by the media for Italian-American *gangsters.* It was also where some of my family members lived. With one bigoted slur, she'd sliced them all.

Amazed by my composure, I retaliated smoothly, "You're right, we're not in Brooklyn. But we're still in the *United States of America.*" Then I did something I never dreamed I'd do. I mimicked my father's words from that soccer match years before. "This is *America* and I am *American!* We outlawed slavery here, even for *daughters-in-law!* So, let me finish my lesson. From *now on,* when it comes to *my* son, you do what *I* say, or else you'll *never* baby-sit for him again!"

She sucked in such a deep breath of outrage at that threat, I thought she'd choke for sure. Shaking her head back and forth, she tried another assault, "You don't deserve my son."

That brought up a point. "*I* don't deserve him? *You've* been making him miserable for weeks. When he tries to talk to you," I picked up a newspaper, smacked it against the tile and she flinched reflexively, "you pretend to read the *goddamn* paper. *Why?* Because he tried to tell you that you could've *killed* your grandson? Is that what you're gnashing your teeth at him for? Must he *always* take your side against mine?"

Recovering from her jolt, she countered smugly, "*Yes.* Because *I* come *first* in my son's life."

Well... she sure was right on that score. I did my utmost though, to make my point. "I come first in my son's life, too. *My* son's only a child, though. What's *your* excuse?"

"I don't need one!" she shot back. "*I'm* Gregori's *mother.* The only thing you can give him that I can't is *sex!*"

Ewww! How in hell could I respond to that? Should I tell her to go ahead and have it with him, as it wasn't nearly as good as she might be thinking?

No. We'd wrestled in the muck long enough. Sick to my stomach, I opened the door. "Remember what I said." I gestured for her to exit. "*Now* you can check on your handbag."

Demetra Gets Her Own Room

"Now you're making me feel sorry for her."
–Gerry's Third Wife

Though I was glad I'd found the guts to stand up to my mother-in-law, I wasn't glad we'd fought so viciously. I'd loved Demetra at one time, if for no other reason than she was Gregori's mother and *he* loved her. I'd also loved her for being a good grandmother to Nick. (Apart from the car-seat incident, that is.) Now that it was out in the open how much of a trespasser she thought I was, I felt awful. Because as hard as this is to believe, I still wanted to have a close relationship with her. And... I actually felt sorry for her. In my heart, I knew I was luckier than she was. She'd been trained for nothing, save keeping house and appeasing her men. These occupations were lost to her when her husband died and her sons married. If I were in Demetra's position, I don't think I'd be able to accept that I was essentially obsolete, either.

On the other hand, did that justify her becoming a manipulative, passive-aggressive control freak, who kept her sons roped tightly to her?

Was it acceptable that she'd strong-armed her way into her daughter-in-law's realm and deliberately squelched the spirit of a younger, more unsure woman, who'd only wanted her friendship and encouragement?

If I accepted the rationalization that Demetra had sad beginnings and got lousy breaks, then I'd have to accept that even murder could be defended, if the perpetrator's sob story harvests enough sympathy. I *did* have compassion for Demetra, but felt crushed by her and disappointed that we hadn't connected. We should have been able to support each other.

Not long after that vile confrontation, Marina died, having struggled for years with illnesses. She didn't suffer, thank goodness, just went for a nap and never woke up. Sotiri was inconsolable, so Demetra, as his widowed sister, moved in with him on a part-time basis. Now she had two helpless men to take care of — her older brother and her eldest son. (After his divorce, Gerry sold the house he'd shared with Doosie and moved back in with Demetra.) The driving back and forth from Sotiri's apartment to hers, the cooking and maintenance for the two residences and men, kept Demetra occupied and out of my hair.

The men gradually recovered from their individual tragedies. Gerry was out on the prowl again and it put a cramp in his style when new girlfriends learned he lived with his mother. And Sotiri could be quite pernickety about his doo-dads being set up 'just so'. His sister wasn't doing things the way Marina would have. As a result, Demetra would leave her brother's house upset over Sotiri's bossiness, only to get home and find her son skulking about, like it was her fault he was single. (I know what you're thinking, but we can't blame her for *everything*.) A solution had to be found.

Gerry set up one. He bought a luxury apartment in Crete and deposited his mother in it. He reasoned she was now in the patient hands of the priest and the *papadia*. She could visit her husband's grave, help *Papa* Elias at the church, or... whatever. Demetra stayed four months a year in her new place in Crete, four months additionally in the now-completed flat on Rhodes and four months back in New York, living with Sotiri.

Some might say this was a privileged way to live. Two gorgeous new apartments — kitchens with top-of-the-line European appliances, new furnishings, views of the sea — the works. Then, exotic excursions to Greek islands and more, and in the wintertime a trip back to the States to spend Christmas with the kids, all courtesy of Gerry. But to Demetra, what was the sense of having two new kitchens, if there was no one to cook for? Besides, let's admit it — she *had* been shipped off and was aware of it.

Nonetheless, she didn't give up. When she came back to New York for her first winter visit, I thought, *Why have hard feelings, as she's so safely out of my way?* That's why, as she was leaving, I made myself say something kind, "Nicky was happy to see you."

She whipped her head toward me. "I can take him to Greece with me. Greece is a better place to raise children than here."

Oh, not again. I feigned a giggle. "That's funny."

She looked at me, deadpan. "I'm serious. Greek children are raised by their grandparents all the time. You and Gregori could come and see us, once a year, in the summers. It would be better for *you*."

I didn't argue with her this time. I merely tittered again. Then said, "Have a safe trip."

But, believe it or not, Demetra's aspirations were going to be met.

About a year after that, nearing Nicholas' fifth birthday, Gerry got married again. This time he'd met someone wonderful. Gerry's Third Wife (nameless at her request) quickly became one of my dearest friends.

Less than a year into their marriage she phoned me upset, saying, "I think Gerry's cheating on me. I found a love note from a girl named, 'Penelope'. Does Gregori know anything?"

I couldn't believe Gerry was up to his old tricks, but I still had faith in my husband's convictions. "If he does, I know he'd tell me," I assured her.

However, I was knocked for six to discover that Gregori *was* hiding knowledge of his brother's latest affair. Thoulah had been right about him all those years ago, after all.

His reasoning was straightforward. "I knew you'd tell her."

"She had a right to know!" I cried.

"Not from me," was his answer, "and not from *my* wife."

Luckily, however, Gerry's Third Wife forgave me my inadvertent role in that debacle and planned a healthier retribution against Gerry than Thoulah had. She packed his belongings into plastic trash bags, tossed them out, then tossed him out right behind them, with no qualms whatsoever.

Despite that, I felt sick and tricked. My husband was a liar and I'd played the unwitting co-conspirator to Gerry-related peccadilloes *twice*. Gregori might still a novice at lying to women, but, *oh* — his brother was an expert. Gerry actually lied about the number of times he'd been married, ('two' instead of 'three') to that latest object-of-amorous-intent, Penelope. He badmouthed 'both' those wives to her, too. Penelope was duped to the point that she became Gerry's mistress (while he was still married to my dear friend, as I've just pointed out) and got pregnant.

And I was so disappointed in my own husband, too. He'd been affronted by my grandmother's multiple marriages. In fact, Gregori's obsession with good impressions had turned him into a repressed, unyielding tyrant, our own "*figura* policeman." I'd feel the muscles of my neck tense as he lectured me and Nick constantly, letting us know by his rigorous critiques that we were sources of unending discredit to him. Now, however, Gregori was readily accepting unconscionable behavior from Gerry, whose liaisons made my grandmother's seem sophomoric.

Well, at least one good thing came from all of this. Between Gregori hiding his brother's affair and the relatives on my mother's side behaving nastily at Nonnie's wake, I no longer gave a fig about *figura*. Fundamental good manners remained with me, but I simply stopped catering to stifling social mores. And once I adopted this manner, I noticed I got a lot more respect.

As for Demetra, all she had to say about Gerry's affair was, "My poor Gerry. I hope he found the right girl this time."

He sure had. Penelope was exactly the right girl, because she married Gerry, *and* agreed to let his mother live in her home and supervise her child. To her credit, though, Penelope recognized she'd made a bad bargain far earlier than I had. Because in the last months of her pregnancy, referring to my friend, Gerry's Third Wife, Penelope asked me this, "What did she say when she learned about the baby?"

I was in a difficult position. I was still Gregori's wife and these were his relatives, like it or not. So I replied, as neutrally as possible, "What do you expect me to say to that?"

Penelope dispelled my antagonism and even had me feeling a twinge of sympathy with her answer, "I bet I know what she said. 'Better her than me.' Right, Patricia?"

She was catching on already, baby not even out of the oven. And after Penelope and Gerry's daughter was born, Demetra moved right in, cleaning her son's house and caring for a grandchild, just as she'd wanted.

In the evenings, Demetra ate with her son and his latest wife, then confined herself to her room in their home, a room with a single-sized bed and watched television, because the couple wanted "some time alone." On the weekends, she still got shipped off, though only as far as her brother, Sotiri's home, where she continued to help him, too, and he continued to be fussy.

This was how Demetra would live the rest of her life. She went through a depression a few years later and had to be given medication for a time. I should feel like there's justice in this, not only for the way she treated me, but for the way she'd pitilessly dismissed Gerry's Third Wife. But I *sincerely* don't. In fact, the whole thing makes me sick. What do we women let ourselves become, how much will we endure in our assorted relationships, because we're too scared, too embarrassed and too *pigheaded*, to make any changes?

I could say that about any number of women in this story besides Demetra, most especially myself. I'd gotten to the point where I could barely tolerate Gregori and his family. Yet, I still remained with him.

Chapter Ten: The Wind Shifts

"Diamonds can be lying jerks.
Skepticism is usually a girl's best friend."
–Amy Alkon, The Advice Goddess

Boo, Hoo, Hoo... I Want to Go to Greece

Now that Gregori's mother was not two blocks, but one continent away, our marriage should've improved, right? Sadly... wrong. To illustrate, here's what he did when he heard about that big argument she and I had. He came home with *flowers*. I thought they were for me.

Then he said, "I'm having dinner at my mother's." And when he left, he took the flowers with him.

I struggled to hold back tears. It was plain to me now that Demetra wasn't the only one who didn't have a husband. Gregori had given his heart years before and it would never be available to his wife.

That belated insight was sobering, but we had marital problems of a more practical nature, too. We had bills, bills, bills. Loans that Gregori had taken for his investments that hadn't panned out, and his business ideas that went bust. To be fair, these weren't the reason I finally balked.

When Nicky started kindergarten, we needed the extra salary, so I had to give up my dream to write fulltime and be a stay-at-home mother. And we still didn't have a house. Thirty-six years old and what I had most to show for it was loneliness and debt. No house, no writing career, and no more children for me. I was an idiot, but not one big enough to have another baby with this man. Nonetheless, I did have one child who was beloved to me, my one precious gift obtained from my ten-year marriage. So I swallowed my despair and went back to teaching for my son's sake. Though it wasn't my dream, it wasn't a bad second choice at all. I enjoyed it, I was good at it, and my pupils stood in for the additional children I'd never have, a perspective that benefited both them and me.

Yet, when I suggested Gregori give me some help with housework now that I was working fulltime, he said he couldn't, because he'd feel he might as well be wearing a *"foo-stah."* ("Skirt.")

All right, then, I hired help.

He didn't like that, either. "Who wants strangers poking around? How do we know the cleaner won't steal things?"

I ignored him and kept the cleaner.

Then the summer came and Gregori decided he'd earned a two month-long trip to Greece.

"*Are you mad?* We can't afford two months in Greece," I told him.

He was adamant. "I want to go to Greece."

I pleaded with him to be realistic. "The flight alone will set us back thousands. Then you'll lose *two* months' wages."

Gregori was the only driver of his taxi, so if he didn't drive, we didn't collect.

"I don't care," he pouted. "I deserve a vacation."

I could feel my insides tightening up. "*You?* What about me? I've been doing two jobs now, the housework *and* fulltime teaching, just so we can make up debts you've incurred—"

"DON'T THROW THAT IN MY FACE! WE'RE GOING TO GREECE FOR TWO MONTHS!" he roared.

"No."

There. I'd said it. And Gregori was staring at me as though a woman he'd never seen before had inexplicably appeared in his bedroom.

"*What* did you say?" He came over to where I stood.

His height intimidated. I only reached up to his chest. A muscle in my abdomen was unmistakably quivering. But I held my ground. Crossing my arms, I glared up at him. "I said, *no.*"

We faced each other like two pugilists. Then, with a look of pure disgust, Gregori shoved me mightily. I flew backwards and banged against the dresser. The porcelain music box Louie had bought for our wedding was set on the dresser, near its edge. Teetering, it fell to the floor with a crash.

Nicky came running in. "*Mama*, what happened? I heard something break."

"Nothing," I reassured him, as Gregori stood by, silent. "Something dropped, that's all."

"*Oh!* It's the music box from your wedding. Maybe we can glue it back together?"

"I doubt it, but either way, don't worry."

Seethingly, Gregori spoke. "I'm going to work. Walk me to the door, Niko*laki.*"

172

I sat down on the bed after they left. *That was a close one,* I thought. Nicky hadn't seen anything. Though I was still shaking, that helped me recover. I went to get the broom and dustpan.

I never liked that music box, anyway.

That night was Friday night. Since Gregori was angry with me, he went straight out with his friends without coming home from work first. I knew he'd discuss the trip with them and they were all big talkers. He'd always return from these weekly testosterone summits and say, "My friends think we should . . ." or "Guess what my friends did?" Afterward, he'd tell me, "You see what a good husband I am compared to them?"

Though he came home later than usual that Friday night, I was waiting up for him. He said nothing at first, putting down his things. Then he faced me where I sat. "My friends think I should go to Greece."

I kept my voice low. "And… are your friends going to pay for the trip?"

He spoke just as softly, this time. "I'm going to Greece."

I'd made up my mind what I'd do if he came home and told me this. I didn't even like him anymore. And he was becoming brutal. "Okay. Go alone, then. I want you to leave."

He faltered. "What do you mean?"

I enunciated each word. "I mean, I want you to live *someplace else.* Not here with us."

He stuck out his chin, reminding me of his mother. "Why should I be the one to leave?"

"If I go, Nicky comes with me. Would you like him to go through that?"

That jolted him. At length, he said, "Fine, I'll go." He took some things and left right then, without saying "good-bye."

After he'd gone, I stayed where he'd found me when he came in, and breathed deeply, trying to stay calm. The room was dark, but I didn't switch on any lamps. The dark soothed me. The dark meant my son was sleeping peacefully, giving me time to think. In the morning, when it got light, he'd wake and ask me where his father was.

And I didn't know what I was going to say.

*** ***

Gregori stayed at *Thio* Sotiri's, who was not happy about it. Sotiri didn't believe in divorce and told Gregori, "Your wife comes first."

When school got out a month later, Gregori and Nicky went to Greece for the summer. We'd kept up a pretext for our son that Gregori was working away from home. Not knowing his parents were separated, he had no reason not to be excited about his trip with his *Baba*.

I explained to my three cousins when we got together one day, why I let Nicky go with him, "I don't know yet, *for sure*, what I'm doing about our marriage. Why should Nicky be upset and in the middle until I do?"

Josephine nodded sympathetically. "Divorce is hard on kids."

Marietta snorted. "So's living in a house where your parents are miserable."

It was important to me that they understand. "Nick loves his father so much. I feel so guilty about him. Since I can't change Gregori's mind, why should I make Nicky stay in Astoria, where it's hot and so far from any beach, just to prove a point?" I spread my hands out. "Nick loves Greece. He'll have a wonderful time. The trip's already costing too much, so what's an extra ticket for him to fly, too? That's not going to make us or break us."

Marie looked at me with no little admiration. "I always believe in keeping a marriage together, if you can. But I have to admit, even *I* don't know if I could send my son over there under these circumstances. You should get 'Mother of the Year'."

"Yeah. She sure should," Marietta said flatly.

*** ***

Going to the airport to see Nicky off, I don't know how I managed to act as if I were just as happy as he was.

"You're going to have so much *fun*," I told him as passports were checked and boarding cards printed. "Now say 'hello' to everyone for me when you get there, okay?"

Nicky looked at me as though a light bulb had popped up over his head. "*Mama*, why don't *you* come with us, too?" He beamed over his sudden inspiration. "It doesn't have to be like *Baba* said, 'Just us men.'"

Wanting to grab onto his little shoulders and weep, I smiled instead, took his darling face in my hands and kissed him. "You are so *sweet* to invite me along. But I have so much to do here before school starts again. You and *Baba* go and spend time together," I winked at him, " 'just you men', and we'll see each other when you get back."

174

It was almost time for them to board. "Could I speak to you a moment privately?" Gregori asked me.

Thio Sotiri had driven Gregori to the airport and I'd come in my car with Nicky. That Sotiri didn't approve of any of this was palpable. He was silent and hard-faced the entire time we were at the airport.

"*Thio*, would you mind staying with Nicky for a moment?" I asked him.

Gregori walked me to a glass partition near the gate, so we couldn't be overheard. "It was good of you to let Nick come. I'll take care of him. I promise."

I said nothing.

He cleared his throat. "I'm sorry that we're having so much trouble these days. There was a time when we had something special." He leaned in closer. "You know, there's going to be a full moon tonight. Will you think of me?"

Oh, this was too much. It was unbelievable that he'd expect *that* to have a softening effect. Before our truly serious problems began, we'd joked that we got on best when there was "a full moon." We'd even chosen 'our song' because it referred to a full moon. And he'd brought up this bit of puerility *now*, when we were on the brink of financial ruin and our whole marriage was disintegrating?

I asked the question to which I badly needed an answer. "Why did you do this?"

He gave me his reason. "You left me no choice. You're never going to tell me what to do."

*** ***

Only when my son was no bigger to my eye than a dark dot bobbing in and out between the other boarding passengers, did I let myself cry. I cried all through the terminal, indifferent to strangers' glances and *Thio's* discomfited stoicism, as I followed him blindly to the parking lot. When he'd delivered me to my car, he hurried off, embarrassed, saying nothing more than, "So long, Patricia," and I sat in my driver's seat with the ignition switched off, crying some more. In the two months that Gregori was on his 'deserved' holiday, swimming, sunning, being served up his favorite meals by his mother, (who'd met them in Rhodes, of course) I cried away almost ten pounds of body weight. Everyone thought I was on some new diet.

I'd told very few people besides my three trusted cousins what was going on. To me, it was too degrading. It meant that *I* was a failure. I worked hard to gain the respect of my colleagues, pupils and pupils' parents.

175

They believed I was capable and wise. If I got divorced, they'd think that if I didn't have the ability to hold my marriage together, how could I have the ability to *teach*?

So you see, it wasn't just my son's welfare or my wedding vows. It was more like I was too big a coward to face everyone and admit that I'd botched-up badly.

"What will people think?" was not the right question to be asking myself. I'd find the right question, but it would take a while, right up until I was standing in a bookshop, in the second week of that July, in fact.

In the meantime, I endured by telling myself, *You made your bed, Patricia. Now lie in it.*

*** ***

"May I help you find something, miss?"

I smiled at the elderly bookshop clerk. "I was wondering whether Judith McNaught has released anything new."

"*Ah*, the romance writer. She's one of my favorites. Let's check the computer." She put on reading glasses and peered at the screen. "Here's a new one. The title of it is *Perfect*."

She read me the plot summary. The main character was a teacher with a son named Nicky. That cheered me up. "Have you got it in stock?"

"We have three hardbacks left," the clerk reported.

My face fell. "No paperbacks?"

"That novel is not out in paperback yet, miss. But the hardback is only twenty-four-ninety-nine and we offer a 20-percent discount."

"Let me think about it."

"I'll hunt one down while you're thinking, dear. You really ought to get it if you're a McNaught fan," she added as she left.

I felt forlorn again. Twenty-four-ninety-nine, with the discount deducted, was still twenty bucks, plus tax. I couldn't afford to pay twenty-five bucks for something we didn't need. I would've loved to have read that novel. It was too bad it wasn't in paperback.

Wait a minute... I wasn't going to spend twenty-five dollars on myself, while I was stuck home alone, because my jackass husband was spending thousands of dollars we didn't have, on a trip? Indignation flooded through me then. I wasn't sure at whom it was directed.

Then I glanced up. There was a woman directly across the aisle, looking back at me. She was in her thirties and reasonably attractive, but she looked

176

pale and dejected. It took just half a second more for me to become aware that I was looking at my own reflection. I stared at that washed-out-looking image, thinking about the multitude of disparities between a woman who worried about spending twenty-five dollars on herself, versus a man who'd spend ten thousand his family couldn't afford and say he "deserved" it. They had one thing in common, though. They were both fools.

In that instant, I knew who I was angry with and what question I should've been asking. I looked at my 'mirror image', again and asked it. "*What the hell are you doing, you stupid girl?*"

The trouble was I'd blurted that *aloud* on the bookshop sales floor and the clerk was just coming back over with Judith's novel in her hand. She stopped in her tracks and eyed me warily. "*What* did you say, miss?"

I apologized hurriedly. "I was talking to myself. *Uh...* is that the book? I'll take it." I paid, dashed out, got in my car, drove home and hurried straight next door to see Colleen. She'd helped me out of my wedding gown. Now, with any luck, she was going to help me out of my *marriage*.

"This is a nice surprise," Colleen said with a smile when saw me. But her expression changed when she took in mine. "Honey, what's wrong?"

"Colleen," I took a breath, "you told me that your brother is a divorce attorney. Do you think he might... talk to me?"

There — it was out.

A Coup is Launched

"It's easy to be brave from a safe distance."
–Aesop

The rest of July kept me occupied with unusual activities and mixed emotions. I conferred with Colleen's brother, now my lawyer, and felt mortified. I stood in long lines at county court and felt desolate. I rang my parents with the announcement and felt ridiculous. I packed up Gregori's things and felt both elated and ill. I read my new hardback romance and cried.

Gregori and Nick returned mid-August. Nick was full of excitement and stories. I had one or two stories of my own. Especially for Gregori. He'd find out shortly that I'd staged a 'takeover'. I'd even assembled some troops.

Of my cousins, it was Josephine who knew best how wretched I felt and what it would take for me to do what I was about to do. She was the first recruit to be present and accounted for, the night Gregori and Nick came home. Her job was to keep Nick occupied while the news was broken to Gregori. Josephine was waiting downstairs at the outside door when Nicky, Gregori and I got back from the airport.

"Nicky, look who's here to welcome you back," I said.

Nick smiled. "Josephine!"

Jo smiled at Nicky, but kept her eyes averted from Gregori's.

"Go up with her," I told Nicky. "I know she has a surprise for you up there. I'll bring your suitcase."

Nick didn't need to be told twice. He ran up to her with a hug and she ushered him quickly up the stairs.

As I took Nick's luggage from the backseat of the car, Gregori went around and got his bag from the trunk. An innocuous looking man with a cane crossed the street to Gregori. I kept my back carefully turned aside, as I heard the man murmur and then Gregori's response, "Yes."

The man handed Gregori a document and limped away.

Gregori read it and turned to me. "What's this?"

Though that muscle in my stomach was quivering again, I spoke steadily. "Exactly what it says."

"You want a divorce?"

"Yes. We don't have a marriage, by my definition. And I'll be able to manage my own money, without having to go through you."

That got under his skin. "This is about the trip *again*. It's worth a divorce to you, is it? I thought it meant so much to you for Nicky to be raised by *two* parents," he said contemptuously.

"I thought it meant a lot to you, too," I responded quietly.

"What about my clothes and other things?" he asked after a moment.

My inspiration had come from Gerry's Third Wife. "They're packed in plastic trash bags and in your car. You can take them all with you when you leave... right now."

Gregori's reaction to this news was not what I expected. He started to laugh. But when he saw that I was sincere, his manner became thuggish again. "Yeah? What if I don't listen? What if I go upstairs right now and take Nick with me, so he doesn't live with *you*, ever again?"

Fury streamed through me at that, lessening my trepidation. "Always the 'tough guy,' aren't you? Don't you *dare* press that button with me. If you try to take my son away from me, I'll call the police. I *mean* it. That's why my cousin's here. In case you give me any trouble."

The bluster drained out of him. He took the car keys I held out to him. When he saw that I'd already removed the ones to our apartment, he just shook his head. "I can't believe you'd do this."

When he said that, I bleakly repeated back to him what he'd said at the airport. "You left me no choice."

His face was ashen, but carefully blank as he put his things into his car. Feeling as though I'd run miles to win a race, only to find my trophy too heavy to lift, I dragged myself inside and up the stairs as he drove away.

Who is 'Mrs. Barella'?

> *"Be bold. If you're going to make an error, make a doozy, and don't be afraid to hit the ball."*
> –Billie Jean King

I had been married for over ten years and Nicky, (who preferred 'Nick' now) was six years old when I filed for divorce. Gregori remained at Sotiri's, but was looking for a place of his own.

Now that it was official, I sat Nick down and asked, "What happens when you and one of your friends are playing together and you each want to do something different?"

Having heard this question from his teacher, he answered automatically, "We compromise!"

"Right." I looked at him solemnly. "But what happens if you can't compromise?"

He shrugged. "Then I guess you can't play together."

"Right again," I said. And using this as my lead-in, I told him about his father and me. He didn't say anything. I don't think the full meaning sunk in right away. Despite this bad news, he and I spent the remaining two weeks of summer joyfully reconnecting and in general, having a grand old time. Then school started again and for the first time, I experienced the gut-twisting challenges of being a single, working parent.

The first quandary was finding someone to pick up Nick from school. I taught across town, both schools ended their day at precisely the same time and it took me fifteen minutes to get from my school to his. There were no after-school programs at Nick's school and it was "against insurance regulations" I was told, to hold him even for those fifteen minutes. I was afraid to let him wait for me in the schoolyard on his own. Also, because I needed to pick him up, I couldn't remain at my own school after day's end, in case a pupil had a question. On the days I had after-school teacher meetings, special favors had to be pleaded, and I was a wreck until I could get home. No one I knew lived closed enough to help. Sotiri was available in an emergency, but I suspected he couldn't see very well. His driving habits were ghastly.

Then the mother of one of Nick's schoolmates said she'd chaperone Nick in the schoolyard for a small fee until I got there. She seemed a blessing, until the day Nick was released to a classmate's sitter, instead. When I ran into the school, frantic, I was informed quite casually, "Not to worry, Mrs. Barella picked up your son."

"Oh? And who might she be?"

It turned out the mom I'd hired never showed up to pick up her *own* children, because she'd been using the babysitting money she earned to buy pot.

At last, I found a reliable woman to stay with Nick until I could get there, but she was on a tight schedule, too. I didn't dare be any later than the fifteen minutes I'd promised her. In November, we had a dreadful snowstorm, which had started in the middle of the school day. Snow was still dumping down when I left work. Someone had shoveled off their driveway and deposited the snow around my parked car, blocking it in. Frenetically, I shoveled, arms aching. I was drenched with sweat, panicked I wouldn't make it back in time to Nick and he'd be left standing in a blizzard alone. When I finally got my car out, the wipers had frozen. I couldn't keep the blinding snow off the front windshield and had to drive back to Nick's school with the driver's window open and my head stuck out, so I could see. By the time I got to Nick's school, the front seat of the car was soaked and I was freezing, as well as late.

Then, there was this:

"My friend, Jeremy, is sad, because his father doesn't live at home anymore either," reported Nick, one day. "But *I'm* not, because I know you and *Baba* will make up. That's what *Thio* Sotiri said. It's true, right, Mom? *Baba's* going to come home?"

I didn't know how to answer. I was becoming uncertain about a divorce again. Gregori and I'd been living apart for eight months and being a single parent was grinding. He'd gone out of his way to be gracious whenever he came by to see Nicky. It was as if he were courting me. He was always on ime with child support payments and was managing expenses better. As a result, our debts were decreasing. His mother had been apprised of our status and was steering clear. *Thio* Sotiri and even some of Gregori's friends, had been talking to Gregori, telling him if he didn't want to get divorced — which he claimed he didn't — then maybe he should change his ways a mite? Even *Papa* Elias had sent Gregori books on marriage within the Orthodox Church.

Nick missed Gregori... and Gregori was being thoughtful, respectful and responsible. Even so, I didn't miss Gregori at that point. If Nick hadn't been involved, I'd have kept things as they were. That was the truth. I'd gotten past the hardest part, deciding to separate and announcing the separation. Couldn't I also manage a career and a child, a child who'd only need full-time supervision for... how long? The next five... six years?

Only six more years, when my son was only six *now*? He'd need my focused attention far longer than that. If I loved him, if I wanted him to grow up in the best way possible, shouldn't I be absolutely certain there was no other way besides divorce?

It took a three-day weekend and a stomach virus for me to make a decision.

The Prince is Reinstalled

> *"Maybe I wanted to hear it so badly that my ears betrayed my mind in order to secure my heart."*
> **–Margaret Cho**

"*Mama*, can *Baba* eat with us? You know he likes lasagna the way you make it."

Our new routine of 'separation without animosity' had progressed to the point that Gregori was in Nick's room, reading to Nick. Now my son was asking that I invite his father to dinner and he was looking at me soulfully, through eyes that... didn't seem quite right.

"Are you okay, Nick?" I touched his forehead. He didn't *feel* warm, but he was unusually quiet, an indication that something was up.

"Yes," he answered, but he put his arms around my waist and lay his head on my stomach, another sign he might be sick. *Oh, no... please,* I thought. It was Saturday of a three-day weekend and I'd been *so* looking forward to three relaxing days.

I kept my arms around Nick and said, softly, "*Baba* can stay for dinner if he likes. But Nick... you understand that *doesn't* mean he's going to live here with us again, right?"

Nick looked up at me and silently nodded.

The three of us ate together for the first time in almost a year. It felt awkward, but Gregori kept things light by joking with Nick. That is, right up until Nick put his fork down and stated, "I don't feel well."

I stopped eating, too. "*Aw*, honey, what hurts?"

"I don't know, but can I go lie down?"

That raised alarm bells. He must have been feeling very poorly to make such a request.

"Go ahead. I'll be there in a minute."

Nick went off to his room and I got up to clear the table. I thought I'd drop the plates when Gregori also got up to help.

"Thanks," I said, uncertainly.

"You're welcome." Gregori cleared his throat. "I wanted to talk to you—"

"Mom!" Nick called from his room. "I'm throwing up!"

Gregori and I ran to Nick's room, wincing at the sounds coming from within. By the time we got there, the room reeked of lasagna and puke. Nick had done his best, poor thing, not get the sick on the bed. Instead, he'd chosen a chair that had a remarkable ricochet effect. I looked around in amazement — it had splashed everywhere *but* the bed, including his turtle tank.

What Gregori said next didn't help. "Why didn't you tell us you felt sick?"

"I *did*," said Nick. And he burst into tears.

"Okay... it's all right," Gregori soothed. Stepping carefully, he picked Nick up.

We placed Nick inside on my bed, gave him some chamomile tea, and when he was calmed, went about tackling the mess.

"It's on every one of his books," Gregori reported. "We're going to have to throw some of these out."

"No, *Baba, please!* Not my *Spider-Man* comics!" begged Nick from the other room.

He sounded so pitiful that Gregori promised, "I'll try my best to clean them."

That's what we did for the next two hours. While Nick slept in my room, Gregori and I carefully wiped down toy trains and comic book pages.

The next morning, Nick seemed better, although he didn't want any breakfast. He sat up in my bed and watched television. Then Gregori came back over with a rented electric carpet cleaner and washed the carpet in Nick's bedroom. Getting everything to rights had taken hours. I collapsed into a chair, worn out. We hadn't eaten, either.

Looking across to Gregori, where he'd slumped on the couch, I asked him, "Want something to eat?"

"Maybe," he said, "But... *not* leftover lasagna, please."

That made me laugh. He laughed, too. That was something we hadn't done together in awhile. It might have been the laughter that emboldened him to say, "Listen, why don't you give me another chance?"

I sat up straight in surprise.

"I know what I did wrong and... I'm sorry. I had a lot of things on my mind... my father died..." He cleared his throat and continued more determinedly, "Just give me six months. At the end of it, if you're not happy... I'll go."

I still said nothing.

Then he said the Three Magic Words:

"Nick misses me."

A mental vision flashed of Gregori the day before, patiently cleaning off Nick's treasured comic books. Gradually, I found myself saying, "I'll... think about it."

Nodding, not wanting to push his luck, Gregori stood up. "I'd better go."

"But..." something compelled me to say this next thing, "if we do it, I want us to see a marriage counselor."

I thought for sure he'd refuse. Instead, he nodded again, "Okay." He went inside to kiss Nick "good bye" and then left.

I stayed where I was for a while. My stomach felt strange. I hoped I wasn't getting Nick's virus.

*** ***

I still can't decide whether I believed we were in the midst of a miracle because I wanted it be true, or because Gregori had enough invested in the marriage that he went as far as he did to make me believe it was true. He moved back in, and I missed the extra closet space.

Six months later, we were still together, still seeing a marriage counselor. Then, I told Gregori that I thought we could start looking for a house. Gregori agreed (finally!) and that felt like another step forward. Nick was elated that Gregori was back and I could breathe easier with another adult there to help care for him. As for Gregori and me, he was being kind and attentive. I believed we were falling in love again. That was a lucky thing, wasn't it? If I were going to go back to him *anyway*, for our son's sake, I mean.

Gregori seemed happy, too. Until Freda, the marriage counselor, *asked* him if he was happy. And Gregori told her, "No."

Me: "No?"

She: "Why not?"

He: "Because I want to go to Greece."

Me: "I thought we were buying a house."

He: "*You* wanted to buy a house. *I* want to go to Greece."

She: "Wait — you want to go to Greece for a holiday?"

He: "No, I want to go to Greece to *live*. I have a good opportunity there."

"What opportunity?" He was asked in stereo.

"Well…" Gregori began.

"*Wait* a minute!" I interceded. I looked at him. "Let's just go home."

As we drove home from Freda's, Gregori talked about his prospect in Greece. He told me that he'd known for several months that his brother and two other partners, who'd started an export business shipping top-brand American house paints from the U.S. to Greece, needed someone who could be based in Greece and liaison between the retail outlets there and the main headquarters in the U.S. He said he wanted to be that person very much.

He reminded me that I'd always known he wanted to go back to Greece someday. He said the salary was good, and we'd be more fiscally stable. He said this would give him the chance to get out of the taxi, which he despised. He pointed out that I'd said it was stressful being a working mom. He said if we moved to Greece, we could afford for me to stay home. He warned that our neighborhood was going downhill, yet in our present circumstances, we couldn't afford better. But the area in Greece, a part of Athens, was much safer, excellent, in fact, and we'd be by the sea. Hadn't I always loved the water and Greece, too, by the way? He assured me that he understood now what'd gone wrong between his mother and me and that when she came to visit from Rhodes, he'd make sure she didn't intrude. Most essential, he told me that if we moved to Greece, it would make him *happy*.

In short, he told me everything I wanted to hear. We'd just gotten back together. I wanted to make it stick this time.

So, if you were me, what would *you* do?

Make the Best of It

> *"Nothing pleases me."*
> –El Greco

Public feedback was varied when I announced I was leaving my teaching post at the end of term to live overseas with the husband I'd almost divorced not too long before. Margie, as always, was encouraging.

"Do whatever makes you happy. I'll miss you, of course," she said over our usual Bellinis. Then suddenly, she looked ready to cry. "Oh, my God! I just realized — this is the first time we'll be separated since we met in second grade!"

My cousins' response was… different. They gave me their "big-brown-eyes treatment" again, only this time as I spoke, Josephine kept her hands spread wide and pressed against the whole bottom half of her face. Marie chewed one of her fingernails. They stayed like that and said nothing.

Marietta did. By the time I stopped speaking, her face was scrunched up in bafflement. "I don't get it. Did you just finish telling us you're *moving to Greece?* But I thought… weren't you and Gregori getting a divorce?"

"He's changed." I hastened to explain. "People can change, if they really want to, don't you think?"

"Sure, they can." "Yes." "You bet."

You had to love those girls. They never missed their cue.

The headmaster at my school, Mr. Longino, was not as diplomatic. "Okay, what's going on? You came back from summer break with your hair shorn off, so skinny and tense I thought you were channeling Winona Ryder. The rumor mill said you were getting a divorce. And now you're *moving to Greece?*"

"It's not as crazy as it sounds, Mr. Longino."

"I hope not. As your supervisor, I feel it's my responsibility to tell you what you're giving up." Mr. Longino ticked the items off on his fingers. "One — you're one of the best English teachers we have and we're thinking of you for administration. Two — you've had such success with your pupils that the mayor came and visited your classroom. Three—"

"You don't have to remind me of these things, Mr. Longino."

He leaned across his desk. "Then maybe I should remind you that you're not tenured yet. If you leave, you lose your seniority and have to start as a new teacher if you come back. Patricia, you've only got *one more year* to go."

I knew that, but hearing it said out loud gave me a jolt. I'd climbed mountains to get my degrees and teaching certificate. I was proud that I'd become a very good teacher. Maybe I *was* making a mistake.

Then again, what was different now than when I'd stayed home with Nick for five years before he started kindergarten? I wasn't tenured then, either, and I hadn't worried. I was safe now with Gregori. We were more financially stable. Maybe I'd try writing again in Greece. It would be fine.

"I appreciate your concern, Mr. Longino."

"It's not just concern for you. We'll miss you. Your pupils will miss you."

I sighed. "Thank you very much, Mr. Longino. I'll miss all of you, too."

But it was my parents' reaction that bowled me over.

"I think you should do it," my mother said.

"You *do?*"

She nodded. "You've had this hanging over your head the whole time you've been married. And since you seem determined to *stay* married to him, you'll have to give him his chance."

I was astonished that my father agreed. "But, if you do this, *make the best of it.* Don't focus on the parts you don't like, focus on the parts you do. Because you're leaving jobs, family, *everything.* Nicky's whole way of life is going to change. I know because I went through it when we moved from Italy. You don't do something this big and then change your mind six months from now, saying, '*Boo-hoo-hoo,* I want to come home.' "

"I won't, Dad," I promised.

He sighed as he admitted, "Greece is beautiful… like Italy. You'll be by the sea?"

"Within walking distance," I enthused. "You'll both come visit?"

"If we live," they said.

*** ***

After Gregori left for Greece, it was just Nick and me again, for six more months. I underwent single-parenting difficulties again, which further convinced me that I was doing the right thing. My main task, though, was to make the transition as easy as possible for Nick. Gregori's new career had him traveling all through Greece. I taped a map onto our refrigerator. We read Gregori's letters and I had Nick circle on the map each city where his father traveled. We also circled the area where we'd all be living when we moved — Glyfada, a suburb of Athens. Nick and I read about Glyfada, too.

Then there was the packing up. I tried to think of everything we'd want that might not be available in our new country. All of Nick's toys went, even those I knew he'd grown out of, just so he'd feel more at home. All our English-language books. We even packed our favorite food staples, as I didn't know what I'd find in the Greek markets. There was so much to pack that some of my students offered to help. When we were done, we had almost 150 crates crammed with possessions, labeled, "Athens, Greece."

Some of our belongings we couldn't take with us, however, like Nicky's turtle, Joe, and his prized set of electric trains. I had to come up with a way to make it less hurtful for Nick to let these go.

My students helped us there, too. One suggested, "When we moved from the Dominican Republic to the United States, I gave my pet bird to my best friend. He still has it. I visit them every summer."

Said another, "I have a little cousin who lives with my grandmother, because his mother is dead. He really wants a train set, but my grandmother can't afford one."

Giving his turtle to his best friend, Jeremy Alexander, and his train set to a needy child made parting with them easier for Nick. Before the trains and Joe made their way to other homes, I videotaped Nick with them and all his other treasures one last time in his bedroom in Astoria.

Everything, including our car, would arrive at the Athens port several months after we got to Greece. The day came that the movers arrived. Less than three hours later, we looked around our empty apartment. Every trace of our twelve years there was gone.

*** ***

Inventive handling made leaving behind our pet and some of our property somewhat easier, but nothing would help when it came time to leaving people.

What do you get when you say "good-bye" to an assortment of Something-Hyphen-Americans, if you're on your way to relocate *permanently,* overseas? An opus necessitating more body clutching and vociferous wailing than one performed at The Metropolitan Opera House, that's what.

Only Nick refused to cry, clenching his hands tightly at his sides to stop himself. He told me why as we headed to the airport, "If *Baba* found out I was crying, he'd feel bad he was taking us to Greece."

Once he and I were on the plane, it was a different story. He lay his head down on my lap and soundlessly let the tears fall. They were even more wrenching because he'd tried to be noble about them. "Don't tell *Baba*," he blubbered.

"Of course I won't," I promised as I smoothed my hands down his hair.

"I'm glad that little boy got my trains, but I wish I didn't have to give Joe away."

"I know. But Jeremy will take good care of him. Turtles live a long time. My guess is Joe will still be around when we come for a visit."

"When can we?"

"Well… maybe next Christmas."

Nick sighed. The tears had stopped, but now he asked, "Mom, why hasn't the plane taken off yet?"

Good question. The plane had mechanical difficulties. They'd made the announcement, but caught up in his sorrow, Nick hadn't heard it.

I soothed again. "There's a delay, but it's nothing to worry about."

Two hours later, we were still on the tarmac. Turtle tears and plane trouble. Our new life was off to a superlative start.

"Oh *brother*," said Nick. "I wish we could get off this plane."

You and me both, kid.

Chapter Eleven: Crossing the Sea

"Once I found myself on the other side of the ocean, I could see where I came from very clearly, and I could see that I carried myself, which is my home, with me. You can never escape that."

–James Baldwin

Red License Plates

And so here I was, in Greece again. Nick and I arrived in Athens August 1, 1995, one week after Gregori's and my twelfth wedding anniversary and two months before Nick's eighth birthday.

Just as Gregori had promised, Glyfada was beautiful and so near to that dazzling blue sea we could smell the salt in the air. We learned Glyfada had been dubbed "The Riviera of the East," because within it are some of Europe's most luxurious beachfront properties. It was originally a fishing town, but because of its waterfront location on the coast of southern Athens, it became one of the choice spots for celebrity residents and affluent émigrés. In other words, we were suddenly living in an atmosphere of very well-to-do.

Temporarily, we were situated in a small, furnished pied-à-terre that Gregori had leased for himself while there on his own. It was built on the roof of a block of apartments. It boasted a large, wrap-around terrace with a sunny outdoor eating area, which was encompassed by pots of jade green palms and lipstick pink bougainvillea. We could sit out there enjoying the sun, or lean on the railings and watch the people down below on *Ioanni Metaxa Street,* one of the main streets in Glyfada. Watching the vibrant life from our balcony was enlivening and walking on *Metaxa* to window shop or eat at one of the outdoor restaurants lining the street was a treat. Despite that, remaining there wasn't possible. Nick was sleeping on a cot in the living room and there was no space for our belongings that were due to arrive within the next month.

So we set out looking for a larger place and found a lovely corner apartment that was much larger than the one we'd had back home. Located on St. Nicholas Street, Gregori and I took the name to be a good omen. On the top floor of the nine-apartment building, it overlooked the mountains from *three* balconies. Living there would be marvelous and I was thankful we could afford it.

Since we believed that the three of us would be making Greece our permanent home, we'd made several decisions with that in mind, not least of which was where Nick would attend school. Several foreign community schools existed for pupils who'd immigrated. There was American Community Schools, which followed the American school curriculum, but we discovered it was comprised mostly of children of U.S. military personnel, or those whose parents were working temporarily in Greece. Nick's education would be easier if he attended *ACS*, but he'd only make friends with classmates who'd be moving in and out of Greece quickly. I also believed he wouldn't feel like he was truly a part of the Greek community, because his lessons would be taught in English and be U.S.-oriented.

The Greece-based partner at Gregori's new firm, George Cristos, recommended a Greek school to us. This school was a short bus ride from Glyfada and contained both a lower and upper school for pupils between the ages of four and eighteen years old. Mr. Cristos also informed us that the upper school was hiring teachers to teach English as a Foreign Language. Gregori and I went to see the school and met with some of the staff. We liked the school very much, and we learned that teaching staff who had children attending received a tuition discount. Mr. Cristos, trying to be helpful, had arranged for me to have an interview at the upper school. I thought it would only be polite if I took him up on it. Gregori said it was, "up to me," if I wanted to work or not.

I liked the head teacher of the English Department, and when she offered me a teaching post, I decided it would be better for Nick if I accepted. I could keep a closer eye on how he was faring. It was important to me that he be happy, so I didn't mind holding off my dream of fulltime writing for a while longer. Besides, I'd enjoy being challenged by a new syllabus, and it would be a good way to meet people, too, I thought.

A job would make things a lot more hectic for me, however. Teaching staff was on duty in ten days after I'd accepted the post, but our new apartment wouldn't be ready for three weeks after that. When school started, we had to remain in the tiny place on *Metaxa*. There was no washer in the flat, and as Glyfada was so posh, not one launderette was anywhere nearby. I had to wash whatever items I could by hand, and wait for our new washer to be delivered to our bigger apartment before tackling anything else. Clothing and school things had been piled up wherever we could find space, and now dirty laundry was adding to the clutter.

When we did move, our U.S. shipment arrived directly afterward and *that* had to be unpacked. Then we were told our car would need a week to pass inspections and clear through customs. Until then, Gregori borrowed a car for me to take to Nick's and my new school, which was located in the isolated countryside of Vari, a farming community. Nick rode a school bus there, but I'd drive. Remembering all that followed after I'd gotten lost in Crete, I took practice runs with Gregori until I'd learned the way by heart. It was bemusing to drive on the one dirt road to the school and see mountains and tumbleweed instead of what I'd been used to seeing on my way to work all my life — the skyscrapers of New York. The only other things out by the school were livestock farms and a soldiers' training camp. I'd occasionally have to stop my car in the middle of that one dusty road to let dozens of marching young men dressed in combat fatigues, as well as shepherds, goats and sheep, cross over. With all these sweeping adjustments, it was a stretch to arrive at school those first weeks, looking poised and ready to teach. But I managed.

Transformations like these in my circumstances were mostly invigorating. But there were inequities I'd encounter that I wouldn't like. One was finding out that our new economic status made me a part of the '*metikisea* brigade'.

'*Metikisea*' was a tax exemption on vehicles, technological equipment, and large household appliances, devised by the Greek government to entice Greek nationals living overseas to return to their mother country. Since Greece didn't manufacture appliances or automobiles, its citizens bought them from other countries, like Germany and Italy. The import taxes imposed by the Greek government for these items were about equal to the entire retail price of the item itself, making the cost of appliances and automobiles very dear for the average Greek. Greece wanted its expatriates to come back permanently, so they'd spend their overseas-earned money *within* Greece. The tax exemption — exclusively for those ex-pats — helped accomplish this. The Greek government also allowed those returning Greeks to buy their way out of the mandatory two-year stretch in the Greek army. By doing this, Greece completely disregarded its citizens who'd remained in Greece, struggling through its dictatorship. This seemed very unfair to me. But Gregori said, "That's the way they do things here."

191

I had a feeling I'd be hearing that a lot.

We decided to buy our household appliances locally. The compact, European-made appliances that fit better in the smaller Greek spaces came standard with the 220-volt electrical plugs and had features that made them a more practical choice. But we did take the government up on the tax-free automobile. It was the prudent thing to do, though this was another thing that made me feel self-conscious. The way the Greek government kept track of which cars had been imported through *metikisea* was to assign them red license plates, as opposed to the usual black ones. That meant when driving around town, every local would know we were of the privileged few who didn't have to pay the same taxes they did.

While our red-license-plate automobile was still on the ship coming over, Nick and I took buses and taxis before Gregori managed to borrow a car for me. We felt asphyxiated when on public buses because they ran on diesel fuel and were poorly maintained. This made the diesel smog in Athens horrendous and created 'acid rain' which ate at the city buildings. It was astonishing to note that since it had been constructed over two thousand years before, the ancient Parthenon in the heart of Athens had been made into a mosque by Ottomans, blown up by Italians in the 1600's, and looted by English in the 1800's. Yet the most damage done to it was by modern Athenian pollution. And a ride in a taxi was even worse than taking the bus. Taxi drivers in Athens were in a secret race known only to them, which they were all hell-bent on winning.

Maybe the sorry state of public transport explained why I saw so many Greeks puttering around on motor scooters. The men steered while standing up, with a five-year-old standing between himself and the handlebars. Wives sat on the seat, holding their infant in her arms. None wore helmets, as they zipped and dipped between speeding taxis and smelly buses. At first I imagined they might all be former Hell's Angels out for a joyride: "Live to Ride, Ride to Live," To-Hell-With-it-if-One-of-the-Kids-Fall-Off. Then I concluded that they were just regular Greek families, who didn't have the benefits of red license plates. Motor scooters were their economically feasible choice to get from one place to another. It looked like a precarious alternative to me, but, *hey* — I was just an *Amerikanaki* — what did I know?

Despite that it was a bit disordered at first, all three of us were handling what we had to, so far, and did what needed to be done. And, for the first time in our married life, Gregori and I were operating as a team. This made me optimistic about our future in Greece.

Looking for Breadcrumbs

> *"Americans and Brits have a different way of saying things. They say 'elevator', we say 'lift'. They say 'President', we say 'stupid, psychopathic git'."*
> –Alexis Sayle

Three months later Gregori and I were still getting along well, but we were more wrapped up in adjusting to our new jobs and lifestyle and observing how Nick was doing than we were in our personal relationship. We'd moved our son out of the city he'd lived all his life, where there were subways and tall buildings, frigid winters and contained spaces, to a place where the children spent ten months of the year outdoors or by the water. All his usual activities had changed. He was in a different school system being taught in a different language. He'd left all his friends and family behind. We'd given an eight-year old a huge challenge, and his well-being was of primary importance. Those first months I never even thought about whether living in Greece was improving my marriage as I'd hoped. But I did notice that Greece was having a good effect in ways I *hadn't* expected.

It was making me more self-aware. I saw that immediately when Gregori introduced me to wives of the men he worked with, who then introduced me to more women who spoke English. Oftentimes, these women were American, too. People assumed this might give us more in common. But the continental United States stretches over three thousand miles and we're not a homogenous society, either. I'm not sure how many people outside the U.S. understand this. It was true that the women who Gregori's colleagues introduced me to, did share superficial commonalities with me. All of us were foreign and married to Greeks and — that was it. There was nothing else to connect me to them. The reason for that was that they were unhappy in Greece and had no intention of doing anything about it. They talked as though they were imprisoned there and doomed as a result:

"You'll be shocked at how everything works in this place. You'll hate it, just like we all do."

"You'll be disappointed in that school you've got your son in. It's Greek, isn't it?"

"Watch out for the Greeks. They're jealous and backstabbing."

Maybe it was because I was afraid they might be right, or maybe it was because I felt they were like crabs in a barrel doing their best to pull down as many as they could into melancholy with them, I didn't want to be near them. Their gloominess affected the atmosphere like paint fumes, and their behavior was obnoxious. They couldn't abide Greek nationals, *including* the ones they'd married. All they talked about was how great they'd had it back home and how Greece was backward in comparison. Of course, this was not true of *all*. There were others of this extraction who lived quite happily in Greece.

But when meeting the discontented ones, it hit me for the first time what I would have become, if I'd stayed within the boundaries of my blinkered upbringing. I'd be exactly like they were: not just slightly xenophobic, but blatantly contemptuous of anyone not part of my closed society.

To make these encounters more unpleasant, the Greeks who'd remained within Greece dismissed the '*metikisea* Greeks' in their usual way, which was to diminish the significance of the offending group by giving them a derogatory title. (Just like their term, '*Amerikanaki*'.) They tagged all '*metikisea* Greeks' — if they were loud, pretentious braggarts — "*Brooklys*." That's right, another swipe at Brooklyn.

I could blame Martin Scorsese films for that particular jab, but I couldn't blame the locals for ridiculing this type of immigrant. I'd met 'Brooklys' types along with the other maudlin foreign women during my early experiences within the fold of 'red-license-plate' foreigners. And when we sat outdoors in the superb weather at Café Oscar in Glyfada, a handsome Greek waiter serving us *frappe*, I saw that vowel inflections were the only things about me and these women that were similar. None of them ever observed how beautiful our surroundings were. They had nothing to say but the following:

"Where on the east coast are you from?"

"What part of Greece are your parents from?"

"They're *not* Greek?"

"Ohhhh... *Sicily*. Huh. I thought you were Greek, at first, but I can see the Sicilian in you, now that I know."

After I'd been classified, they'd then issue me admonitions:

"I can't believe you married a "real" Greek and came *here* and you're not even Greek. What did your husband bribe you with to get you to do it?"

"Just remember... the Greeks are not like us."

"Not like us." I couldn't believe I'd traveled six thousand miles to hear *that* again.

194

I'd come home from these outings discouraged, already missing my cousins and Margie. *Were these the only women I was going to meet here?*

No. I'd made up my mind I'd be happy in Greece. I'd make new friends, for sure. It was just going to be a little harder than I'd anticipated.

And I knew if I wanted to meet new people in Greece on my own, I'd have to improve my spoken Greek. It was still dismal. Nick wasn't faring well on that score, either. Though we'd arranged for him to have Greek language lessons while we were still in New York, my doubts on whether they'd been as successful as his tutor claimed were proven accurate on Nick's first day of third grade in Greece. One of his new classmates asked him which was his favorite soccer team and Nick's reply was, "I was born in September."

This exchange was reported to me by Nick's new teacher, Mrs. Anastasia. She also mentioned that the school administration hadn't informed the teachers there'd be new pupils in their classes who couldn't speak Greek. Only three other children in the lower school besides Nick were in that category. When we picked a Greek school, we knew Nick would struggle with communication at first. However, we hadn't considered that his teachers might feel ill prepared to deal with a pupil who needed to learn lessons being taught in a language he could barely speak.

Fortunately, Mrs. Anastasia was the first of the many dynamic women I'd ultimately meet in Greece. She was resolved that Nick would learn to speak Greek fluently, make friends, and assimilate. By the end of term, she'd helped enormously in bringing all that to fruition. We still had a ways to go until then, however.

You could tell that as soon as we sat down to do his math homework. Word problems. I was lousy at them, even when they were in English. Regrettably, Nick was, too. But I strived for optimism as we worked.

"Okay," I intoned cheerily to Nick. "*Enas manah-vees.* Do you know what a '*manah-vees*' is?"

"It's a 'fruit-seller'," Nick responded, already bored.

"That's right. *Good* for you. Okay, now, this 'fruit-seller', he goes to his... '*apoh-thee-kee.*' What's an '*apoh-thee-kee*', Nick?"

Nick sighed. "Who knows?"

"That's alright. We'll look it up..."

Out came the "English-Greek Dictionary," in which we'd find that the word meant "warehouse." After several other hunts through the dictionary for more words we didn't know, we'd decipher the problem as: "A fruit-seller goes to the warehouse, where he buys two dozen plums for twenty drachmas apiece, then sells them for fifty drachmas each. What's his profit?"

We had five of these problems per evening. It'd take us twenty minutes to translate and complete each one, unless Gregori was there to help. That wasn't often, as he was still traveling for business. Sometimes the Filipino cleaner, Lita, was there, and she'd translate. Many Filipinos immigrated to Greece to work as housekeepers or gardeners and they all spoke Filipino, English, and Greek. What a paradox. Lita was multi-lingual, but a *house cleaner*, while I was an English *teacher* who struggled through my son's third grade homework. If Lita or Gregori weren't there to help, Nick's homework occupied our whole evening.

If my son's language struggles were dire, mine were even worse. Even everyday things, like going to the market, were a challenge. Greek markets have plenty from which to choose, but I was familiar with only a few of the imports and most of those, as you might expect, were from Italy. Hardly anything was imported from the United States. No *Kellogg's Special K*, no *Nabisco* graham crackers, no *Bisquick*. The cunning businessperson who'd imported *M&M's* to Greece was making a killing. I thought with a pang of the foodstuffs we'd packed from home. Once those ran out, I'd have to find substitutes.

Apart from being mysterious to me, food items were marked in units of drachmas and grams or kilos. As I perused shelves, I'd mumble, "one kilo equals 2.2 pounds, one dollar equals 245 drachmas."

One day at the market, I consulted my list: 'breadcrumbs'. Where to find those? I looked in the bread section. Not there. How about the... um.. spices section?

After fifteen minutes of hunting, I knew I'd have to ask. I didn't want to, because I didn't know the word in Greek for 'breadcrumbs'. I did know two words in Greek, however, that might help me get my meaning across — 'bread' and 'stuffing'.

I spied three shop clerks standing together, chatting. Taking a deep breath, I walked over and said, "*Sig-noh-mee.*" ("Excuse me.")

They stopped talking at once. By my pronunciation, they could tell I was foreign. This should break up their routine.

"Can we help you?" said one of them in Greek.

Well, that sounded promising. Haltingly, I attempted to describe what I needed in Greek. "I'm looking for 'bread', but... not really 'bread'. I don't know the word in Greek. It's bread we use for stuffing."

"Stuffing?" said one in Greek. "You mean, 'rice'?"

"Not 'rice'." I tried again. "This is 'bread', but *Italians* use it for stuffing."

"What kind of 'bread' is used for stuffing?" asked another, in bafflement.

Why couldn't I remember the darn word for 'breadcrumbs'? I'd heard it hundreds of times. *Wait* — I'd thought of another word that might clear things up — "*scoh-nee*". That meant, "powder". I could say, "bread powder", and maybe they'd get it.

"It's like 'powder', but it's 'bread'," I tried again.

"*Ah* — so you want 'flour'?" said the first.

Damn! Naturally they'd assume I'd meant 'flour'. "No," I shook my head, feeling like an idiot.

Let's try hand signals. I spread open my hands wide and held them together, palms up. This was to indicate where a loaf of bread would be.

"You have a loaf of bread, very *dry* bread," I began again, "and you do this—" I mimicked pulverizing bread, by slapping one hand repeatedly on top of the other.

"Then..." They watched me raptly, as I mimed picking up the crumbs of imaginary bread I had squashed, "you pick up the bread and now... it's like powder. See? And... you 'stuff' it in." I curved one hand into a bowl-like shape to indicate a whole vegetable and used the hand that held the imaginary breadcrumbs to mime putting them into that vegetable.

After I was done with this mimicry, I was winded. The three stood looking at me, with their arms crossed and eyes narrowed. I held my breath. Did they get it, or would I have to repeat my vaudeville skit?

No. They'd had their fun. The first one I'd spoken to looked at her colleagues, rolled her eyes, turned to me, and asked, in English so flawless, even The Duchess of York would be impressed, "What do you need?"

I blinked once. *Why, she'd scammed me, the little brat.* Nonetheless, I replied slickly and in English now, too, "Breadcrumbs". She nodded snootily and continued in English, "Right. 'Breadcrumbs'. Down that aisle, next to the *flour* and across from the *rice*."

I grinned at her impishly. "Thanks." I held my head high, too, as I turned away. The breadcrumbs were just where she'd indicated they'd be. Wrapped in clear cellophane printed with bright blue letters, sold in quantities of 425 grams, at a cost of 285 drachmas per packet. And right on the package was the word in Greek for breadcrumbs. Though she'd mocked me, the Greek clerk helped me learn another Greek word I'd *never* forget again:

Breadcrumbs = *Free-gahn-yez Tree-men-nehs.*

But, not every Greek national had fun at my expense. Nor were they all "jealous and backstabbing," as the red-license-plates gals had declared. Nick had a personal guardian angel in the form of his third grade teacher, and I met one of mine in my new neighbor, Sofia. She found me sitting on the communal steps of our apartment building at half-past eleven one night, sobbing, because of our new German washing machine. By the time we'd bought the appliances and moved into our new apartment on St. Nicholas Street, I had heaps of clothing to be washed, and then neither Gregori nor I could figure out how to work the washer properly. The instructions were written in every language *except* for English. Gregori could read the instructions in Greek, but he'd never done a load of laundry in his life, and didn't know what the terms in Greek translated to in English.

Even the symbols on the dials made no sense. There were cycle settings marked 'A', 'B', 'C', but every one of them was a cycle that lasted three hours. *Three hours* to wash one load and I couldn't stop it once it'd started. No matter what knobs I pushed or pulled, the water refused to drain out of the machine unless I allowed the cycle to complete. Cursing and praying, I rifled through the instruction booklet, hoping directives would appear like Moses' epistles.

By the time Sofia found me in hysterics on the outside steps, Gregori and Nick were asleep and I'd been washing laundry for twelve hours straight, held prisoner by a Deutsche creation that was as unfaltering as Rolf Milser.

"Patricia, what's wrong?" asked Sofia.

After my gibbered expositions, she said in her precise English, "Oh, that's right, you got the *Bosch*. We saw them bringing it up. You'll love it, once you know how to use it. Don't worry. Come to my place and bring the instructions with you."

She patiently translated as I scribbled it all in the margins of the booklet. She helped me that evening and many times after that. She was also right about the *Bosch* washer. 'Rolfie boy' was great, once you knew how to handle him.

And, as if learning Greek weren't enough, Greek membership in the EU gives additional incentive to study within an EU country. As a result, study guides and textbooks for practice in English proficiency, as well as English-language exams, are all developed in the United Kingdom. What this meant was that both Nick and I had to exchange our American English for British English, since he had to utilize it in school and I had to *teach* it. It was another challenge for both of us, but I had to be doubly heedful. After all, it would've been painful to be corrected more than once by my own pupils. So we both relearned spelling and vocabulary variations like "post" instead of "mail", "colour" instead of "color". Even grammar rules were inconsistent with those in American English. I learned this the day an 8th grade pupil asked me if I had an "extra rubber". When Americans make mistakes on paper, they 'erase' them. When the British make mistakes, they 'rub' them out. Hence, a 'rubber' is an 'eraser' and not at all what you might've assumed it was if you're an American who's unfamiliar with British terms.

I mentioned this to another American English teacher at my new school. Smiling she said, "You'll get used to it. I've lived here so long I use British English without any thought. And do you know what happens when I write to my mother, who's never left the States? She sends my letters back with the spelling 'corrected'. She says using European English is unpatriotic."

The British were no less territorial in their construal, I discovered, when I was introduced to another colleague of Gregori's, who was British. When she heard I was American, she tittered loudly, "I suppose that means you use the word, 'eggplant'. Why do Americans use a *fake* word like that, when we all know the correct word is 'aubergine'?"

It wasn't very big of me, but I couldn't let this one go. " 'Eggplant' might be a 'fake' word, and 'aubergine' the 'correct' one, but do we all *also* know that 'aubergine' is *French*, not English?" I countered.

The banter amongst those of the Republicanism versus Colonialism spirit could be humorous, sometimes, but after a while, linguistic politics just got stupid and annoying. Nick and I grew accustomed to British English, just as we grew accustomed to using drachmas, then Euros, and to crossing our "seven" when writing our numbers. We got used to a twenty-four-hour clock and said "seventeenth hour", instead of "five P.M". And we spoke more and more Greek every day.

And an odd thing happened. We started to forget the American phrases we weren't using. Since I was teaching English to beginners, as my Greek improved, my English vocabulary shrunk. I couldn't spell in either language without the help of a dictionary. My English articulations went *way* off, sometimes sounding neither British nor American, but Greek. Nick had the same problem. We were like changelings, not Greek, not English, but no longer solely American.

People started to say, "I hear *some* American east coast, but yet, you sound almost English. Where are you from?"

"*Where are you from?*" Same old, same old.

The good news was, after a bit, nobody would ever say, "They're not like us," when talking to me again. They couldn't place my English, my spelling was British, I swore in Greek, and I cooked Italian. I wasn't any particular "us" anymore.

The Little Saint Nicholas

"What is a rebel? A man who says 'no'."
–Albert Camus

Less than six months living in Greece and I was evolving rapidly, as I met new people and encountered new situations. I gained the courage to ask for help when I needed it, without worrying about how it would appear. I was developing the ability I'd admired in *Thia* Popi — to laugh at complications, instead of being overwhelmed by them. My life in my new country was making me less ethnocentric and more adaptable. I was thirty-nine years old before I was able to achieve all of this. Yet, for my son who'd just turned eight, they were surprisingly simple milestones. He demonstrated this to us in an extraordinary way.

At the end of our new road, there was a little white stucco church. It had a clay tile roof and was no bigger in its entirety than Nick's new bedroom. It was Saint Nicholas Church, for which our street had been named. As the community grew, a much larger Saint Nicholas Church was built, but the tiny original remained and was open every day. There was no staff in attendance, but you could go in whenever you wished, to light a candle and leave a donation in an unlocked donation box. It was such a tiny space, there was no room for seating. So if you wanted to pray, you'd have to do so standing. It was a unique kind of place and Nick was captivated by it. He'd go inside and stay forever. I'd wait for him outside, in our parked car. I could see him from there, just standing in that little church. Once in a while, he'd move his arms as though he were speaking to someone, and I wondered if he liked being in there because he thought it was the perfect place to talk to God.

One morning after Nick left for school, Gregori pulled me over to our television. "Look at this," he said.

The news report was showing our little church. A group of protesters had thrown a Molotov cocktail into it. Everything in the interior was burned to ash and the pretty white exterior blackened with soot.

"Oh, *no*," I said. "Nick will be devastated."

Nick surprised us when we told him what'd happened, however. He didn't get upset. He just said, "We'll fix it. Right? *Baba* works for a paint company. He can give the priest paint."

I didn't know what to say. I looked at Gregori.

Gregori said, "The church needs more than just paint to fix it, Niko*laki*. All the icons and candles are gone. Everything inside is destroyed."

Nick waved his hand dismissively. "Those are for other people to get. *We* can get the paint. *Baba*, you'll ask George Cristos for the paint?"

Gregori didn't have the seniority to request that his company donate paint to a church. He was probably thinking the same as I, because he was looking at Nick dolefully. But Nick was looking back at Gregori with such hope. I held my breath as they stared silently at each other. I was looking at two identical profiles, one a child's, one a man's.

Suddenly Gregori said, "Of course, I'll get you the paint. Tomorrow after school, you and your mother will go see the priest. Give him my card and tell him to call me at my office."

The look on Nick's face was worth whatever this would cost us. "*Thank you*, Baba," he said.

After he'd gone to bed, I asked Gregori, "Do you think George will donate the paint?"

Gregori made his favorite hand circling motion. "We're talking about a *lot* of paint. Stucco's very porous. It'll need many coats to get rid of all that black smoke stain. I hate to ask George such a thing. But it's important to Nick. Worse comes to worse, George will give us the wholesale price and we'll just have to pay for it ourselves."

I was proud of the way he'd handled this. "Okay, Gregori. That's what we'll do."

If I was happy with Gregori, I wanted to give George Cristos a medal the next day. As soon as Gregori told him what the paint was for and that Nick had requested it, he said he'd donate it. Furthermore, Nick was right — other people did contribute everything else. Soon, the little Saint Nicholas Church was prettier than ever. I'd never seen anything get done as fast in Greece.

We later found out that the suspects were 'The Anarchists', a anti-establishment group that expressed their sentiments by destroying things. They threw homemade bombs into empty buses that transported pupils to *private* schools, because they were "against elitism." Then they threw them into buses that transported pupils to *state* schools, because they were "against group-brainwashing." In short, they blew up everything, because *everything* was what they were against. They offered no replacement alternatives; they just left behind a mess. Every November 17, in "tribute" to the brave students who'd been slaughtered by the junta, the Anarchists broke into the current day Athens Polytechnic University. Faces covered with black cloth, so these 'fearless rebels' couldn't be identified, they'd climb over the university gates, smash the windows of the buildings and tear the school apart, causing millions of drachmas in damage each year. But they weren't arrested for it, because the Hellenic population had vowed never to forget the slaughter of those students, and the new democracy in Greece declared that *all* government-owned school buildings would from then on be a political asylum for *any* protesters.

I wonder if anyone besides the little American noted the contradiction that a group who professed *anarchy* was being protected by a *government* decree. As you can tell, I wasn't impressed by Anarchists. To me, they were just glorified hooligans.

But Nick never once concerned himself about the people who'd bombed his favorite church, or what their purpose or values were. He just said, "Let's fix it."

And we all did. The most powerful statement that came from the bombing of a church was made by an eight-year-old boy.

I was proud of Nick for that and everything else he was achieving. I was proud of myself, too. Instead of crumpling under all our new challenges, we were meeting them straight on and blossoming as a result.

I *so* wish I could say the same for Gregori.

Chapter Twelve: Mutiny

"He who is not content with what he has, would not be content by what he would like to have."
—Socrates

Barking Dogs and Beggars

I didn't get it. I just didn't get it. Gregori still wasn't happy.

Why not?

He'd gotten what he'd dreamed of — we *lived in Greece,* in a beautiful, wealthy suburb. The communal garden of our apartment building was filled with breathtaking bougainvillea, roses of all colors, olive and citrus trees. We could walk to the seashore, if we wished. He had the career he'd chosen that, while not without its challenges, was gratifying to him. It paid well, another one of his prerequisites. He could afford all the designer accessories he wanted now. He traveled to remarkable places, met interesting clients. He also got that month off every year he'd said he needed. He could use it to go to Rhodes and swim, his favorite past time. In fact, now he got to swim six months out of the year. He was healthy and still relatively young. He had everything he'd said he wanted, so *why* did he still carry on as though he'd been cheated out of something big in life?

When I'd come home from the market and laughingly told him about the clerk and the breadcrumbs, he said, "You should have slapped her."

And when I responded, "But I know the word now — listen — '*free-gahn-yez tree-men-nehs*,'" it was as though he didn't hear me. He was still focused on the clerk's actions.

"That ignorant bitch," he said.

Then came March. We'd been in Greece seven months. The weather was glorious, warm enough to go to the beach, so we headed off, taking Nick, and a friend of his, Kostaki, who lived in our building.

Boy, oh boy, had things changed since 1980. Evidently, plenty of young Greek girls had adopted the practice of bathing topless that most of modern Europe enjoyed. On this particular day we found out what the older Greeks thought about that, because on the beach was an elderly Greek woman, who, despite the heat, was wearing the traditional black that announced her as a widow. Stretched out on a towel near her was a teenage granddaughter, basking in the sun — topless.

Suddenly, the granny shouted to her granddaughter in Greek, "Don't you know the sun will scorch you? You're going to worry me to death with your habits and your ideas! For the love of God — will you *please* put on your *sun hat!*"

This really tickled me. Laughing, I said to Gregori, "I guess we can thank globalization for that."

"Oh, yeah," he replied sarcastically, "Greece has really become modernized. They're so backward in so many ways, but *that* they've adopted."

I looked at him curiously. "You sound like you don't like it here."

"I like it — okay?" he snapped. Realizing his tone, he composed himself. "The weather's great. But you can't tell me everything about it is perfect. You said it yourself — there are stray dogs everywhere, people driving like maniacs, and no restaurant to eat where everybody isn't smoking."

I sighed. "Okay. That's all true. And I admit I hate those things, too. But they were under a dictatorship only twenty years ago. It's understandable that Greeks don't want any restrictions. Complete freedom is their cherished ideal right now. I'm sure some of these things will change once they feel more confident that someone's not going to invade or take their independence away."

He wasn't finished with his list, however. "What about the gypsies begging everywhere? The socialist system?"

"We were aware that Greece operates under a socialist system before we moved here," I pointed out. "You were the first to say every society has its good points and bad. The system's not so terrible. And as for the gypsies, maybe if their children were allowed in the public schools, they wouldn't be begging on the streets."

"Why are you defending Greece?" he asked, sulkily.

"Because I can't see the point of focusing on things I can't change. Because every time I get frustrated with something here, I think of all the winters I spent shoveling snow and all the summers I spent trying to find a parking space back in New York."

This time it were as though he'd purposely misconstrued what I was trying to say. "You're right. It's not like New York. New York was run *much* better than this place is."

I couldn't believe what I was hearing. "I'm sorry, did I maybe misunderstand you?" I retorted, succumbing to his moodiness now. "You *hated* New York when we lived there. You never stopped comparing it unfavorably to Greece. You're finally *in* Greece, Gregori, and *now* you're saying you prefer New York?"

He didn't respond. He just kept a petulant look on his face, as I continued, "Just look at your son, Gregori. He's thriving here. He's going to a prestigious school where he has a teacher who's devoted to him. He's learning to speak Greek so quickly that it's amazing. He's making nice friends. He's learned to swim so well that he's even thinking of joining a team."

"Yeah, but he still can't play basketball," Gregori replied condemningly. "And *everybody* plays here. He *has* to learn."

Well, what do you know? Seven months in Glyfada was still not enough sunshine to brighten my husband's ubiquitously Stygian soul. It was fortunate that Nick came running over at that moment. I'd been about to say something nasty.

"Hey, *Baba*, why don't you come swimming with Kostaki and me? We'll see who can hold our breaths the longest!"

As Nick ran off with Gregori following halfheartedly behind, I thought, *Can I play, too, Nick? I'll be the one who holds your father's head underwater.*

*** ***

Later that month, one day after my fortieth birthday, in fact, I was lounging in a chair on one of our balconies, facing the mountain with the cypress trees swaying in the slight breeze. Nick was downstairs playing outside with Kostaki, who'd discovered a tortoise living in our garden. Their laughter floated up to me and I wanted to bask in Nick's successful integration into Greek society. Instead, with despaired recognition hanging heavy on my chest, I was thinking about that conversation Gregori and I'd had at the beach.

Not once had he said, "You and Nick are doing a great job here. Thanks for trying so hard. Thanks for making it easy for me to live here."

Nor did he concern himself any longer with what I might be struggling with. I still had no friends, besides Sofia. We chatted every time we ran into each other outside the apartment building, but I didn't know her well enough yet to confide my troubles. Most teachers I worked with were much younger and single. The few who were my age appreciated me as a colleague

205

they could count on, but they weren't looking for close friendships at work. Margie and I still communicated every day, by email now, instead of phone. But I didn't want to tell her too much because I didn't want to worry her.

I'd counted on Gregori being my friend. He'd worked on our relationship for the promised six months in the States. I believed we'd reached compromises with which we could both live. Now here we were in Greece and I had gotten an 'extension', an additional six months in which we behaved more like the united couple I'd envisioned when I'd first dreamt of our marriage. But it was only an *extension*. Once Gregori saw that I was adjusting to Greece, he reverted to being the same as he'd been before we almost divorced. He disregarded me unless something came up that vexed him. Then his resentment would rear up.

Like when I tried to explain my frustrations with my new teaching post. I didn't agree with the Greek methodology for second language acquisition. In my opinion, it was mind numbing and not as effective as it could be. I loved my pupils and they were so eager to learn, it was a teacher's paradise to work with them. They deserved a better system. And there was that head teacher. It was increasingly clear that she had her own agenda. She'd hired the best teachers and after picking their brains for ideas systematically destroyed them. She had the school owner's ear, who didn't speak English, surprisingly, so anything she told him in Greek, I couldn't dispute. The other teachers in the department who did speak Greek did what they were told, needing their jobs too much to go against her. Though the head teacher didn't intimidate me as she did my colleagues, I could foresee trouble with her, ahead. As for the administration, it took ages getting approval for classroom projects that in the States I would have incorporated effortlessly.

When I'd brought up these disappointments at my birthday dinner out the night before, Gregori got upset.

"How can you not like it?" he protested. "It's a beautiful school and a nice, steady job."

"My ideas are being used, but credited to the head teacher, so I have no chance for advancement. And being foreign, I can never legally be appointed," I attempted to explain.

"Why can't you tutor private English lessons, then? They pay good money."

"I don't want to tutor. It's boring and I don't believe in the teaching approach," I repeated for the umpteenth time.

"It's good *money*. You can make your own hours," he persisted.

"Why do we keep going over this? I've explained how I feel about teaching. It's more than just a job to me. Why can't you accept that I don't think the way you do?"

Oh, it was draining and useless to confide in him. Especially if he thought whatever I was talking about would affect him personally. I had to conduct myself the way *he* would. Adjustments were *my* task, not his. He'd told me that it was my choice whether I worked or not in Greece, so why was he giving me this grief? Why could he never say, "Do what makes you happy"?

I decided to stop talking about my work with him. It served no purpose. I wasn't ready to make changes yet, but I was assessing options. I'd had a glimmering of an idea that I was mulling over based on the enthusiasm I'd received from my colleagues whenever I presented a new teaching idea. They found anything different interesting, including materials I'd brought from the States. They'd want to know how I was utilizing them in my classes and if they could try them, as well. These were the times when I felt competent and whole — when I was teaching or conferring with my colleagues. Though most of the English teachers had less teaching experience than I, they were on their way to becoming brilliant educators. That they admired me as a teacher was a compliment and made me feel less like an outsider. In truth, I felt more valued by a group of women I'd known less than a year, than I did by my own husband.

I'd been contemplating all this as I relaxed in the sun. The day before, my colleagues had all wished me "Happy 40th birthday", but in Greece, turning forty is not the big deal that it's made out to be in the States. I liked that Greek attitude. Still, I *was* forty; not that old, but not that young, either. I needed to find something fulfilling to do and soon. If I came up with something professionally appealing, I'd go for it, no matter what Gregori thought about it. The way things were going between us, I'd go mad here otherwise. We went home straightaway after dinner, and he instantly fell asleep in a chair, before we'd even cut my birthday cake.

My thoughts were abruptly interrupted by ferocious barking and a terrified scream.

Oh, no! Not that dog again! I jumped up, leaned over the balcony rail, and shouted down, "Nick! Kostaki! Stay *out* of the road!"

On the street below, I saw a couple with a young boy, who was shrieking, because a large, stray mutt had cornered them. They cowered together as the dog curled his lip back and revealed sharp, unfriendly teeth. His ears pulled back to the sides of his fierce-looking face, as he prepared to strike.

Before I could think of what I might do to help, our neighbor from the apartment below, old Mr. Telly, ran out and chased the dog back with a thick branch. *"Fee-yeh apoh thoh, koh-proh-skee-loh!"* ("Get lost, you filthy mutt!")

The dog backed off from the trio a bit, now directing his attention to Mr. Telly, though he continued to bark frenetically.

The dog recognizes Telly, so he won't jump him. It's only people he doesn't know that he wants off the street. That's what Gregori had told me and I prayed it was accurate.

He was right. The dog still growled at Telly, but didn't attack. The hapless strangers saw their chance and hurried away. As soon as they were off the block, the dog stopped barking and, as though nothing were amiss, withdrew behind some bushes to lie down.

The resident mongrel that patrolled our side street believed in his doggy brain that he was protecting those who lived there and fed him. He chased anyone he couldn't identify. If they couldn't run away fast enough, he'd strike. This dog was one of a huge population of stray dogs in Greece. If there was a dangerous animal on the street, like the one we had downstairs, there was no local resource to phone for help.

Gregori and I found this out the hard way when we'd first moved into Saint Nicholas Street. None of our neighbors thought to warn us about the dodgy canine being fed by three Greek families who saw him as their private security guard. They'd named him 'Zeus'. Like his namesake, he was fiery and pitiless. The first time Gregori stepped out onto 'Zeus' road', the dog lunged and took a bite out of his leg. Nick and I were upstairs in the apartment, when we heard a dog growl outside and a bellow following that sounded like Gregori's. We ran to our balcony, looked below, and spotted Gregori hobbling on the street, swearing.

A woman across came out on her porch and shouted, "Zeus! Down!"

The dog obeyed.

Holding his injured leg, Gregori asked her incredulously, "Is this your dog?"

"No," she replied, "but he watches the street for us."

"He just bit my leg!" Gregori scolded.

"You see how he protects us?" smiled the woman. "Don't worry — if you live here, he'll get used to you." And into her house she went, leaving

Gregori alone with a dog that'd just chomped on him. Still swearing, Gregori limped in, his calf bleeding steadily. The dog had punctured skin.

"You'll have to get a tetanus shot. Is that woman mad? That dog is dangerous!" I said, aghast.

"She said he's not hers." Gregori was shaken. "I'll get my leg taken care of and then go to the police."

When he returned, he had the strangest news. "The police said they have no jurisdiction to pick up the dog and nowhere to put it, even if they did."

I was speechless as he continued, "The only possibility we have—" he pulled out some official-looking papers "—is to get the neighbors to sign this, which says that they all believe the dog is a health hazard and needs to be removed. If it's in writing, the police can help. But they warned me that there's a good chance they won't sign. They said with the new laws that state the police can't pick up strays, people are training stray dogs to be guard dogs."

I was shocked. "People don't leave guard dogs out on the street."

He snorted. "I guess they do *here*." Then he leveled me a look. "Guess what else the cop told me? He said, 'I can tell you've been out of the country for a while. Only an *Amerikanaki* would report this to the police in Greece.' Can you *believe* that?"

Clearly this affronted him. But he had more revelations. "One of the cops there took me aside and told me that the only way to get rid of the dog is to poison it."

I put my hand up to stop him. "Let me get this straight — a *police officer* said we should *poison* a dog?"

Gregori nodded as though he couldn't believe it either. "That's what he said. He said to get a '*foh-lah*', a piece of poisoned meat."

"A '*foh-lah*?" I repeated, appalled. "You're saying poisoned meat is so routinely used that they've created a *noun* for it?"

Gregori answered gravely. "No, poisoning an animal is a serious crime. You go to jail for it. The cop warned me that if we did it, we'd have to be *very* careful that no one suspected us."

I covered my face with my hands. "This is lunacy. There are so many laws to protect animals, that people feel compelled to kill them, in order to protect *themselves*?" I looked at him again. "You know what? If it's *real*, what you learned today, I can't do it. I can't *kill* a dog. I mean, even if we shot it, it'd still be awful, but at least it would be quick. Do you know how horrible a death by poisoning is?"

"Yes." Gregori looked sincerely disturbed by the thought. "So... should we move?"

"What would that accomplish?" I replied wearily. "If people train dogs like this, how do we know there won't be another somewhere else? The only logical thing to do is stay far away from that side. And I guess they're right — the dog will get used to us being here."

Gregori's laugh was short and harsh. "And the hell with everybody else who comes down that road and doesn't know any better, right?"

*** ***

Now from my balcony watching Mr. Telly chase Zeus, I wondered how long the dog had been here and how many people he'd bitten. I'd seen him manage one successful strike for every two months we'd been in the flat and attempt many others. Yet he was still being fed; he was still "free". Free to terrorize, get hit by a car, or be poisoned.

It occurred to me that there were more laws in Greece protecting homeless dogs than there were protecting gypsies. Just like the dogs, gypsies were running loose all over Greece, living out in fields, squatting in condemned buildings and begging on the streets. They could use some assistance or at least, compassion. But they were eyed more suspiciously than was the grungiest canine. A stray dog could be in a schoolyard, but not a gypsy. I wished there was something I could do about that, and about the stray dogs, too.

Well, I could envy Zeus, at least. He certainly wasn't dissatisfied with *his* work.

Gregori came home and was downstairs with Nick and Kostaki, all listening to Mr. Telly's report of the episode. Provoked by years of chain smoking, every word Telly set forth sounded like it was being ground through pebbles. Some of what he said graveled up to me. "My wife is so sick... frightens her every time... spoke to the police... jackasses..." and so on.

I saw Gregori nod commiseratively. All our hands were tied. There was nothing we could do.

"... I'd Have Been a Ninny Not to Kill Him ..."
–Scarlett O'Hara, *Gone With the Wind*

"Oh, that costume is perfect! Let me take a photo of you."

In Greece, *Apokrias* is the celebration similar to 'Carnival' in Rio. It's three weeks of revelry and people dressing in costumes before Lent, the period of serious pre-Easter fasting begins. *Apokrias* usually starts in the middle of February, but the pupils in the lower school were having a special *Apokrias* party in late March as a reward for getting good grades. Here was Nick, thrilled with his get-up we'd made ourselves of "The Riddler," a character in one of his favorite *Batman* films.

"I want to go wait for the bus now so my friends will see me as they pull up," he said. "Do I look like Jim Carrey did in the movie?"

"*Exactly* like him," I affirmed, smiling. "I'll tell you what. You go on own. I'll grab a cup of coffee and sit on the balcony, so I can see how everyone's dressed, too. Would you like that?"

"Sure!" said Nick. And off he went. The marble hallway stairs brought the sounds back up to me, as he clumped down in his 'Riddler shoes' humming one of the songs from *Batman Forever*. I went into the kitchen to prepare my coffee.

Nick's disguised today. He's waiting for the school bus on the side street. That's where Zeus is.

Why had that ominous thought popped into my head?

I set my empty cup down and gazed through the window over the kitchen sink, which faced Zeus' street. There was Nick, his back to me, in his jaunty green hat and cane with the question mark handle. He was still singing the U2 song. I recognized the lyrics, "Hold me, thrill me, kiss me... *kill me.*"

My body stiffened with eerie dread. I turned my head to the right of Nick and peered closer at the bushes that lined the outside of our garden fence.

There.

Crouched beneath the shrubbery, haunches and stomach touching the ground, Zeus was crawling toward Nick. Silently, stealthily, his teeth bared and his ears pulled back in his standard stance of aggression, he inched his way closer. He was going for a surprise attack.

On Nick. *My baby.*

I bolted. I ran first to Nick's room, grabbed his baseball bat and then ou the door. I ran and jumped down three flights of stairs. *Please-God-don't-let him-hurt-him.* I jumped the last three steps, slid and righted myself, as hea surged across my ankle. Ignoring the pain, I continued in a wobbled sprin and crashed open the entryway doors. How many seconds did I have left?

I honed in on Zeus, practically able to *smell* him. I didn't dare shou a warning to Nick, for fear that would accelerate the animal's intent. Th fastest way to him was to run between the rose bush and the bougainville vine, I saw. The dog heard me crashing through and was distracte momentarily.

"GET AWAY!" I roared. Whether it was to the dog or the boy didn matter. At my shout, Nick cried out in fright, turned and saw me swingin his baseball bat at the dog behind him.

Zeus, thwarted, howled in frustration. *Good God — he was huge.* I never been this close up to him before. Nick's yelps shifted the dog's attentio back to him. "I SAID, GET BACK, YOU *BASTARD!*" I screamed a secon time and swung the bat once, twice. Zeus backed away somewhat, thoug he was still growling and barking.

I don't know what alarmed Nick more, Zeus, or me, screeching an demented, but I couldn't worry about that now. I'd bash that animal t bloody bits with Nick as witness, if it meant he wouldn't be harmed. "YOU SON-OF-A-BITCH! YOU THINK I'LL LET YOU TOUCH HIM?" swung wildly at the dog.

"Mom!" Nick exclaimed. "What are you *doing?*"

At the sound of Nick's voice, Zeus stopped barking. Heaven help me he didn't look both shocked and shamefaced.

"OH, *NOW* YOU RECOGNIZE HIM? YOU'D HAVE TORN HI APART, WOULDN'T YOU?" I circled him, the bat still swinging.

Zeus stood down. I lowered the bat, but we kept our eyes locked o each other and both of us were snarling.

"*Mom!*" said Nick again. "The bus is here!"

I whirled to see a coachload of pupils and a driver, all staring out th windows down at me. *Just great.* By ten o'clock that morning, the enti school would hear about the maniac American teacher.

Taking a breath, I turned to Nick and said calmly, "Go on then, so get on the bus."

"But what *happened?* What did Zeus do?" Nick wanted to know.

I was still panting, but I managed to keep my voice even. "He was doing his regular thing. I'll tell you more about it later. Don't worry about it for now and go... have fun. Okay... sweetie?"

Nick kept his eyes on me warily, even as he climbed aboard the bus. He and some of his friends were still peering out the windows as the bus drove out of sight.

Zeus had trotted off down the road and I was left alone with a swollen ankle and several bleeding gashes where thorns scraped when I'd pushed through the rose bushes. I held the bat brandished even now, as I watched him go. Somehow, confronting a wild dog hadn't been nearly as terrifying as my run-in with those flying cockroaches sixteen years before.

Battle sore, I hobbled back inside and phoned Gregori at work. When he answered, my voice shook, "That dog has *got* to go."

*** ***

"Don't put that on your face! It's ridiculous!"

Gregori and I were fighting again. This one was a first, though. We were arguing over the particulars of our reprehensible conspiracy to do away with Zeus.

After I'd filled Gregori in on the near catastrophe, we talked forever about alternatives. But there was no way of getting out of this situation with our sanity and integrity intact. In addition, there was further disturbing motivation for our decided course. Gregori came home from work the day after my battle with Zeus, furious.

"Do you see what the family across the way is doing just now? They're training another one to attack, a German shepherd this time. My God, they're like *Nazis*. And they're getting away with it because the law is on their side." Gregori continued inexorably, "We *have* to get rid of Zeus. It's our only choice."

Brave words, but now that the time had come to act on them, Gregori was falling apart. Starting with the fact that he'd taken black clown paint from one of Nick's old Halloween make-up sets, and was smearing it on his face.

"We have to disguise ourselves! If they recognize us, I'll go to jail. You'll be deported and God only knows what'll happen to *Nee-cky*."

I could tell he was anxious because his accent in English was becoming more pronounced.

"Let me tell you something, if you put black paint on your face and somebody sees us out there, they'll know we're doing something we

213

shouldn't. Because *nobody* goes for a walk in black face paint, unless they'r
Al Jolson, or they're up to no good!"

We conducted this entire conversation in whispers. Nick was asleep
but we were scared deathless he might wake up and see what we were up
to. Unbeknownst to him, Gregori and I had done everything required
including assembling the *"foh-lah."* When I asked Gregori where he'd gotten
the poison, he wouldn't say. That was probably for the best. I'd gotten the
meat, slit it open, and stuffed the toxins in. It was now in the fridge, tightly
wrapped in foil, on which I'd marked boldly, "DO <u>NOT</u> EAT."

Everything was set. Gregori said, "It's after midnight. Are you ready to
do this?"

I shook my head in torment. "I'll never be ready. But we said we'd do
it, so let's get it over with. We have to wait for him to take the meat and eat
it, you know."

"What! *Why*? We never said that. We *never* said that we'd have to wait
for him to eat it!" This last minute addendum to our machinations had
agitated Gregori.

"I know we didn't. But I was thinking about it and we have to. What
if he doesn't eat it, for some reason? Something else could get it, or, God
forbid, *someone* else, like a baby," I asserted.

"You're worried that a *baby* is going to pick up a piece of dirty, raw meat
from the street and swallow it?"

I retorted waspishly, "I'm not debating this with you, *got it*? I'm only
doing this because I've been *pushed* into a corner and my son's life and other
children's are at stake. I'm *not* about to take any chances that we don't get our
mark and get him *quick*. I want to be sure we harm *nothing else* but him."

After that homily, Gregori said dourly. "Okay, we'll do it your way *this*
time. Just don't get all 'teacher' on me. I'm not one of your students."

After we'd finished admonishing one another, we set off.

*** ***

Less than an hour later we were back home, lying on our bed. We'd
changed, washed, and cleaned our teeth. But "great Neptune's sea," wouldn't
do it for us, either. We'd always feel soiled by what we'd done.

There had been no cause for worry on Gregori's part. It had been so
pitch black that we could barely see Zeus when we stumbled upon him.

Gregori's eyes were much better than mine in the dark, so I'd whispered
"Are you sure it's Zeus?"

"It's him," he whispered back.

Zeus had no doubts about our identity, though, because there was no barking or biting this time. We were part of his beat now, part of the despicable humanity he'd believed with all his canine heart he was defending from harm.

We leaned down towards where he lay under a bush and gave him his last meal. Then, like the thieves we were, we skulked away. In the morning, no one would know what we'd done, except us. The only other witness would be gone.

We said nothing for a while, as we thought about the night's events.

"Do you suppose they'll know it was us?" I asked.

"Maybe. Maybe not. That dog upset a lot of people."

"But only one of them went after him with a baseball bat."

"So what, in any case, if they know? They can't prove it, and if they're not completely ignorant, they'll get the message and they'll stop."

We were silent again, thinking about what the aftermath might be. The street would be safe now. That was one good thing.

"Gregori? How many dogs do you think are killed like this in Greece every day?"

"Probably a lot."

"I feel sick."

"Me, too."

We lay there in bleak, but complete communion with one another. How unexpected. In all the time that Gregori and I'd been together, I'd longed for a true bond with him and him alone. But I'd only felt that twice. The first time was when he'd held my hand as they cut our baby out of me. And the second was now, when we'd jointly done murder.

Mindful Solely of Sea Urchins

> **"The need for change bulldozed a road
> down the center of my mind."**
> **–Maya Angelou**

It was late July of 1996. Short of only one year in Greece and there was no getting around it. I'd made a big mistake in giving Gregori a second chance.

The problem wasn't Greece. Though stray dogs might have been a mark of an underlying madness, there was so much else about it that was perfectly sane and marvelous. For example, I loved that the society as a whole considered children a blessing. Women with babies were assisted by strangers, young and old. Even the speed demon taxi drivers dallied to lend them a hand. I recalled how I'd struggled with strollers and packages in New York when Nick was a baby, while people waiting to get past would huff with impatience. But in Greece, children were never a nuisance, never shushed or hidden away. They were the center upon which life was based.

When children became teens, they did their share of 'rebelling', but typically against government or society, rarely against their families. They might get piercings and color their hair green, but these same 'radicals' held hands with their grandmothers while walking outdoors. I loved to observe how teens, adults and seniors would all discuss politics, each age group sharing their differing opinions, listening with genuine interest and deference to one another.

I also loved that in general, the Hellenes had a high regard for education and sought new ideas with a thirst. At every "café-nee-o" ("coffee shop,") one would hear juicy debates on philosophical, social and political issues. On the more volatile issues of current events, conversations could escalate into loud disputes, though never physical violence. Greeks were as ardent about their political beliefs as they were about their children. Given enough Greek coffee and cigarettes, these conversations could go on for hours. And sometimes, given enough ouzo, they'd all end up sounding a bit like Homer. The one married to Marge, that is.

These fresh encounters were opening my eyes. When I'd first met Gregori, I hardly ever picked up a newspaper. Now I was reading them daily and with the help of a dictionary, could manage them in three languages. Previously, I'd deferred to Gregori's analysis of current events, but in time, I felt confident enough in my knowledge base to formulate my own opinions. If I had questions, I could ask anyone for answers. Even a second-year high school student in Greece knew more about world politics than some of the adults I knew back home.

There was more to life in Greece than intellectual high-mindedness and family values, however. Hellenes also shined at play. Shops were always closed, it seemed, for yet another national holiday. With my capitalist attitude, I missed my 24-hour *Walmart,* but there was something to be id for knowing that on holidays (and Sundays, of course,) I *had* to relax, ecause even if I wanted to, I couldn't do any chores involving shopping.

And those many holidays were an elation, commemorated with ageantry. The start of Lenten season, Clean Monday, the skies in Athens ere filled with colorful ribbon and paper, as each family took a picnic inch up to the mountains and flew a kite, specially purchased or made y hand for the occasion. On Good Friday, the streets were flooded with riests holding a flower-covered, symbolic coffin, soldiers carrying guns, id believers gripping lit candles. They all marched together in a solemn rocession of thousands, mourning the death of Jesus. But Easter Sunday ie mood turned jubilant, as neighbors on balcony after balcony on the uildings in Glyfada, roasted lamb on a spit and called out to one another, Christos Anesti!" ("Christ has risen!") Hellenes celebrated their holidays tterly, and I followed their lead gladly.

Living in Greece was having a positive effect on me in countless ways. could've been happy there, if the man who was my husband weren't so erpetually discontent. Some who'd moved back to Greece after having ved outside it told me that this was a common bane of immigrants. "Half our heart's in one country and half's in another," they said.

In view of that, I tried to have compassion, but when Greece couldn't e the panacea Gregori had expected, he became withering in his treatment f me:

"Why do you take your job so seriously? It's just a *job*. You make it into ich a big deal."

"Why don't you use the washer after eleven at night? I told you, *here*, iey charge us less for water at that time. Everyone else does it like that, hy do *you* have to be different?"

He belittled me in front of others:

(While taking a cousin of his sightseeing) "What do you mean, that's een 'reconstructed'? How dumb is *that?* It's the original marble. I thought ou studied this in school."

And when we were alone:

"You are heavier now than you've ever been in all the years I've known ou. I can't stand the sight of you."

It's incredible to me now how much of my self-image was tied up in hat he felt for me and said about me. I became adapted to feeling sick iside. I had too much pride to confide in anyone I'd just met in Greece id I refused to tell people back home how things were between Gregori

and me. Six thousands miles away, what could they do to help? So I l
myself become isolated. I spent every day at the Greek private scho
unhappy, doing a job I no longer believed in, working for someone I r
longer respected. In the early evenings, I'd enjoy my son's company, b
once he was off to bed, Gregori ignored me completely. That was far wor
than his disparagement.

Then Demetra came to stay with us for a week before she went on
Rhodes for the summer. It was as though Gregori had completely forgotte
the promises he'd made. I came home one day and couldn't find anythir
in my kitchen. She'd rearranged the cupboards and moved the silverwa
to another drawer.

"You *keetchin ees* much better now. You like *eet?*" she smile
guilelessly.

No, I *goddamn* didn't, but when I took Gregori aside to tell him
speak to her about it, he groused at me loudly enough that his moth
could hear us from the balcony where she was sitting, "You're such a pa
in the ass! Every little thing bothers you!"

For the life of me, I still don't know how I grew to accept so passive
our relationship as it was. Slowly, somehow, I formulated a theory th
husbands in *general* had to be this way, that women *everywhere* had bee
duped and we just had to put up with our "difficult men" or not get marri
at all. That bizarre hypothesis was what got me through each day. I sa
myself as "strong" because I could *endure* my marriage. So when Grego
directed his hatefulness toward me, I was actually pleased with myself th
I could receive it stoically. It was only when his venom started spreading
our nine-year-old son that I reacted fiercely.

This particular July afternoon, the three of us were having our lunch
one of the delightful, outdoor *tavernas* on the beach. As always, the weath
was perfect, the food was delicious, and Nick and I were having fun. The
several bees decided to join us, going directly for Nick's food. Nick jump
back, swishing his hands over his plate. Taking exception to this, one b
flew straight at Nick's face. Letting out a yelp, Nick ran from the table.

Gregori demanded angrily, "Nick! Get back here and sit down!"

Nick didn't comply. "I'm not sitting back there. I *hate* bees!"

Heedless of the other patrons, Gregori shouted furiously, "I *said* —
back down, you little *weirdo*!"

The look on my son's face at that moment crushed me. Calmly I said
Nick, "It's okay, son, we'll wrap the rest and bring it home. You can go play."

218

When he left, I turn to Gregori, enraged. "You call your son a name like that? *You're* the 'weirdo'. How do *you* like it when people call *you* names?" *Oh*, I was just *waiting* for him to throw another tantrum. I'd have dumped Nick's plate of calamari right in his lap, if he did.

He didn't. My vehement defense of Nick brought him back to his senses. But predictably, he had to place blame for his bad behavior. Bitterly he said, "Why does he react like *that*?"

I leaned towards him and hissed, "He doesn't *like* bees."

He made a scathing face. "Doesn't *like* them? He's *afraid* of them, you mean."

"Big-*fucking*-deal." Gregori eyes widened. He wasn't used to me swearing at him. "What does that signify about him to *you*? He's a great kid, he's doing well here, and *you* should be proud of him."

"I didn't expect any son of mine to be afraid of bees."

"Just like you didn't expect 'any son of yours' to like a different soccer team than you do? You made him feel bad about that, too. He's not your *clone*. He's your *son*. I'm your *wife*. We are your *family*. Treat us right." But even as I spoke, I was thinking to myself, *You're wasting your breath.*

I was right. When I stopped talking, he said scornfully, "You still don't get it, do you? Sure, Nick is my family. And my mother and my brother are my family. But, *you*? You'll never be on the same level to me as they are."

That's what it came down to. His son, his mother, and his brother were his family. I was just his property. *What was wrong with me that I hadn't seen it?* Now that Nick and I were exactly where he wanted us, in Greece, he was saying it outright. *Holy cow*, I'd made some bonehead choices in my life, but sticking by this man all these years topped them all. Revolted by him and myself, I got up. "I'm going for a walk."

I walked down to where Nick was playing in the sand. He'd seen Gregori and me arguing and looked worried. "Are you alright, Mom?"

It wouldn't help pretending that it hadn't happened. "I'm fine, Nick. I'm just going for a walk. Make sure your father is nearby if you go back in the water, please."

I walked along that beach, as far away from Gregori as I could get. Wading to one of the massive, black rocks protruding from the water, I climbed up, watching the crevices for hidden sea urchins. I'd always remembered Gregori's warning on that first trip: "They sting if you step on them." I'd been careful. All this time and I'd never once tread on one. I'd gotten stung, anyway, hadn't I?

219

I sat there alone and let myself cry. As I did, the surrounding loveliness taunted me. I was in such a splendid place, yet I just felt desolate and wanted to go home.

But if I returned to the New York City Public School system now, I'd take a salary cut to almost half of what I'd been making when I'd left. In what hellish part of New York City could Nick and I afford to live on a wage like that? Even if we could go back, how would Nick feel about it? He was just getting used to things here. He was still so young. Leaving Greece was not an option. Gregori knew I'd take no chances with Nick's life. I stopped crying and started chuckling a bit madly. Because there was not a *single* thing I could do.

And then suddenly, I was furious. Out of desperation and panic, I'd deceived myself into believing Gregori had *changed*. He was the same as he'd always been and I was *stupid* for convincing myself otherwise. And now, *I'd fucked up my whole life.*

Hearing those words in my head was like being smacked full force by a soaring wave. My body went rigid with cold. No wonder I hadn't dared ask my mother what she'd meant when those anguished words burst out of her at Ester's wake. I was terrified I already knew. Had *fear* caused my mother to make poor choices in her past, as it had with me? Was that what had turned her into such a sour little martinet? Is that what *my* future held?

My crying stopped for real. *"No."*

I said it out loud. I still had a chance to transform my existence. From now on, I'd deal with Gregori for who he was and not for who I wanted him to be. And I might think he was a *prick,* but he was also Nick's father. I witnessed today that Gregori's absorption with his own ego, an ego so weak that he worried incessantly about what others might think, could actually harm his child's own sense of self. But I still needed Gregori financially and physically right now, to help raise that child. So, I'd stay with him, for Nick's sake, but when they were together, I was going to watch Gregori *very* carefully. And since it was now patently plain that he'd never wanted anything more from me than my participation in an expedient marriage, conformance to social expectation, he'd get it. *My* way.

I sat on that rock for a long time, thinking, but I couldn't sit there forever. Making sure I left no trace of tears on my face, I climbed down and waded to shore. Then I walked back to my son.

Chapter Thirteen: The 'Little American' Opens a Business

". . . Because in Poker, Sometimes Stupid Wins."
–Pete Davis

Goosebumps

When some women are unhappy in love, they make radical physical changes, like dying their hair red. I decided to do something else: create my own corporation. *And* I dyed my hair red.

I'd been formulating my idea since the previous March. That fight on the beach was all I needed as an impetus to make my business plan a reality. My plan was multifaceted, but I knew it could be done and that I was the person to do it. I was dismal at love, unmistakably, but I knew *for sure* I was exceptionally good at teaching. Since my enterprise would be based on that, it had every chance of being successful. It doesn't take a psychology degree to figure out why I didn't just quit my job at the school and pursue my lifelong dream of writing. A burgeoning part of me knew I'd leave Gregori someday and I needed to get financially solvent. I was deprived of joy in my marriage and didn't feel fulfilled in my job at the Greek school. But if my idea worked, I'd begin making money immediately, and at least feel significant and useful in another area of my life besides motherhood.

My goal was to move Greece away from language teaching which was grammar-based and get as many teachers nationally to see the benefits of a literature-based methodology. If you're not an English teacher, that might sound like "all Greek" to you. The bottom line is the teachers I'd worked with in Greece observed that my teaching method was atypical, but they also acknowledged that my pupils responded well to it and found it more appealing. The supplemental materials I was using also attracted my colleagues' interest. If my present colleagues were an indication of the caliber of educator teaching in schools across Greece, it was possible my methods would be welcomed in other classrooms throughout the country. So I contemplated, *What would it take to bring these techniques to all the teachers and schools in Greece?*

I'd also need sufficient quantities of the materials I was using. American teaching materials weren't stocked in the few English bookshops there were in Athens, nor did they have much of a selection of children's books from the States, either. In New York, Nick and I would go the library every Friday after school and borrow books for the weekend. He often chose *Goosebumps*, a children's mystery book series. When we moved to Greece, Nick's second-grade teacher from New York, Mrs. Macchio, sent Nick the latest in the *Goosebumps* series every month. I blessed her for it each time it showed up, because Nick was thrilled. It always made me sad that he was missing out on those trips to the bookshops and libraries back home. It would be great if, in addition to the teaching materials I and my colleagues loved, I could get children's books from the States, also.

Then I realized that the *Goosebumps* series was published by Scholastic Inc., the same publishing company that created many of my teaching materials. This led me to thinking: If Gerry and his partners could import paints from the U.S., why couldn't *I* import Scholastic books and teaching materials?

My idea blossomed from there. I imagined having my own retail book outlet, where I could have children's events and demonstrate my English language teaching methods. I could promote the materials by conducting teacher workshops at schools. My excitement mounted as I pictured my son smiling over all the stories we'd been so fond of, all back in his life again. I'd be able to introduce those books to his new friends. My pupils would love learning to speak and write English, if they could only read it from not only the *Goosebumps* series, but *Clifford the Big Red Dog*, *The Baby-sitters Club*, and more. I was certain Greek educators would find Scholastic teaching materials far better than the dated materials currently available. Just the vision of being able to give something back to Greece after I'd gotten so much from it, and to see my son recapture some of the delights he'd been missing from home, made it worth the effort to organize this. The more I thought about it and researched it, the more confident I became that I could pull it off.

I didn't ask Gregori's permission. I just told him what I was going to do. In August, a month after the beach fight, Gregori and Nick were again in Rhodes with Demetra serving them home-cooked meals. This time I wasn't crying over it; this time I was using their holiday away to fly to New York and write up a viable business plan. I had the help of my good friend, Gerry's Third Wife, who, apart from that 'claim to fame', also happened to

222

e an outstanding CPA. Then I spent another week negotiating with Scott Bowker, the sales manager of Scholastic's International Division. I had to convince him of my competence, the merits of my plan, and then we had to parley terms. It was nerve-wracking and grueling, but exhilarating, too, because it paid off.

When I got back to Greece, Gregori didn't like my business idea, or my new hair color. I didn't care. I'd done both for me. With my red hair and Scholastic's contract, I was armed against his disapproval.

"You have a good job at the school," was Gregori's same old recording.

"I'm not sticking around to watch the head teacher destroy the whole department."

"Why the hell can't you mind your own business and just work here?"

"Is that what *you* do?" I countered.

He changed tactics. "What makes you think you can do this? It sounds impossible to me."

"It's *not* impossible. Your brother did it with his two partners. If they can bring paint here from the States and distribute it all over the country, why can't I bring books here and do the same?"

His next device was sarcasm. "If *they* can do it, you can? *You*, one little foreign girl, who's been in Greece for *one year*, can do the same job that three Greek men, all professional businessmen, all nationals, are doing?"

I didn't even blink as I replied, "No, I'm not saying that I can make the same job of it as they can. Given time, I can do a *better* job. George Cristos said he thought my idea was excellent and from the way I'd talked about it with him, he wished that he and I could be partners in the paint business. What do you think of *that*?"

The insult took the wind out of his sails a bit, but still he argued, "You're just going to give up teaching at the school?"

I'd planned to leave before the start of the next term. Instead, the head teacher had suggested I continue at the school for two days per week until my business built up. She even promised she'd advocate the books, so I could have my first sale at the school where I taught. I suspected she wanted to keep me there a while longer for her own purposes, but telling Gregori that I'd still work there two days per week would give me a bargaining chip. At the same time, I'd have a perfect place to begin promoting my materials in earnest.

223

Gregori's relief was evident when I told him, "They've invited me to work there part-time."

"You *see*? They *like* you there. You're giving up a sure thing…"

"Don't start this again, *please*, Gregori. It's not a 'sure thing'. I am *foreign*. I can *never* be appointed there. They can fire me *anytime* they want."

"Where will you get the money for it?"

I was prepared for that, too. "I have some money saved and you'll give me the rest."

"No I won't."

"Yes, you *will*. You *owe* me. You made all kinds of promises to me before we got back together and you haven't kept *one*. I'm not going to be unhappy for the rest of my life. If you don't give me the money, I'll leave."

Of course, I wouldn't leave. Nick had already been through enough harrowing change. But if my luck held, Gregori wouldn't suspect that I was bluffing. It was his move now. Would he fold or call?

He 'called'.

Smirking, he said, "All right, if you're determined to do this, and if even George thinks it's a good idea, I'll give you money. But you give me fifty percent."

My own husband was trying to negotiate much tougher terms than my new sales manager had. I looked at him seriously. "Do I get fifty percent of the taxi and the apartment we bought in Rhodes? Another promise you made when we got back together was that you'd put my name on those things."

He shook his head. "Nope. Nick's name is on them. That's all that should matter to you."

That shouldn't have hurt by this time, but it did. Nonetheless, I said gamely, "Then I guess what's yours is yours, and what's mine is mine. You give me money and my new business is mine alone."

I got a resentful stare, but when he saw I wouldn't back down, he forced one word through his teeth, "*Fine.*"

Well, how about that? Considering I was a rookie at this, I'd played some decent hands. Though it'd been hard won, I got what I wanted. Both my sales manager and my husband would be impressed by what I'd accomplish.

Serafim Books

> **"For the things we have to learn before
> we can do them, we learn by doing them."**
> **–Aristotle**

How fitting that Serafim Books, like the universe in Greek mythology, was born out of the chaos of my life.

Gerry's Third Wife and I had chosen the name while I was in New York. "Seraphim" was the name of an angel, and our motto was, "a good book is like a guardian angel." I needed a logo to go with the name. Nick, then going into fourth grade, designed a brilliant one. In doing so, he changed the spelling from 'Seraphim', to 'Serafim'. He said it made more sense that way to the Greek eye.

Then I had to hire a shipper, a customs agent, and an accountant who knew the minutiae of the Greek socialist system. It imposed *so* many regulations on how and when the books could be brought into the country, which books weren't considered educational and were therefore taxed at a higher rate, and even the types of invoicing required. Often I felt we were importing lethal substances rather than books.

On my own, I found the shipper and customs agent, but it was Gregori who recommended the accountant. "Why don't you use Eris from my office? She'll charge you less."

I chewed on my lip, debating. Sofia was an accountant and I'd wanted to ask her. But it was a positive thing that Gregori was taking an interest. So I decided, "Okay, I'll ask Eris."

Now I had those helpers in Greece, but I also got assistance from the States. Some orders to Greece could only be posted, some only shipped, and there were evils to conquer with both methods. Terry Miller and Carl Wassman from Scholastic's offices spent *hours* on the telephone with me, helping me circumvent the bureaucracy that frustrated my customers. And as we did, sales grew. I wrote reports to Scott monthly on every landmark sale made and every obstacle overcome. As sales increased, Scott became just as keen on my territory as I was. Sales went so well that, after the first six months, he made me Scholastic's official representative, able to promote Scholastic Book Clubs and Book Fairs *and* he renewed my distribution contract for the following year!

After a while, it made no sense to import only American books, when Scholastic in the United Kingdom had wonderful teaching materials, too. Soon, I was importing books from other publishers, like Penguin and Random House. I could recommend these to pupils studying English at a higher level of proficiency, while increasing my offerings to foreigners in Greece who wanted a bigger variety of books in English.

With this excellent selection, I began educationally-themed 'events' at schools and other locations. Every participant received a relevant book and worked on a subject-related craft or other literature-based activity. As my network grew, I observed that Greek families spent piles of money for their children to have tutors or attend language schools after their regular school day. In these programs, rote repetition was the basis for foreign language attainment. Learning other languages, particularly English, was necessary but dreary and expensive. I was determined to change those last bits. I had confidence my techniques worked, although I anticipated that there'd be some who'd oppose them.

What I didn't expect was that the majority of educators would *embrace* them. For me, that eager acceptance was overwhelming. The first time I gave a workshop at a *TESOL Greece* event (*Teachers of English to Students of Other Languages*) the room was packed, and the chairperson of the *TESOL* board asked me if I'd "mind" conducting the workshop a second time. Can you imagine? On the contrary, I felt honored. The teachers who came to hear me speak were exceptional educators with excellent credentials. And most of them were *Greek*. In all the time I'd lived with Gregori and known his relatives and friends, they'd continued to reject me as alien and beneath them. Now I was having an encounter that was far removed from that.

As Aristotle said, "it is the mark of an educated mind to be able to entertain an idea without accepting it." Even if the teachers attending my workshops disagreed with some of my theories, they listened to, thought about, and discussed them. Being in their company was so unlike being with Gregori and his family, or even the head teacher at my school. These were the Hellenes who thought like the ancients I'd admired for so long.

The name I'd chosen for my enterprise soon signified more than I'd originally foreseen, because I met numerous 'angels' who loved Serafim Books and helped it grow. Some became the friends I'd been looking for in Greece. They were my biggest surprise yet.

Nothing in Common

"There are two kinds of women: those who want power in the world and those who want power in bed."
–Jacqueline Kennedy Onassis

They were "not like me," the women who began buying my books, attending my workshops and setting up events for their pupils and children. Nor were they like each other.

One used to be a fashion model. One used to be a naval officer. One used to clean houses for families. One had family in the House of Lords.

One had skin so translucently pale, her veins came up blue when she walked into the sea. Another had skin so glossy and dark; she looked just like the olives that came from *Kalamata*.

They were Muslim, Jewish, Catholic, Baptist, Orthodox, Atheist, Republican, Democrat, supporters of *Nea Dimokratia,* and followers of Trotsky. They spoke Greek, Italian, French, German, Arabic, Hebrew and every English that exists, from Sydney to Glasgow, from Belfast to London, from Newcastle to New York, Louisiana and '*Tex-ass*'.

Some said "biscuits" were fluffy and drizzled with gravy. Others said "biscuits" were sweet and served with tea. The girl from Scotland learned, "*poh poh poh,*" the Arab learned, "*y'all,*" the one from Newcastle, learned, "*don't bust my chops,*" and the Italian-American learned, "*mashallah.*" Their children called them, "Mom," "Mum," "Mam," "*Mama.*"

On their tables at night, you'd find everything from grits to goat, haggis to hummus. Together, they celebrated Thanksgiving, *Eid al-Fitr*, Guy Fawkes, Passover, and *Apokrias.*

They laughed about each other's weaknesses and rejoiced in each other's distinctions. They were artists, accountants, activists, social workers, businesswomen, librarians, and teachers. They offered their brainpower, their time, their food, their religions, their languages, and their dedication. They helped children who had life-threatening illnesses, worked at the American Embassy in Athens, in a division of Scholastic International, or built a children's theater. They owned schools or taught at them; they spayed stray animals or painted murals. They read stories to children, protested war, got food to the hungry, or went camping with Girl Guides.

It was momentous to me noting how unalike we appeared on the surface, but that we all had similar values and purpose. We had nothing in common that didn't matter and everything in common that did. What mattered to us all were our families, our friends, our integrity, and our quests to be creative. We shared a determination to leave our spot in the world — at this point in our lives, that was Greece — just a little bit better than we'd found it when we arrived.

I was inspired by these women. The girls in my past, like Margie, my much-loved cousins, and me too, of course, would suffer our plights in helplessness, sighing, "That's just the way it is." And the ones I'd met when I first came to Greece sat and grew fat on their own malcontent. But my new female acquaintances were neither submissive nor sullen. They were driven by the challenge, "If you don't like it, *don't* settle for it."

There was Angela, a Girl Scout leader and the only African-American living in Glyfada who'd made her way to Athens via the US military from Louisiana. She'd met and married Gianni Papadopoulos and remained in Greece with him.

On the subject of their union, she astonished me once when she said, "Yep, I stick out here like a sore thumb. When my husband and I are out together, Greeks come up and ask him did he marry a black woman because I'm 'good in bed?' Can you believe *that*? I told him... he'd *better* answer, 'Yes!'"

Not only was Angela ten years younger than I, she was from a Southern state in the United States I'd never had the opportunity to visit. If we'd each stayed in our separate parts of our native country, we'd never have met. Instead, we came across each other in Greece and bonded over a common love of books. She and I organized *Baby-sitters Club* book series literature events for her troop. Angela would eventually work at the American Embassy in Athens. I didn't know then that having her at the embassy would help me later on down the road.

It was Angela who introduced me to Nancy, another Girl Scout leader, apart from about a hundred other things she did for the community. Nancy was the stepdaughter of Abbe Lane, the singer, and she had a heart as big as her wallet.

"So, *you're* the new kid on the block," she said to me when we met. "About time somebody started selling English books around here. Let's see whatcha got!"

Nancy bought books by the bagful for her kids, her friends' kids, her scouts and her theater group. She didn't just chaperone at Serafim Books' children's events, she hunted down the venue and the attendees. Nick got to go to these events, too, and met children at them who'd been born in many parts of the world. He enjoyed that as much as he enjoyed his now endless supply of *Goosebumps*.

And there was Randy, a teacher at American Community Schools. She was a child-rearing expert and one of the most dedicated, brilliant teachers I've ever had the benefit of meeting. She was also a huge Scholastic Book Club customer, ordering so many books for her pupils that she was able to get a computer for her classroom just from the bonus points.

When I introduced myself, she remarked, "Scholastic's finally got a rep in Greece? Well, maybe *now* I'll have less trouble with shipping."

She was so no-nonsense that she came across as a bit intimidating at the start, but I'd discover just how kind and helpful she was.

Then, a lovely blonde woman approached me at a Boy Scouts event, "Got any books on bugs? My son, Dimitri, is obsessed with them."

This was Pam, a Canadian. I'd started an education service, but *she'd* started the Greece affiliate of Make-A-Wish International. Pam invited Serafim Books to be present at her next Make-A-Wish fundraiser. It wouldn't be the last time we'd work together. I can't think about all the children in Greece with life-threatening illnesses whom Pam has helped without getting teary-eyed.

Through Pam, I met Eleni, a Greek-Cypriot from South Africa, who was Pam's 'right-hand-man' at Make-A-Wish Greece. Eleni became one of Serafim Books' staunchest groupies, sending her daughter to every event and buying as many books as she could. It was through Eleni I met Kim and Josie, two artists who added their talents to children's events.

This list of women would grow larger as time went by. When I got to know them better individually and they talked about their own struggles with husbands or mothers-in-law, with being foreign or with finding their place in Greece, I thought my trials paled in comparison. I don't think they knew how extraordinary they were and they probably still don't. They weren't always successful in their endeavors. But, they'd made a home so far from home. They'd not only adapted to a faraway community, they'd enhanced it. They never let themselves be hampered by disappointments, but focused on their joys and goals.

So I guess I can say, like those whores back in Naples, they made something delicious out of limited choices. And now I'd learn to do the same.

To discover this about myself was a gift to me from all those women. Bu the woman who'd be my biggest 'angel' in Greece was Joan Maragoudaki. About a year after I started Serafim Books, I needed part-time assistance Eleni from Make-A-Wish told me she knew someone who was lookin for "something interesting to do." That's how Joan materialized. Born i England, she'd also married a Greek and had been living in Greece for mor than twenty years. She loved children, was an experienced English languag tutor and social worker. A perfect candidate. It was also nice to discove that her son, Alexi, was the boy in Nick's class about whom I'd been hearin so much. This gave Joan and me more to share.

Not only was Joan smart, diligent and honest, she was *fun*. We had th same quirky sense of humor which not many in Greece seemed to get. enjoyed the glances we'd receive from strangers when she'd say outrageou things in public, such as this, to her son:

"*Hmmm*, Alexi, you're hanging around with Nick too much. You'i starting to sound American. I'm going to have to beat that out of ye."

Of course, she was being droll. When I hired her I said, "Some Gree teachers are still a bit skeptical about our materials because they're not a British. They might be more amenable to them if you're pushing then since you're English."

She set me straight. "You'll be disappointed there."

I didn't know what she meant at first. Then I witnessed her have th same experience I'd had when I first got to Greece. One of our Britis clients asked her, "I don't recognize your accent. Where are you from?"

"Newcastle, England," answered Joan.

"You sound Scottish," sniffed the Brit.

"I'll take that as a compliment," quipped Joan.

That was when I learned that because of her northern 'Geordie' accen regional-linguistic superiority complexes were aimed at her, too, just by differer teams. We shared a derision for them. She made no bones about hers.

"Thank you for that elucidation, Ms. Expert-Knickers," she'd say t whoever corrected her diacritics. "If it's vowels that are botherin' ye, e some prunes, why don't ye?"

It wasn't only her sense of humor and life perspective that bega to endear Joan to me. It was also how much she'd been affected by he exposure to the Hellenic culture. The noise in her home was one exampl Though she held English protocols, like standing patiently on a queue while everyone else in Greece elbowed her aside, she permitted her childre

230

o shout as much as their 'pure-blood' Mediterranean counterparts. And her dog, whom she'd named 'Bob', barked as much as any other Greek dog without her shushing him too harshly. Another example was her cooking. Using plenty of garlic and fresh vegetables, Joan cooked genuine *fish*, the kind with the bones still in, not that white stuff her countrymen ate, that reminded me of the 'fish sticks' Donna's mother used to serve. Joan had also obtained awareness of 'the evil eye' and would be the first to jump in and fake spit', "*Toof-toof-toof*," just in case it were lurking.

However, what I enjoyed most was watching Joan with her husband, Manoli. They restored my faith in enduring love. Initially, Manoli seemed just like Gregori, yelling as loudly and complaining as often. But one day, he did something that flummoxed me. I'd gone by their place to go over some book orders. They'd just finished dinner. Joan was relaxing in front of the TV while Manoli was doing the dishes! He wasn't at all embarrassed by my catching him at it, either.

"Hello, Patricia. How are you? Sit down over there with Joan and I'll bring you some wine. My wife's had a rough day, poor little bugger. Maybe you can cheer her up," he said, pleasantly

It hit me then, *He adores his wife.*

He must have wondered why I stood there staring at him after that. He couldn't know another of my idiotic, sweeping perceptions had just been crushed. *All* marriages were *not* a misery.

Suddenly my life in Greece was filled with positive people. I had constructive things to accomplish. My world was opening up in a way it never could have, had I stuck with the sheltered safety that Gregori maintained I should.

Even Eris, the accountant Gregori had recommended, was helpful. She had a big personality and a way of accomplishing business at the municipalities that would've taken me twice as long on my own. When she came by the apartment each month to do my books, she and Gregori laughed a lot together. She made Nick laugh, too.

One night, as Gregori sat in the kitchen helping Nick with his homework, and Eris and I were in the dining room going over accounts, out of nowhere, she said, "I never noticed how beautiful you are. I wonder... does your husband appreciate you?"

That commentary was surreal. She was my accountant and a colleague of Gregori's. We'd never exchanged personal observations about one another and we hadn't even been having a conversation.

I didn't know what was going on, but... *something* made me land he
one of my "you're-being-impudent" looks that I'd perfected as a teacher
"I've no complaints," I returned nattily. "And... I'm done with this invoice
You can add it to the total."

We finished our work in silence. When we were done, Gregori offered
to drive her home, so she wouldn't have to take the bus.

After they left, I thought, *What's up with her?*

A Literary Haven

*"... I applaud you for your outstanding dedication
to education."*
–First Lady of California, **Maria Shriver,** *in a letter written to Patricia*

As I'd promised Gregori, I started my enterprise part-time in September
of 1996, working from a home office and storing books in the spare
bedroom. Six months later, orders of books had taken over that room and
part of our living room. We had to build shelving to hold them. Gregori
bitched about it, but he built them.

Gerry's Third Wife, back in New York, was my financial guide. During
one phone meeting, we looked at numbers and concluded that it was time
for me to resign from the school and pursue Serafim Books exclusively.
Now I could travel to schools in the provinces. I got to see parts of Greece
I never would've seen and meet more teachers who shared my vision. I felt
less like a gatecrasher in Greece by the day.

Those school visits resulted in more invitations to conduct teacher
workshops and more book orders. Due to the time difference between
Athens and New York, the fax machine whirred all night long. For me, that
signified my enterprise was working.

For Gregori—

"*Gamoto!* (Fuck it!*)* What the *hell* is that noise, Patricia?"

— it was just another disruption to contend with, aggravating his regimented life.

By December, even with shelving, there were far too many books in the
apartment. Clients had to step over and pick through cardboard cartons. I
didn't want to appear unprofessional. I also worried that the child welfare
people would come after me. Ten-year-old Nick was lugging heavy boxes of
books up and down our stairs. It was time to find new headquarters.

It was also time to determine how involved in this venture Joan wanted to be. I crossed my fingers and asked her if she wanted to be my business partner and open up our own location.

Lucky, lucky me, she said, "Yes."

We had limited funds, so we had to be resourceful. We hunted for five months. In May of 1998, right before Joan's birthday, Eleni rang to tell us, "I found something that might do. It needs a little work, mind."

Nick and Alexi were in Nick's room when Eleni phoned. They wanted to see the building, too. It wasn't too far, right on Themistocleous Street, next to a Lotto shop. When Joan and I walked through it, we exclaimed in delight. It was precisely what we'd hoped for and at the right price, too.

But Alexi and Nick exchanged horrified glances. "*This* place!" they said in unison.

Then Alexi said, "Mum, this is ghastly!"

And Nick said, "Mom, this is gross."

"Nonsense," we told them. "It just needs some fixing up."

It had three levels. The main level boasted marble flooring that was stained and cracked. The top level was a third the size of that main floor and overlooked it through a balcony railing, which clearly needed to be replaced, or we'd fall to our deaths. The basement walls were covered in mold and the toilet in the miniscule bath was the digs for all sorts of hideous little beasts.

We spent the entire summer getting that place in shape. As Joan said, "It was bloody back-breaking work, but we're *so* glad we did it."

We opened in August, shortly after my fifteenth wedding anniversary. The front of the shop was freshly painted in shades of forest green and the entranceway was flanked by two white ceramic pots filled with red geraniums. On our pristine white awning, the name "Serafim Books" had been painted in black.

Caringly Joan said, "We have to keep Nick's logo, it's very clever," so that was painted on the awning, too, right beneath the lettering.

Inside, the main floor was now gleaming and painted in tones of butter and sage, and boasted a spectacular collection of English-language books shelved according to reading level. It also contained the largest assortment in Athens of stickers, puppets and other creative playthings, all theme-related to the various children's titles.

The balcony floor was now our office and where we kept our selection of teachers' materials. We could work up there and look down through the new, sturdy rail whenever someone came into the shop. Teachers could join us up in the office, where we'd discuss their classroom needs over cups of coffee or tea.

The filthy basement was now sparkling clean, the unsanitary fixtures in the bath all replaced. One of the walls was painted in chalkboard paint, so children could use it at events, and another wall covered in cork, where we could pin their artwork or photographs we'd take at workshops.

Our new headquarters looked so welcoming, that even Spiro, the taciturn, chain-smoking man who owned the Lotto shop next door, complimented us by whistling in appreciation at the new exterior. We smiled, because from him, that illustrated great approval.

In between events and workshops, I visited schools throughout Greece and Cyprus, while Joan, back at the shop, kept track of materials, bookshops, book fairs, book clubs, the dates of events and... she could probably still list all the rest. Neither of us could have been so productive without the other. My acuity was improving. I'd chosen a better business partner than I had a mate.

Chapter Fourteen: The 'Agonists' Collide

"A man is in general better pleased when he has a good dinner upon his table than when his wife talks Greek."
–Samuel Johnson

'Mr. Bean' Cooks for His Family

By the end of that year, Serafim Books was in the black, with a smidgeon ft over to allow ourselves a small wage. That September, we had a party for 'ick's eleventh birthday in the basement events room that we all enjoyed. veryone involved with Serafim Books loved it. Everyone except Gregori.

Though I kept it to myself, all throughout our workday there was a incessant chorus at the back of my mind lamenting my tragedy of a lationship. That chorus couldn't be ignored in the evenings. It wasn't bedtime when it became impossible, as one might expect, when the moteness between my husband and me became dismally apparent in the rm of our absent love life. No, it was earlier, at dinner.

Nick helped me with the laundry and Lita and I managed the rest f the housework. But as time went on and I was at the shop for longer ours, I didn't have the energy to create a meal every night. Salads gave me e most trouble. Dinner salad was the microcosm of Gregori's bumptious eal, a pictogram to him of his control over his home life. But I only ought he was meticulous about his vegetables and after a decade and a alf of living together, it was starting to wear a bit thin. I'd had fifteen years hearing, "You don't like onions in a salad? Who *doesn't* like onions in salad?" "What the hell kind of olives are *these*?" Or, "*Dammit*, Patricia, ese tomatoes are not ripe!"

I could whip up something easy and nutritious. But make salad? I just *uldn't* anymore.

Sometimes when we had to work late at the shop, I'd hear Joan on the none with her husband, "Manoli? Could you put the chicken in the oven d cut up the salad, please? I'll be home in an hour."

So I tried that with Gregori. I'd ask him, politely, "Gregori, would you ind making the salad?"

Gregori's response was the same each time I asked. There was th brutal, vibrating pause. His eyes would freeze, his jaw would clench, ar after breathing hard once or twice, he'd say through his teeth, "*Fine.*"

And as I cooked and set the table, he'd silently, but wrathfully, rust open cellophane bags holding salad ingredients, slam vegetables down ne the sink, pull a salad bowl out of the cupboard and bang that down on the countertop, too. He'd forcefully wash and *smack* those vegetables dov on the cutting board and then *bang* the knife, *chop* hard on the vegetabl and *slam* the salad bowl onto the table. And every "*Chop!*" "*Bang!*" "*Slam* "*Smack!*" was his statement of what he thought of me, as loud as if he we shouting it.

That's how it was at our house at night. Though we exercised civili in our interactions for the most part, we'd gotten to the point where v couldn't stand each other. That feeling oozed its way out through o management of lettuce greens.

Our son, who loved us both, never suspected there was a lot boilis under our thin crust of amicability and that it might crack and burst for at any moment, because of a thing as simple as fixing dinner. I'm su he wasn't oblivious to the fact that *Mama* spent a lot of time alone o the balcony, staring out at the mountains. Or that *Baba* spent a lot time watching soccer matches and swearing at the players, who served my stand-ins. Still, I think... I hope... there wasn't enough open hostili between his father and me to cause him any real stress. He did notice son things. When he heard his father "*chop-chopping*" and "*slam-slamming* he'd look up at his dad, then over at me and wiggle his eyebrows, as if to sa "Hmmm, somebody's having a bad day." Then he'd smile at me.

That smile kept me centered. Gosh, he was *sweet.* It had been difficu for him, but he'd adjusted to everything in Greece, including my new caree He was, as the Greeks say, my little "*palee-karee,*" a "fine young warrior."

Could I be any less than he?

Yet, with all that I was doing for him, I knew I wouldn't be makii dinner with the zest I had in the past. But we'd get used to that change, to

As Joan and I made headway in our work, I started judging myself l my own standards, not Gregori's. If he wanted a home-cooked meal, l him make it himself. Much to my incredulity, that's what he did. His fath rest his soul, would have been horror-struck.

However, Gregori would only cook *beans.* He cooked white bea red beans, *fava* beans. He cooked beans because they were "healthy" ar economical". Most significantly, Gregori cooked beans because he knew I hated them and he was using them to make another statement. There was an additional benefit for him, too. The inevitable result of eating so many beans had me sleeping most nights in the spare bedroom, as far away from *him* as possible.

When Nick exclaimed one night, "Oh, no, not 'Mr. Bean' cooking again!" Gregori grudgingly gave in to an evening or two per week of helping me make salad or boil up pasta. It was my son who'd rescued me from a diet consisting solely of legumes.

The War with Me

> *"I don't move on logic — I move on my gut.*
> *And I have a good gut."*
> **–Oprah Winfrey**

It was an act of willpower to ignore that background din in my mind which insisted ever more adamantly that I address the state of my marriage. Just as it took discipline to avoid thinking about all I missed from back home.

One of the best things about emigrating from the United States to Greece was that it gave me a basis for concrete comparison between two societies. I suddenly appreciated things like 'free enterprise' and 'separation of church and state'. I'd always taken them for granted, until I tasted what life was like without them.

Though Greece is technically a democracy, the Constitution establishes the Eastern Orthodox Church of Christ as the "predominant" religion. Which means that Greece generally respects the right of its citizens to practice whichever faiths they prefer. But non-Orthodox are treated with misgiving and told that they're "not truly Greek" if they're not Greek Orthodox. Things like business licenses, car registrations, and requests for electric bills in your name — which in Greece, are tricky enough — were even more difficult to obtain for non-Orthodox. They also faced some harassment in the form of arbitrary identity checks and had difficulty burying their dead.

The other "American" thing I uncovered about myself while owning business in Greece was my keenness for capitalism. I felt hampered by government restrictions on commerce. There were so many regulations fo private businesses; it was a miracle anybody managed to sell anything.

I ranted endlessly about this to Joan, "We wouldn't want anyone t make any *real* money. That would be *bad*."

Having said that, there were some government regulations in Greec I wished we *did* have in the States. For example, every month, a crank little civic worker came into our shop to collect money for our medic coverage. We *had* to pay, or we couldn't have a business. This frustrated m at first. Then I learned that every fulltime or part-time employed person i Greece retired with full medical coverage and a *decent* pension, which thes payments included. Unlike social security benefits in the United State pensions were never threatened by government cuts. I wondered if th policy was the reason I never saw homeless elderly people in Greece, as did back home. In fact, the only living creatures who slept on the streets i Greece, were either tourists or four-legged. Even the gypsies had somewher to sleep at night. Still, I never got past the detail that they weren't allowe to go to school, another illustration of my American mind-set. In the U.S federal law dictates that *everyone* between the ages of five and sixteen mu attend school. The gypsies couldn't even read in Greek, let alone Englist They spoke their own language, a form of Sanskrit.

One day I said to Joan, "I bet we could find a Greek teacher who'd b willing to teach gypsy children at Serafim Books. It probably wouldn't co us that much."

Joan laughed, an incredulous look on her face.

"What?" I countered, "You don't think it's a good idea?"

"I think it's a marvelous idea," she replied. "I just can't figure out you're a fascist or a bleeding-heart liberal. One minute you're bellyachin about socialism and the next you want to teach gypsies."

There was no doubt that by having so many new experiences, I wa becoming conflicted about some of the principles I'd always held as fixec One of the signs of this internal turmoil was that my stomach hurt a the time. I figured maybe it was the beans. Then one day, as I sat o my balcony alone again, clutching my midsection, something sagaciou Nonnie once said came back to me, "Don't trust *anything* but what yo stomach feels like."

That long-ago caution was summoned up, because a part of me kne that my stomach was struggling to convey something to me. I sifted throug clues as to what it might be. My stomach felt fine while I was at work, b

238

when I got home and saw Nick, it ached in a peculiar way. This bleak pain diffused as I kissed him and asked him about his day. Later, when Gregori turned his key in the lock, my stomach would lurch and feel progressively worse as the evening wore on.

At length, it came to me. It wasn't the beans. My bellyache was letting me know that I was at war with *myself*, trying hard to pretend I was happy when I knew I wasn't. I was gratified and productive professionally, I was entertained socially, but I was not *happy.*

That truth and the reason for it hit me with a pang whenever I observed the bond between Joan and her husband.

Sometimes she'd come into the shop incensed, saying, "Manoli's being a *pig* today, I hate him!"

But you could tell she didn't mean it.

Then Manoli might come by, to help us with a new computer program or fix something for us and I noticed that no matter what he was doing, his head would turn towards Joan whenever she walked into his line of vision. It was an automatic reflex for him. Manoli and Joan also make each other laugh, but laughter had vanished between Gregori and me.

It was toughest to discount these sentiments after I'd had a glass of wine. I didn't drink much, but occasionally, I'd have a glass while preparing dinner. *One* glass was all it took for my self-restraint to crumble. I'd leave the kitchen and lean against a wall in the dining room, where Gregori sat with his evening paper. His back would be to me, so I'd be watching him from behind as he read, holding my near-empty wine glass and thinking:

Gregori, why can't we be friends? I'm struggling so hard to make a life for myself here, but I miss home. I miss Margie and my cousins, Reese's Peanut Butter Cups, children knocking at our door, saying, "trick-or-treat," and trips into Manhattan to see the Christmas tree and the World Trade towers. I miss the delight on Nick's face when we did those things, and when he ate at his favorite Chinese restaurant, where the waiter taught him how to say, "thank you," in Mandarin. I could've lived without these, though, if only you'd loved me.

Have you noticed I'm not a "legitimate" person, anymore? I'm a foreigner, assessed with suspicion. Even Nick's friends tell him I "talk funny" and cook strange food. I bet you went through that in the States. Why can't you be my ally as I go through these changes here in Greece, where you said you had to be in order to be happy? You aren't, though, are you? Poor Gregori, you got taken in, too. All you wanted was someone who'd make you hot meals every night. Neither of us got what we hoped for, did we?

After a while, Gregori would sense I was behind him. He'd turn around "Why are you standing there, staring at me? Is the food ready? Are we eating yet?"

Was this enough for me to accept that I should end my marriage? Not yet, but it was enough for me to admit that I should skip the glass of wine. Or maybe, double it.

At Last — a Talisman

> *"All men are mah-lah-kahs (jerks)*
> *to a greater or lesser degree."*
> **–Joan Maragoudakis**

My tumultuous feelings were getting stronger and had to be evaded aggressively. One was especially tenacious — *Would it really be so wrong to leave Gregori?*

I had to fight that contemplation the hardest. Despite my resolutions on that rock at the beach, I still believed that since *I'd* chosen this marriage, if *I* couldn't fix it, the only way I could save myself from being an abysmal mother and a discredited failure, was to bear it. Otherwise, there'd be humiliation, as well as my son's anguish and resentment. A stomach lining being eaten away by acids was a preferable feeling to those. So, I battled my thoughts with unrelenting work. It was one area in my life where things were now going well.

Joan and I were on the same page in all significant matters. The education and well-being of children was vital to both of us. I know she suspected there was a problem in my home life because she'd witnessed Gregori's waspishness towards me. But I never talked about it with her. I thought she'd worry that my domestic troubles would be bad for our business. Pretending all was well worked for a while, until the day I phoned her from the shop to say I'd stored the large shipment that had arrived the day before. I'd kept counting and organizing, until every bit was neatly away. I was so jubilant over this feat; I didn't notice she'd answered the phone very sleepy-voiced, or her taut silence after my pronouncement.

Then she said, "Have you gone *mad*? It's flipping six o'clock on Saturday morning! You got back there at six o'clock last *night!* Go home and go to bed!"

And — *click!* The line went dead.

I was taken aback by her reaction. Then I looked out the small window we had in the basement where I'd been working all this time. *Good Lord,* he was right. There was light out there. I'd been working for *twelve* hours. Well, there was no sense going home now. Nick always slept in on Saturday. He and Gregori could have breakfast together. I still had some work to do, why not just stay until Joan came in, so I could apologize in person? She'd be pleased. I made a pot of coffee. When Joan came in at ten sharp, I was already on my third cup. I'd scrubbed the toilet, dusted all the shelves, swept the floors, watered the plants, cleaned the dog poop off the front lawn, and started on a new window display.

"Hi," I said with a smile.

But, *surprise.* Joan didn't smile back. In fact, she looked hopping mad. I'd never seen her lips and jaw set like that, as if she were trying to hold a spoonful of foul-tasting liquid in her mouth.

She nodded once. "Still here, I see. *Right,* then. You and I have to *talk.*" She pointed up the steps to our office. I followed her up, feeling like a youngster. Was I going to get a lecture? She sat down in her chair and I sat in mine. "Now, then…" she began. And she held her arm straight out, her hand palm up, like a traffic cop signaling "stop."

Uh oh. I knew that position. Joan assumed it whenever she was about to tell her children or her husband off. I *was* going to get a lecture. I'd have to let her have her say. I was prepared to say I was sorry for waking her, but I wasn't prepared for what the content of this talk would be.

"Listen, Patricia, I am *exhausted.* I cannot work any harder than I have been. When I signed on for this, I knew it would be hard work and I'm willing to do it. But I cannot work twelve hours a day, seven days a week!"

I was confused. "Who's asking you to?"

"You are!" she exploded. "By working like *this.* It's an implication that you don't think I'm doing my fair share!"

I was mystified. "Wait… you're not angry that I woke you up this morning? You think *I* think *you're* not working hard enough? Joan, you were here for ten hours yesterday. When are you supposed to see your husband?"

"When do you see *your* husband?" she returned.

She had me there. I hadn't been open with her on the state of things at home, had I? So being the conscientious person she was, she assumed that if I could be at the shop for a twenty-hour stint, I'd think *she* should be, too.

I sighed. It was time to come clean. "Maybe I don't want to see him
I put my two hands together in the shape of a circle. "*Zero*. That's what I
and I have. I only have my son and…" I stood up and spread my hand
wide "…*this*. My marriage has gone from bad to worse. And I just deplete
my savings account — *totally* — to start a new business at the age of *for*
because I left my career in New York!"

I shook my head in disbelief at that foolhardiness and Joan watched m
bounce around as I raved, like one watches the little silver ball in a spinnin
roulette wheel, trying to guess where it's going to land.

Spreading my hands wide to encompass the enormity, I raged, "I le
everything. Did that make my husband happier? Did he love or *apprecia*
either Nick or me, any more than he had before we'd come here with him?

I looked at her as though I expected her to have valid replies to m
rhetorical questions. Judiciously, she said nothing. I lamented on, "An
now, I'm here. How can I drag Nick back there, after I'd dragged him her
Tell him… *what*? 'Sorry, I've made a mistake'?" I took a deep breath. "N
I'm going to stay here and be happy—" I banged my fist on the desk "—
it *kills* me. I'm going to do well by my son and the other children wh
come in here, because… that's what's important." I slammed my fist dow
on the desk again, "Serafim Books is going to be the *best* education cent
in Greece! So… I'm sorry that I'm here all the time. But, Joan, I just *have*
be. Everything else in my life is a *mess!*"

Joan's eyes were so wide open that the bright blue irises had whi
circling all around them. From not knowing much about my anomalot
marital life, in minutes, she'd been apprised of it *all*. If she asked me to bu
her out of the deal at that moment, I wouldn't have blamed her.

Before she could say anything, the phone rang. I picked it up, still o
of breath. "Serafim Books. May I help you?"

"*Are you still there?*" Gregori bellowed through the phone. I knew I
could be heard across the room to where Joan was sitting. He continued
roar, "*There's no milk and I have no underwear! Are you coming home to
laundry?*"

"I'll be home in an hour," I snapped back. He banged the phone dow
on his end. I was sure Joan heard that, too.

I put the receiver down quietly. I didn't like the look on her face. It w
too much like pity. *Oh, God*. I clenched my teeth together. I wasn't goir
to cry, even if, to stop myself, I had to keel over dead. We were partners in
business with lots of potential, a business I'd started on my own. On tho

herits, I was going to maintain my dignity. "What do you want to do?" I asked, evenly.

Joan was silent as she held her hands in her lap, tapped her foot and looked at me. At length, she spoke. "Right. I'll go downstairs, make us some tea, and then you can show me where you've put everything so's I now where to find them."

The time she was making tea, I used to collect myself. *Oh, well.* Whatever was going to happen would happen.

Except, as she came up and handed me my tea, she did something I'll never forget. She patted my shoulder. "That's the tea you like best, isn't it – the orange one?"

"*Um...* yeah. Thanks," I said.

"*Mmm-hmm.*" she replied as she sipped. Then, "Looks lovely downstairs, the way you've organized everything. I like the display window you've started, too."

I swallowed some tea. "Thank you very much." I held my teacup like a talisman. Though I've tried, I don't think I'll ever manage to express to her how much her tea and her manner towards me that day meant. It's one thing to be in a strange place feeling wholly alone and another to have a purpose here, with a worthy associate to help you accomplish it. But don't you agree that it's entirely something else to learn that associate is a true friend?

I finished my tea. "I think I'll go home and have a nap." I said.

That wasn't going to happen. Gregori was waiting at home as he'd made plain, angry, thirsty, and apparently, nude. The woman sitting next to me new that now, too.

Still, all she said was, "Good idea."

There was Everything Else, so Why Not This?

> **"Only time will heal your broken heart. Just as only time will heal his broken arms and legs."**
> **–Miss Piggy**

If chronic matrimonial sufferance was not a dire enough justification for my leaving Gregori, my accountant, Eris, provided me with one that was.

She was some gal. I'll never forget the time she advised me, with a big smile on her face, to "wear a skirt" if I had to go to the tax bureau. Some of the clerks there would push my paperwork through more quickly, as sign of their appreciation, she'd said. Joan's feminist spirit was outraged t that suggestion, but I confess to trying it, and Eris was right. Governme red tape was cut through more quickly whenever I treated the dispensatio employees to the sight of my knees. I was thankful to Eris for telling n that, *and* I was thankful for her help when I first started Serafim Books. Sh did something else I'm indebted to her for, too. She saved my life. Thoug I'm pretty sure that wasn't her intended objective.

I don't remember which public agency she and I were headed for th day, but it had something to do with another groundless regulation, th time regarding the setting of the cash register we kept in the shop. For thi we needed to cart the actual machine to some official somewhere and hav our accountant with me, so she could sign… whatever it was she neede to sign. Like I say, the details of our trip with the till are murky, but th conversation I had with Eris afterward, as we drove home, I rememb clearly. She started it off by telling me that Gregori had told her he and weren't happy together.

My *husband* told Eris, who was a worker in his office and my accountan that he wasn't happy with me, his *wife*.

It was a betrayal, all right, but I stayed calm and kept my eyes on th road. I had the car radio switched on, and The Katzimihas Brothers, m favorite Greek folk singers, were harmonizing the words to one of the signature ballads, "Laugh, little bird of mine, life is a crazy woman.. How apt.

I had to chuckle then, recalling Gregori's words when he suggested use Eris as my accountant, "She'll cost you less."

Eris chuckled, too. In fact, the entire tone of her telling was jolly, whic prompted me to conclude, "And it's *you* he prefers, instead."

She smiled a duplicate smile to the one she'd worn when she'd advis me to wear skirts to the tax office and said, "Yes!"

You'll be surprised by what I did then, I think. I glanced at the clo over the car radio and said, "We've plenty of time to get back. Why don't buy you a beer?"

We sat at another *taverna* by the sea and drank our beer, and Er was beaming, reveling in her role of bad-news harbinger, as she presente me with details of Gregori's duplicity. I don't know why some wom think catching the romantic attention of another woman's husband is a exceptional feather in their caps of sexual appeal. But some do, and Eris w one of them. She told me that Gregori had chased her around his desk and smacked her on her bottom. How cliché can you get?

To this day, Gregori maintains that what he did with Eris "wasn't cheating". I don't know if he says this because he really believes it, or because he wants others to believe it. I do know that a married man chasing a woman around his desk and smacking her on her ass isn't literally "cheating", but he is, to use a Greek expression, "stepping on his wedding crown."

How about that? Just as when I'd climbed on the rock at the beach and cried, I was being hit with this new shattering blow while surrounded by glorious scenery. And when Eris finished talking, she said, "This is on me," which is just what Thoulah had said, after she'd told me *her* devastating news. This whole episode had a sense of the familiar about it, perhaps even the inevitable. I think that's why I was able to remain calm throughout. I let Eris pay for our beers. Then we chatted about inconsequential things as I drove her to her apartment, smiled, and waved good-bye.

In every Greek tragedy, there's a point called the 'agon', when the protagonist and antagonist finally clash and the story climaxes. Gregori and I weren't exactly 'protagonist' and 'antagonist', but our two different perspectives on marriage had ultimately collided. We'd reached our own 'agon', but if I had any control over it, it wouldn't be an 'agon' with violent ramifications like the ones in literature. I'd maintained my dignity through every other degradation in my marriage, and I'd do so through this final one.

That night, after Nick was in bed, I kissed him good night and asked, "Do you know that I love you *very* much?"

He answered, "Of course."

Once he was asleep, I went to bed myself and lay there, waiting for Gregori. When he got into bed and switched off the lamp, I said quietly, "I had a chat with Eris today." I told him what she said and finished with, "…I'm leaving you."

He said nothing.

We didn't fuss. Not then, nor from that night on, until the time Nick and I moved out. However, I *did* ask Joan the next day at the shop, "Would you mind if we let Sofia do our accounting from now on? Here's why . . ."

Joan got that "I-taste-something-foul" look on her face again. "*Eris?*" she said, with repugnance. "She smells like she doesn't bathe."

I admit that her judgment was gratifying, but Eris was my reason for finally conceding defeat in my marriage, so I prefer to remember her as a person who did me a great favor.

Leaving Gregori was the one time in my life I genuinely valued being a successful pupil of *figura*. After practicing all those agonizing good manners for so many years of my life, they didn't desert me when I needed them most. And I needed them very much at the end. Because on the day I left him — it's somewhat amusing really — the last thing my lover, my husband, and the father of my child, said to me:

"Have you got time to do one more load of laundry, before you go? I don't know how to use the machine."

Moving Downstairs, or Why I Loved the Poly-katee-kee-ah

> *"By all means marry; if you get a good wife, you'll be happy.*
> *If you get a bad one, you'll become a philosopher."*
> **–Socrates**

Whatever good or bad thing was going to happen in my life, Greece wasn't going to let it happen on a less than perfect day. The day I left Gregori was no exception.

We separated in January of 1999, but a legal divorce while I was in Greece would've invalidated my alien's residence card. It'd be a huge bother to apply for another without a Greek national husband as 'host'. That's why, for the first time in all the years we'd been together, having Gregori as my husband served as a convenience for *me*.

And this is what I explained to everyone back home. I bit the bullet and made the long-distance phone calls, because they had to be told.

The main consensus from Margie and my cousins was, "Well… you can never say you didn't try your best."

And that was comforting, because it was true.

My parents added something for which I honestly couldn't fault them. They said, "But — you're *sure* this separation instead of a divorce is just for convenience? You're not going back to him again, are you?"

When I exclaimed, "*Hell*, no!" I think I convinced them.

Donna, I didn't have the nerve to phone, I admit, but I sent her an email. She was very sweet and supportive in her reply, yet I noticed my heart squeezed a little when I read what she wrote at the end:

246

I wonder if this is a good or bad time to tell you Kurt is getting married. He met a French girl while he was living in Paris. My mother is thrilled. She'd given up on ever having grandchildren since both her kids stayed single for so long. Now she's taking French lessons!

For Nick's part, because he was older and wrapped up in his own life, he was as blasé about this separation as he'd been when he was four and I'd handed two strangers into his life, telling him they were his grandparents. Either the kid had an incredibly resilient constitution, or the other shoe would drop someday with a very loud *thump*.

With that possibility in mind, I was determined that I wasn't going to move him out of the *poly-katee-kee-ah,* which is what an 'apartment building' is called in Greek. We both liked where we lived and the people who lived there. So we took a smaller apartment on the ground floor. If Gregori felt uncomfortable having me underfoot, *he* could move to another building. We hardly ever ran into each other, anyway. He kept to himself, having nothing to do with the neighbors. I was the one who'd sit with my morning coffee, on my new, garden level balcony that was next to the building entranceway, and see everyone as they left for the day. Our neighbors were warm and always had time for a chat.

There was little Maria, Sofia and Gianni's youngest, who'd perform her nursery school songs for Nick and me. There was Mr. Telly and his ailing wife, Mrs. Kleopatra. There was Kostaki, of course, who lived with his parents and sister in the apartment across from Nick and me. Kostaki's parents were musicians. Every Sunday, around noon, we got to hear them playing classical music on their piano. Nick had also made friends with Sofia's oldest, Eva and with Kostaki's sister, Vlasia. All four would sit out on the front steps together. Sometimes the girls sat just with me, so they could practice speaking English.

Nick and I still had all that good company, because we'd moved downstairs instead of to a new building. If those neighbors were surprised to see that Gregori stayed up in in the other place, they said nothing more than, "Oh, a new home for you. Enjoy it in health!" ('In health' is th[e] equivalent of a blessing, in case you were worried about 'the evil eye'.)

There were two exceptions. One was Sofia. I'd asked her and h[er] husband, Gianni, who was her business partner, to be the accountants f[or] Serafim Books. She wanted to know why we weren't using Eris anymor[e] so I told her. Sofia felt comfortable enough with me by that time [to] express the same sentiment Joan had, "*Af-tee? Mah, vroh-mai af-tee*[.]" ("Her? But she *stinks!*")

It was nice to know my girlfriends supported me in my time of crisi[s.]

The second was Mrs. Kleopatra. On my way down the inside steps a[s I] was transferring some of my things, I ran into her talking with the wom[an] who cleaned the common areas for us. I said hello to them and continu[ed] on down.

Mrs. Kleopatra was hard of hearing and didn't realize how loudly s[he] talked. That's why I know she didn't mean for me to hear what she sa[id] about me to the cleaner:

"Patricia will never get married again at her age."

That stopped me, mid-stride. Now that I'd overheard *that*, I f[elt] compelled to hear the rest.

"I *know*," replied the cleaner.

Then they both said, "*Kai-men-ee.*" ("Poor thing.")

People in Greece say "*kai-men-ee*" when they see a starving beggar, [a] sickly child, or bedraggled stray cat. But I was "*kai-men-ee*" to a near[ly] deaf, crippled, elderly lady with a heart condition and a toothless, Albani[an] refugee, who cleaned houses for a living. And all because I was divorci[ng] Gregori. It made me laugh so much I wondered why I'd ever worried abo[ut] what people would think.

To Nick, the idea of running up and down the stairs to two differe[nt] apartments and two different bedrooms of his own was a perk. Now th[at] we weren't together, Gregori dropped the pretence of being able to co[ok] only beans, so Nick would eat with whichever parent was preparing wh[at] he fancied having most.

The arrangement worked. I had my son, my work, my friends, and m[y] own place. I felt established and secure in Greece. I wasn't leaving.

Chapter Fifteen: Turning Back

"Security is mostly a superstition. It does not exist in nature...Life is either a daring adventure or nothing."
–Helen Keller

Real War

Late one night, I woke up to a loud banging on our door.

"Py-ohs ee-nay?" ("Who is it?") I called sleepily, tying up my robe.

"Ah-stee-noh-mee-ah," came the reply.

The police? I looked through the peephole to see a man in full uniform, holding up a badge.

I opened the door. "May I help you?" I asked him, in Greek.

"Immigration police. I need to see your papers, please."

"One moment, I'll get them," I said.

When I came back with my residency permit and my passport, the officer asked, "What is your business here?"

My insides jumped as I thought about what the best response would be. "I'm married to a Greek citizen."

"You have a Greek husband? Where is *he*?"

Now how to explain? "Ah... he's upstairs in the flat on the top floor." I hesitated. "We're... separated. I'm staying in this flat with our son."

The police officer said nothing. He just studied me.

God help me, I prayed silently. *Don't let them deport me. If they do, don't let them make me leave Nick here with Gregori.*

At last, he pointed at my papers and said, "Your residency permit expired one month ago."

My eyes widened. "Oh! I must have forgotten. I went back to the United States for business last month. They stamped my passport..." I babbled, "...you can see the stamp on my passport."

He flipped through, found the stamp, and examined it. It seemed to satisfy him. After another moment, he handed me back my things. "Make sure you get your permit renewed."

"I will. I *promise*, I will," I assured him, fumbling with my papers, light-headed with relief.

Without another word, he left. I closed the door and sagged against i
Then I started to cry. After everything else, this was just too much.

*** ***

My separation was the first in a series of life-changing events tha
would take place in 1999. In February, Turkish troops captured th
Kurdish rebellion leader, Abdullah Öcalan, as he sought asylum in Greec
The Greeks, long-time political enemies of the Turkish government, we
sympathetic to the Kurdish cause, and the Greek government was caugl
in the middle. If they gave the Kurdish leader sanctuary, there'd be wa
with Turkey. If they didn't, the Greek people would riot. Öcalan was bein
transported for safekeeping to Kenya when he was captured by the Turk
Conspiracy theories abounded and mayhem reigned throughout Gree
and the Kurdish community in Turkey.

If this didn't make the mood volatile enough, there were religious/ethn
wars raging at the northern border of Greece in Kosovo. The *NATO* allian
had sent American and British troops into the region as "peacekeepers," v
northern Greece. Their presence in the north was not welcome by Gree
citizens. The Greek disapproval of American and British intervention too
a humorous form originally. When British troops went into upper Gree
with tanks, bogus signs that detoured the unsuspecting soldiers back in
the center of Thessaloniki (Salonika) had replaced the street signs directir
traffic to the region of Macedonia. The tanks ended up right in the midd
of an outdoor produce market.

Joan hooted at this, "They went to catch Albanians and Serbs ar
ended up with vegetables and fruit!"

Then things got vicious. In March, *NATO* began a bombing operatic
against Yugoslavia that lasted several months. The legality of the atta
was disputed by many nations because electric lines, water supplies, ar
television stations were destroyed. Not to mention the train full of civilia
who were blown to bits when the bridge they were traveling on was hit.

As refugees from the bombed areas surged into Greece, the situation
the border worsened. Greeks there were trying to keep out of the confli
so anger within Greece against the *NATO* forces grew, creating more ant
American sentiment in Greece. *NATO* forces at the northern border
Greece weren't the only cause of escalating political tensions. There we
scuffles popping up everywhere around us, even in neighboring Turkey ar
Cyprus. Problems in those two countries always leaked into Greece.

250

That July, I experienced what happens when emotions boil over and people perceive their political freedom threatened. It was during the protests marking the 25th anniversary of the Turkish invasion of Cyprus. Cyprus is still divided, and this occupation is one of the most violently contested in the region. To observe the anniversary, Greek-Cypriots gathered in marches everywhere around the world. The most passionate march took place in Cyprus, to the blockade that separated the northern part of the island taken by the Turks from the south. It was televised live in Greece and Nick and I will never forget what we saw.

As the Turkish soldiers watched warily from their post on the barricade, the Greek-Cypriot citizens, chanted and yelled, pressing themselves against the barrier. The camera zoomed in on one young man who was shouting zealously, the cords of his neck sticking out as he yelled. He raised his fists and pounded on the divide. This started a precedent. Other young men began banging with fists and open palms, their outrage escalating. The Turkish soldiers were looking distinctly uneasy. We saw them tighten their hold on their guns.

"My God, what are they *doing*?" I exclaimed. "Something terrible is going to happen, I know it."

"Are they trying to break the wall down?" asked Nick. Neither one of us had ever witnessed anything like this.

The camera panned back to the first young man, still shouting and banging on the barrier. We gasped as he did something perilous. He hoisted himself up on the barrier so he could shimmy up the flagpole on the other side, upon which was flying the Turkish flag. As he made his way up, he stretched one arm out to grab the flag. The Turkish soldier nearest him shifted his gun, called out something and motioned agitatedly for the protester to get down.

The din was unbelievable. People screamed to the young man on the flagpole both fearful admonition and reckless encouragement. News microphones reverberated with noise and the newscaster blasted commentary fervidly in Greek. The camera dipped wildly from one part of the pandemonium to another. Greek-Cypriot youths tried dragging the climber down, while others waited edgily, poised to jump up themselves. The Turkish soldiers' agitation increased.

Nick and I stood petrified, unable to look away from the scene. And so, we watched the inevitable happen.

Just as the climbing protester managed to grasp the flag, another Turkish soldier further away shot him. The one soldier who'd warned the Greek Cypriot to climb down flung out his hand instinctively to help the youth who'd been shot. Realizing what he'd done, he quickly jerked it back to his side, but he couldn't mask the horror on his face. The young Greek-Cypriot lost his grip on the flag and pitched backwards from the shot. He toppled over the divide, into the crowd of protesters. The camera zeroed in on his face. The blood on him was appalling. Some had splashed on the lens of the camera and showed as dark splotches on our screen. The screeching crowd held him by his arms and legs, face up. He wore a startled expression, as though he truly hadn't expected this pitifully predictable end. He was dead. The entire event had unfolded in less than fifteen minutes of real time.

That incident only added to the unrest in Greece. My friend, Angel at the American Embassy in Athens, warned me that the situation on the northern border was getting troublesome for Americans. Even though the British were part of that *NATO* offensive, it was the Americans with whom the Greeks were most furious, because the killing of the young man in Cyprus during the protest against the Turks stirred up unresolved hostilities. The Greeks support the Cypriots in their desire to get the Turks out of Cyprus, but Turkey is an ally of the United States. The suspicion that the United States was involved in the Kurdish leader Öcalan's capture, along with the interference at the northern border, and the televised death of the young Cypriot, all fueled resentment. As a result, Americans in the north were being harassed, and the United States government was evacuating the American Embassy up in Thessaloniki for the time being.

*** ***

Likely, this was why the immigration police had come to my door. There was a family of Albanian refugees who lived in the apartment adjacent to ours. As I sat on the cold marble flooring, leaning against the inside of our apartment door, I heard the police officer knock at their door, too. I was still sitting in the same spot an hour later, when I heard that whole family in harried whispers, hastily gather belongings and take off into the night.

I didn't know what to do next. Nick and I were scheduled to go up north together for a very important book exhibition not too far from the border. Gregori was traveling for business, and I didn't want to leave Nick with Joan and Manoli again. But if we went, we'd be perilously close to the fighting and the vehement anti-Americanism. Rescheduling wouldn't help unless I planned on canceling until there was peace in the region.

252

The fact was, I was losing my nerve for running a business in Greece. wasn't just the political climate. There were other obstacles.

By this time, several *Scholastic* book titles had been placed on the overnment (state) school list of accepted titles to use in English-language aching, an unheard of occurrence for American books in Greece. Our aterials were in every private school and every major bookshop in Athens d Thessaloniki. We'd been featured in magazines and newspapers. Soon, e were expanding to Turkey.

But as the business grew, so did its complications. Some were just iisances, such as the man who let his dog soil the front lawn of our shop cause he didn't like foreigners owning businesses. But other issues were ore trying, like the wily new sales manager in the States, who'd tried to botage our entire operation for self-aggrandizement, or the disgruntled okseller who, when we'd closed her account for lack of payment and no les, spread vicious lies about our integrity.

Those who worked closely with Joan and me knew we were industrious d honest, so none of these distractions had succeeded in destroying us. it they sapped our energy when we were already exhausted. We needed to ke on a new partner to add manpower, but no one we'd interviewed so far emed up to the task. Add all this to the fact that I was a single, working other again, and that Joan was feeling guilty she was spending less and s time at home.

The immigrant police pounding at my door had been the limit. ombined with everything else, that simply shattered my determination.

So I did something you'd never expect. Still crying, I got up off the or and called my father. I guess I wanted sympathy. I didn't hear what I pected, though. With my father, I never did.

*** ***

"Okay, so it's tough to own a business and be on your own. You knew that. , why are you crying?"

"I think Nick and I should leave Greece. I think we should sell Serafim oks."

"Just because the police showed up? They have to do that. That's their ."

"Dad!" I wailed, sounding just like a little girl. "Didn't you hear what I d? We're supposed to go *up* there where there's a *war* going on and I don't ow if we'll be *safe*."

And all at once, my father was laughing at me. "*Ha ha ha! 'Safe'? C[...] my God — you're so American. You want to come back to the States, wh[...] you'll be 'safe'. Yeah, okay — move to Colorado. You can send Nicky to sch[...] in Columbine.*"

That hit me like a brick. He was right. The high school shooting h[...] happened only a few months before, too.

I got hold of myself. "You're right, Dad. I'm sorry. I don't know wh[...] come over me."

"*You're upset. It's understandable. If you want to come back, come ba[...] But not because you're afraid. Like your grandfather Appollonio used to say–*

...Oh, Lord, not another parable...

"*—the only time we're ever 'secure' is when we're dead.*"

After we hung up, I thought about what my father had said an[...] remembered a story he'd once told about seeing bombers flying overhe[...] in Sicily. He said he stayed outside in his garden, eating his spaghetti wi[...] *salsa puttanesca,* nonetheless. I thought of Gregori's father hiding Itali[...] soldiers in his basement on Rhodes, and then Gregori himself, looking [...] for spies when the junta took over. I thought of Nick, insisting we help [...] a church back together.

If they could be brave, so could I.

*** ***

Nick and I went up to Thessaloniki as scheduled. We sold plenty [...] books, and he made me laugh with his silly jokes. We visited the muse[...] that housed the artifacts from the tomb of Phillip of Macedonia. We [...] the steamed mussels for which Thessaloniki is famous. And everywh[...] we went, we saw armed American and British soldiers, whose guns look[...] fierce, but whose faces looked barely older than Nick's and Alexi's.

Not long after we got back to Athens, a Greek bus was seized by t[...] desperate Albanians who held the travelers at gunpoint. In an exchange [...] gunfire between the hijackers and the Greek police, a 28-year-old Gre[...] male passenger was killed. It happened on the same route to the north th[...] Nick and I'd just taken.

Nonetheless, I remembered my father's sage words. Joan and I h[...] Serafim Books through political, business, and personal trials for two an[...] half more years after that, all the way through July 2002. We were sorting n[...] stock at Serafim Books, in August of 1999, when we heard the news abo[...] the devastating earthquake in neighboring Turkey. We were there again [...]

254

llowing month, when we *felt* that Greece was having an earthquake of its wn. We sat together in our office, biting our nails, listening to reports of Iilsovec's violent ouster in the northern regions of The Balkans, and the calation in hostilities between Israel and the Palestinians in the southeast. nd when the World Trade towers in New York City fell in 2001, Joan as the first to phone me. All of it had its impact on us, but as exiles made eir way into Athens from Israel, Lebanon, Albania, Turkey, and more, e and I made sure we had books to suit *everyone's* children, and we sat own to read to them *all*. We traveled wherever we needed to and sold our lucational tools throughout Greece and Cyprus, until it was time for us go home.

Dog Again, and Spiro, the 'Manga'

> *". . . You really do have to love yourself*
> *to get anything done in this world."*
> **–Lucille Ball**

"You're martyring yourself for your son. That's not being a good mother."

I was at the shop, on the phone to Randy, the incredible teacher and ook club champ', who taught at American Community Schools. But we eren't talking about business. As one of my angels, she'd decided to give e some wise advice.

"You're telling me that I should start dating for *Nick's* benefit?"

"That's one good reason. The other reason is for you. *It's almost two years nce you left Gregori. Don't you want to at least* see *if there's a man out there ho could be your lover, your true friend, your life mate? If you have no one and othing else, that'll put your son in another bind. He'll always feel responsible r you, particularly as he's an only child."*

"You're right, Randy. And I know you and Joan both have found that appiness. I just haven't met anyone here that might suit. Every decent man y age I know is married. The rest smoke so much, they'll probably all get ing cancer."

"You don't have to date, then. But go out, at least — see a play with friends, aybe. Especially when Nick's with his father. Let your son see that you'll be right, that you have a life besides your work and him."

The whole time I'd been listening to Randy's counsel, Joan had be(e)
going in and out of the shop, carrying paper towels and a plastic trash ba(g)
muttering to herself.

I put my hand over the receiver and mouthed silently to her, "*Wha(t's)
wrong?*"

She shook her head back and forth, a cross look on her face.

I went back to the phone. "Randy, thank you for caring about me. (It)
means a lot. I have to go, though... something's come up over here. We('ll)
talk again, soon."

When I hung up, I thought about what Randy had said. Here was mo(re)
momentous advice given to me over the telephone. I knew that sooner (or)
later, I'd have to curtail my work hours and get back to having a life outsi(de)
of Serafim Books. Joan had been saying the same thing.

And speaking of, I went downstairs to see what had upset her. She w(as)
stamping books with a vengeance, still looking stern.

"Joan? What's up?" I asked, glancing at the calendar. Joan had on(e)
or two days every month that were not her best. Her family and frien(ds)
knew, our workers knew, even Bob, her dog who worshipped her, kne(w)
and steered clear. The date was wrong to be the cause of her consternati(on)
today, though.

"Oh, Patricia, it's that *horrible* man again with that little white do(g.)
He's let him run all over the front garden. It's a mess out there and we'(ve)
got Giannopoulos School coming in for a workshop later."

"Him *again*?" I said, riled, now. "I've had it. It's about bloody time (I)
told him off."

"You're just wasting your breath," she warned, as I marched up t(he)
stairs. "He does it on purpose."

I stopped short, however, when I saw what was going on outside. (I)
ran back into the shop, and whispered hurriedly down the basement step(s,)
"Joan! You've *got* to see this, you won't believe it!"

It was Spiro from the Lotto shop next door, giving the man with t(he)
white dog 'what for'. Usually Spiro was so unruffled, the epitome of wh(at)
the Hellenes call a "*manga*", which loosely translated, means "one cool, h(ip)
dude." Spiro embraced the whole "*manga*" spirit. He had the "*Rembetik(a)*"
music playing in his smoke-filled shop, and the cigarette dangli(ng)
permanently from his lower lip. He made the monosyllabic respons(e)
whenever customers came in to buy Lotto tickets. He lifted his eyebro(ws)
up for "hello," if he liked you, but kept them level and impassive, for "(...)

256

away quickly, you bore me," if he didn't. In short, he turned 'haughty' into an art form.

Now, however, his Greek was energetic. "*Kah-les gee-nay-kehs, eenay!*" he was shouting.

"Who does he mean, 'they're good women'?" I muttered to Joan to translate.

"Be *quiet,* for once!" she snapped back in a whisper. "I can't understand it all either, if you're going to talk over it."

"*Ow!*" I said, rubbing my side. She'd pinched me. I hated when she did that. Maybe I'd better check the date again. And what did she mean, *"for once"*?

Spiro had restored to his composed self. Now that he was speaking more slowly, I could get his drift.

"You make me sick. You come into my shop and spit obscenities about them, because the 'dark one' asked you politely not to let your dog shit all over the lawn. She asked you because they have *children* going in and out of there, all day long. Do you know how many times I've seen little ones step right in it? Then, they cry. Because of *you.* You disgrace us all. You don't want them here because they're foreign. They're good women, I *told* you. The 'blonde one' buys Lotto tickets from me. They smile and say, 'hello' to everybody on the block, they give little toys from their shop to my son."

Spiro took his cigarette out of his mouth and used it as a pointer to illustrate his rebuke. "I don't like your dog's shit on the front lawn, either. You let him loose here again, or come into my place to speak ill of them *one more time*, you'll regret it."

With that, he turned his back and in his 'hip, cool way' sauntered back into his shop. So we wouldn't be seen eavesdropping, Joan and I scurried down the stairs.

She spoke first, "I'm *gob smacked.* I had no idea he liked us."

"I had no idea he even *noticed* us," I replied, awed.

The "dark one" and the "blonde one". The "good women" of the bookshop. Not brands, like *Amerikanaki* or *ksen-ee* (foreign woman), but reasonably legitimate identities. It was a sign of recognition by the natives of Glyfada. I'd been accepted as a full-fledged member of Greek society.

Wouldn't you know it would happen right as we were leaving Greece?

The 'Blonde One' and The 'Dark One' Have Left

"The 'mangas' don't exist anymore.
They've all been hit by the train..."
–Greek Rembetiko folksong

"Have we got everything?"

"Yes, Patricia. Stop fussing."

"Well, I was just wondering, if we wanted to take anything... a book, some stickers, maybe. We'll leave her the euros for them. It'll be her first sale."

"It certainly won't. We've booked orders all the way through October. That should give her a nice start."

"Yes."

Joan and I looked at each other. There was nothing more to say. Serafim Books had been sold. Joan was on her way to England. Manoli had been transferred, and the plan was that they'd remain there for the next four years. Joan was on board with it, but Manoli had made one grave mistake. He'd tried to convince her that Bob should be left behind. That would happen only if he left Joan behind, too.

The sale of the shop, the divorce, the moving of furniture across the seas, even the transfer of my car ownership, had been achieved only through typical, hair-tearing, Greek means. As you'd expect, Gregori had driven a hard bargain. If I wanted to take Nick back to the States with no legal hassles, I'd have to give up all claims to our joint property. I left a 20-year marriage with some old furniture and a used car. And selling that car in Greece had been quite an experience, too. At the Motor Vehicles Department in Glyfada, I ended up yelling long and hard, just the way my now ex-husband had taught me, in order to get that sale accomplished.

But all that was behind me now. I had the most important thing — my son. And I'd discovered who I was. Whatever would happen, I wasn't afraid. There'd be no sense in that, because security is only an illusion. Unless you're dead, of course.

The last thing left was to say good-bye. That would be tougher than anything Joan and I had already accomplished. We closed the shop door one last time and left the key where we'd promised. It was cataclysmic, walking away. Still, like everything else we'd done since we'd been partners,

258

e did it unflinchingly, although I wanted to break down like, as Joan ould say, "a big girl's blouse."

For us, there'd be no more Serafim Books. No more Spiro next door the Lotto shop, or peevish Greek man and his little white dog. No more eing each other every day, sipping our tea, debating current events, and scussing sales strategy. No more children smiling through story hour, teachers jotting notes at our workshops. No more book conferences or sits to schools.

I'd said good-bye to Mrs. Kleopatra, Mr. Telly and everyone else in our uilding. I'd hugged Sofia. They'd all given me farewell gifts. But it was ly Joan and I who drove to the airport. A team, as always.

And here it was, time to board. I had to say farewell to the one person 1 met in Greece who'd meant the most to me.

The last glimpse I had of her, she was walking away, head up, shoulders ack, pretty, blonde hair like a sparkle glittering on the Greek sea.

Good-bye, Joan.
Good-bye Greece.

Chapter Sixteen: New Colors

"Every perfect traveler always creates the country where he travels... You have your brush, you have your colors, you paint paradise, then in you go."
–Nikos Kazantzakis

I left Greece in summer of 2002, seven years after I'd moved ther Nick came back later, at August's end. Naturally he wanted to spend tl rest of his school break with his father and his Greek friends. We'd h: a farewell party in the garden and all of them, including those he'd m through Serafim Books, were there. I knew he'd miss them all.

I also knew it wouldn't be easy for him starting afresh in *another* ne place. Yet, he'd proven how adaptable he was. My fondest hope was tl he'd take away from our seven-year experience what I had, the knowled; that he could live *anywhere* and be happy there, if he kept his heart ar his options open. I didn't want him to feel he needed to stay huddled one corner of the earth with just one group of people, being only "Greek or "Italian," or "Something-Hyphen-American." I wanted him to feel I could be a citizen of the *world*. Most of all, I hoped that living in Gree had been good for him, as it had been for me.

I believe that the more societies we learn about, the more people v meet, the more shades we collect in our paint set, giving us that many mo colors with which to paint our days. Life is a lot more interesting when v gather as many colors as we can. My grandmother understood that.

You might be wondering — with so many women to choose from, wl was the heroine of this story?

That's easy. The heroine of this story was Greece herself. Like tl mother every human being longs for, she gave me everything she ha both the bad and the good, and stood by as I strived to learn from it a No matter what happened to me, she always reminded me that there w beauty to be found around me if I'd only stop for a minute and see it. SI accepted me for myself, but she challenged me to grow stronger. And whe I was strong enough to stand anywhere on my own, she applauded me ar set me free to go out into the world wherever I would.

And that's why you shouldn't think for one minute that I regi marrying Gregori. Our relationship was bound to fail. If I'd been strong nd believed in myself, I'd have been able to accept that much sooner. ut it took meeting him, marrying him, moving to Greece with him, and ourishing there, to change what I needed to change inside myself, to leave im. I now can consider the good our marriage brought me. Because of y association with him, I gained important knowledge about our world. ll always remember how he cried at his father's funeral, and the joy on his ce the first time he held our son. I'm able to think well of him, at least r these, because I'm content now. I know who I am and I stay true to yself.

A loving partnership should be a joining of compliments, not pplements. Those compliments can become, as my friend, Randy oukissas, said, "Lovers, true friends, and life mates."

I'm keeping my fingers crossed, because this time... I think I found im. Or rather, we found each other. And you'll laugh when I tell you – he's a "Real" American. Just as I expected, we have nothing in common. hat is, nothing in common that doesn't matter, yet everything in common at does. But that's a subject for another story.

Explanations and Apologies

Writing *Harlot's Sauce* gave me the opportunity to take a fresh look at parts of my past, through older and more accepting eyes. It took me almost half a century to see the humor in many of these incidents that I experienced the first time around as heart crushing. Their value was in their *inanity* rather than their calamity. This was the view held by the priest's wife in Crete, and if I'd developed her knack to see this sooner, it would've taken that much less time for these occurrences to have the positive effect on me they eventually had. I still don't have the technique down yet, but I keep practicing. I also tried to focus on the sameness, rather than the differences of people throughout the story, and make it apparent that we all have comparable fears. That's why bigotry in all its forms is nothing more than downright silly. But if I didn't achieve this lofty aspiration and managed only to offend, I'm sorry that I hurt your feelings.

To my son, Nick, even though you've read and approved of this memoir, I still want to say that I know I presented many of the people you love in ways you've probably never seen them. What I wrote does not invalidate what you think of them, or what they mean to *you*. They all have some wonderful qualities, which is why I got involved with them in the first place, and why you love them all so much.

It's also important to note that I've changed some of the names here. Greece is a small country, and I'm not out for revenge. So, for example, 'Penelope' is not the name of 'Gerry's' fourth wife, nor is 'Eris' the name of the woman who helped end my marriage to 'Gregori'. In fact, some who've read Greek mythology might recognize that Penelope was actually the long-suffering, faithful wife of Ulysses in *The Odyssey,* and Eris is the name of the Goddess of Discord, who threw the Golden Apple that started the Trojan War. (Okay... maybe there was a *little* revenge in picking those names.)

Also, for editorial reasons, I had to make composite characters of Margie and Donna. I was blessed to have more than two friends in my past who helped me through tough times, and to write about them all would've taken far too many pages. So the things that happened and the things that were said by Donna and Margie in this memoir *did* happen and *were* said, but sometimes by more than two friends. I'm also respecting the privacy of a few people I care about by writing them as composites. Not everyone wants to have their personal actions, like secret religious ceremonies, discussed

with the general public. Nonetheless, if you think you recognize yourse
here, no matter where, and it appears I'm making fun, I ask you to pleas
look again, because the one I mocked mostly was myself. I needed to writ
this story very much, because it was one of the most important journeys c
my life, my own "diaspora", if you will.

The story also reads as though I'm an only child. I actually have tw
siblings who were present for some of these events, but again, for brevity
sake, the editors thought it best they not be developed.

As for the historical events, dates, and figures, to the very best of m
knowledge they are all accurately described. There is still a discrepanc
about whether Abdullah Öcalan was on Greek soil or Kenyan when he w.
captured, but the rest was all verified by several sources.

For those who wish to learn more about Greece and Italy, obtain
some great recipes, see some fun videos, and even hear actors' podcaste
readings of *Harlot's Sauce*, they are all posted on my website at
www.patriciaVdavis.com. *Harlot's Sauce* has its own Facebook Fan Page
and would love for you to be its friend at:
http://tinyurl.com/harlotssauceonfacebook

I'll close by leaving you with one recipe. The best one
- *Harlot's Sauce*:

Harlot's Sauce
(*Salsa Puttanesca*)

The Neapolitan prostitutes became known as "culinary sirens", because the delicious aroma of this spicy dish coming from the houses of ill-repute in Naples would lure potential clients off the streets. It was inexpensive and quick to make, keeping the interruption of their 'business' to a minimum. Another saucy explanation is that *salsa puttanesca* was cooked by married women who'd spent all day with their lovers and needed to prepare a fast meal before their husbands came home.

The original recipe (below) was created with only garlic, anchovies, and basil, cooked along with ripe, chopped tomatoes, yet it's flexible enough to add anything you prefer. Whatever ingredients you choose, be sure to stir them together with a passion!

7 tablespoons good olive oil
1 large onion, chopped
4 garlic cloves, minced
1 cup (200 ml) water
2 anchovy filets, mashed with fork
8 Roma tomatoes, peeled, seeded and diced
10 Italian or Greek oil-cured olives, pitted and sliced
fresh chopped oregano, fresh chopped basil, dried red pepper flakes, salt, and pepper

Sauté the onions and garlic and anchovy filets in the olive oil. (Anchovies are usually not sautéed for a long time, in order to avoid a strong, fishy taste.) Add tomatoes, a bit of water, and sauté again. When the sauce comes to a boil, add olives and any other ingredients you've chosen. Reduce the high heat, stir the sauce occasionally as it cooks, adding more water if it becomes too thick. Sprinkle with herbs, pepper flakes, salt, and pepper, to taste

Mmm... Delicioso.